SUB WIFE

A Memoir from the Homefront

SAMANTHA OTTO BROWN

MILSPEAK BOOKS

An imprint of MilSpeak Foundation, Inc.

Author's Note: This is a work of nonfiction. I have done my best to represent all events, places, submarines, and people to accurately represent within the power of my memory and lack of security clearance. Some names have been changed.

Manufactured in the United States of America

Library of Congress Cataloging-in-Publication Data

Brown, Samantha

Library of Congress Control Number: 2021947282
ISBN 978-1-7378676-0-9 (paperback)
ISBN 978-1-7378676-4-7 (epub)

Editing by: Margaret MacInnis
Cover art by: www.BoldBookCovers.com
Formatting by: www.BoldBookCovers.com

MilSpeak Foundation, Inc.
5097 York Martin Road
Liberty, NC 27298
www.MilSpeakFoundation.org

For all the ones waiting at home. It's time to tell your story.

And my Sweet P, that the world be wide open for you and your curls.

"But such things happened to every one. Every one has friends who were killed in the War. Every one gives up something when they marry."

-Virginia Woolf, *Mrs. Dalloway*

"I always wondered why the makers leave housekeeping and cooking out of their tales. Isn't it what all the great wars and battles are fought for—so that at day's end a family may eat together in a peaceful house?"

-Ursula LeGuin, *Voices*

CONTENTS

CHAPTER 1

Silent

A glossy female mannequin with no face posed atop the display table in a Santa hat, a shredded miniskirt, and a bright red Christmas sweater. She was off kilter—one leg rotated out, one arm slack, chin down at an angle—as if she'd been bumped and never righted. It worked for her, in a plasticky sort of way. Her body language read as unbothered and cool. For that I envied her deeply. I was down below, worrying about death.

My friend Michelle brushed up against me sideways, pressing her shoulder against mine and speaking low. "I know I probably shouldn't be asking but…have you heard anything?"

I shook my head almost imperceptibly. "No. You?"

"Nothing."

"Shit."

"Don't say shit. Shit means something bad happened." Michelle kept her eyes fixed on the table of stocking stuffers below the mannequin: coffee mugs, novelty socks, and reindeer antlers with bows and jingle bells. It was a week and a half till Christmas.

Our husbands had deployed three months earlier on the USS *Georgia*. When they left in late September 2017, they'd been projected to be home by now, around Christmas. Instead, it had been many days since we'd gotten any word at all from them or their submarine. I'd been sending an email every

1

day to absolutely no reply for almost two weeks. It isn't unusual for submarines to go quiet. In fact, many are quiet for their entire time underway. Silence and secrecy are a sub's greatest defense. Their silence should not have rung any bells.

But about a month prior, November 15, 2017, in the South Atlantic during routine operations, the Argentine submarine ARA *San Juan* had gone quiet too. First, there'd been reports of a "seismic anomaly" in the area *San Juan* had been transiting—a sound consistent with an implosion. Then, a string of failed satellite calls that may have come from the vessel, or perhaps not, were detected. The sub's crew, the government said, if the boat were in distress, should have oxygen enough for seven to nine days underwater, which was reassuring for the first seven to nine days. By day ten, it wasn't anymore. Day after day, the world media broadcasted images of submariners' families camped behind chain link fence, wrapped in blankets and flags, waiting for answers, holding homemade signs for their loved ones. *Te queremos, te extrañamos. We love you; we miss you.*

For almost two weeks now, whenever I closed my eyes even to blink, I wondered if we, the spouses of the USS *Georgia* Blue, would be the next ones mourning on a pier. Yes, it was fairly routine for submarines to go silent, but not the *Georgia*, I thought. Not my husband. Both his first deployment and this current one, he'd emailed almost every day, even if just a few lines, so I'd know he was all right. Now, nothing.

Whatever I was doing—driving, teaching, brushing my teeth—the *Georgia*'s continued silence rested like sandbags on my chest. A nightmare I couldn't wake from. As a wife, my job was to be strong and placid. I'd been biting back the mounting panic, trying to logically work my way through worry with the few facts I did know: *The San Juan is diesel powered, the Georgia is nuclear; which means all different systems, all different scenarios. The San Juan is smaller by more than half. Their different crews carry out different missions. Right? If something*

2

has happened, the Navy wouldn't hide it. Right? But nothing bad happened to the Georgia. *Right?*

Every time I refreshed my email and didn't see my husband's name in a sent-by field, I felt one step closer to breaking down completely. I refreshed it exponentially more with every passing day.

Waiting was all-consuming.

Michelle and I weren't supposed to be talking about it. Not to our friends, our families, or even each other. The *silent* of *Silent Service* applies to spouses and families just as much as the sailors themselves for the safety of everyone. But we, the wives of the *Georgia* wardroom, were finally all together for the first time since the *San Juan* disappeared. Tonight, we were celebrating early Christmas with dinner, drinks, and a little shopping in a swanky town center. A small, welcome Band-Aid over the gaping absence of our loved ones.

"Do you think anyone else has gotten an email?" I spoke barely loud enough to be heard over the store's speakers. Michelle shrugged.

"*Ay,* did you say you got an email?" The Weapons Officer's wife, a tiny hummingbird of a woman grabbed my wrist and yanked me toward her. "Did you say you got an email?"

"No, no have you?"

She shook her head and pressed her hand briefly against her forehead as if she had a headache. "You got my hopes up." Then, she popped up on her tiptoes and leaned behind me, tapping the Navigator's wife on the shoulder. "Neither have they."

She pursed her lips into a forced smile and shook her head laughing. "Damn."

I looked around the store for the other half of our group. "Where's Emma and everyone else?"

We found them in the back, between the fitting rooms and bralettes, clustered into their own tight circle. Emma, another junior spouse like

Michelle and me, waved us over to their group which included four others, all with phones in hand, refreshing for emails. They opened their ranks, and we huddled together speaking only as loud as necessary to be heard.

"I guess you guys haven't heard from yours either?" the executive officer's, XO's, wife asked, already knowing the answer as we shook our heads. On the outside she remained, as she always was, cool, collected. "I wouldn't be too worried. It happens." Of all of us, she had the most experience, the most deployments under her belt. She'd met her husband, now the second in command of the boat, when he was on his junior officer— JO—tour, as several of our husbands were on now. She had at least ten years more with the Navy than I did—I was sitting at a measly three-ish. I'd been hoping her answer would be a little more rousing or inspirational, but she never faltered. I wondered if it was real or if she hid her worries behind smiles and nonchalance like I so wanted to. She was like a living mannequin, a model of what the perfect sub wife should be: always outwardly brave and resilient, never crumpling or giving in to speculation as we were now. If I'd told her that, she would've laughed me off because the model sub wife is humble too.

"Were they scheduled to *do* something?" Emma asked, implying more than she said. My thoughts turned to tomahawk missiles and covert missions in enemy water.

"I thought so," said another JO's wife, before quickly adding, "I mean, not that I really *know*, but with all that training, I'd assume." Prior to deploying, the crew spent hundreds of hours running drills for operations they'd carry out underway. "A proof-of-concept thing," Doug had called it months before, unable to tell me much else, even in the relative safety of our home. All the spouses nodded, remembering the late, late nights the sailors spent in trainers.

"Well, that was before all the breakdowns, right?" someone else chimed in. "They lost so much time right off the bat."

"Don't remind me!" Michelle laughed and tossed her head back in mock exhaustion. Her husband's division had been hardest hit when the *Georgia* required urgent repairs just hours out of their overseas port. Many members of the crew sacrificed days' worth of sleep on the repair. For a while the damage appeared so extensive, there'd been talk of them being towed home. "Can you imagine that?" We'd said. "A sub being *towed* back?" That casualty alone had cost the boat over a month of operational time and lost the families back home any chance of Christmas and New Year's together. Now their return home was predicted to be in late February or early March, but none of that was relevant till we knew they were still alive.

"Should we ask someone in the FRG?" The question floated out delicately. The Family Readiness Group was made up of all the crew's families, hundreds of spouses, parents, and children. Were they as worried as we were?

Another wife shook her head. "No. Keep it quiet. Don't cause anyone to worry or panic. That's the last thing anyone needs—a rumor. Quiet is normal."

"How often have you had this happen?" I asked the XO's wife across our circle. "How often are you waiting on an email like this?"

She rocked back on her heels. "I really can't remember. And honestly it depends on what boat they're on, what they're doing. The BNs don't transmit any messages while they're underway, you know? The fast attacks do their own thing too."

"Yeah, I guess." The *Georgia* was a GN, a "guided nuclear," distinguished by the type of payload she carried—guided missiles. Though she was equal in size to the subs carrying nuclear warheads, the Boomers, *Georgia*'s missions called for different levels of communication with the surface. Fast attack submarines were smaller, stealthier boats, and their transmissions were known to be in and out, making them more difficult to track. But that almost made it less nerve wracking, I thought, because at least you knew they'd be off and on, right? It was expected. I don't know why I wanted to speculate. It'd been a long time since a sub had gone missing anywhere in the world. None of us here had ever had to worry through that before, and I doubted any submarine spouse of any class of boat felt better for it.

"Are you doing ok?" The XO's wife eyed me steadily, seemingly ready for whatever answer I gave—whether I put on a brave face or owned up to the hysteria.

I didn't know what to say. This was only my second deployment. I looked at Michelle and Emma, on their third and first deployments, respectively, and half shrugged, half laughed. "I *guess*?"

"I'm not!" chirped the Weapon's Officer's wife, breaking the silence and throwing up her hands. "I can't sleep! I don't know what to tell my kids! I can't turn on the news!" She was technically on her first deployment. Her husband's time on submarines had been limited to shipyards and sea trials, but never an actual stint overseas.

"Me neither!" shouted someone else. "I've been taking Ambien to sleep. Haven't said a word to the kids."

"I'm stress-eating like hell. So many Oreos."

"My mother-in-law calls me every fucking day about the *San Juan* like I've got the answers."

"I thought I was being smart by watching all the *San Juan* coverage on the Spanish channel. But I guess the phone calls with *tia* have my kids picking up more than I counted on. They're not the anxious types though. They're better than me."

"So tough, so strong," someone interjected, and we all nodded at the strength of military children.

"We're still sending him emails every night. I think it helps."

"So glad mine doesn't understand any of this yet; I only have to console myself."

"I've cried so much my dog told me to see a therapist."

Our whole circle dissolved in laughter. Other shoppers were watching us now, but no one minded. All the secret talks were over. Now we were just women laughing—something resembling normal. I felt the weight rise off my chest, buoyed up by the commiseration of these wives, this group of women I'd so dreaded becoming one of. Until Michelle had asked, I didn't know if I was the only one without emails. Until we'd gathered, I thought I was the only one coming unhinged. *What would I do without them?* I wondered.

As we left the store and walked to dinner in the balmy evening air, the XO's wife stayed beside me. "It really will be ok," she said. "Every deployment has some crazy stuff happen and it's never the same as the one before. Eventually, nothing surprises you anymore; so, you have that to look forward to!" The prospect of a whole career, a whole twenty years married to the Navy, still made me shudder but, with support like this, it seemed less impossible than before.

At dinner, we toasted to the holidays, to one another, and to the *Georgia* for bringing us all together. We paused for our spouses wherever they were, whatever they were doing, and prayed for their safety. We prayed for the missing *San Juan* and all her loved ones. I prayed silently for an email. It felt selfish, but at that point, I'm sure we all did. And I was so, so thankful to be part of that *all*.

CHAPTER 2

Wife Stuff, One

"You nervous?" my husband asked, just outside the bar. Tonight, Doug was being hailed—officially welcomed to the USS *Georgia*. It was late November 2016.

I didn't answer. Of course I was nervous. I wasn't ready for this at all.

"Don't be. You've got nothing to be worried about."

It was so like him to say something like that: so sweet and reassuring, yet completely out of touch. What did *he* know about my nerves? He was the sailor. He had a place here. He had been called upon. I was just the spouse. What did he know about meeting the other wives for the first time? What did *I* know?

The first submarine wife that came to us was a whirl. She was supermodel tall, had stunning dark eyes, and spoke so quickly I didn't catch her name. Immediately she took my phone right out of my hand and created herself a contact with an anchor emoji beside her last name—"so you can find me easier later"—then looked herself up on Facebook, requested herself as a friend through my profile, and accepted from her own phone, all as she and her husband were calling to check on their babysitter. She wished me a Merry Christmas and said she'd see me in a few weeks. For what, I didn't know, but my husband Doug and I were barely inside and already we'd been flooded.

Doug was being hailed in a dingy bar in downtown Jacksonville, Florida. It was our first wardroom party, and technically a Hail and Farewell, which also saluted—farewelled—the boat's departing officers, moving on from the USS *Georgia* to their next duty stations, at the same time it welcomed the new ones, like Doug, who had checked into the boat just a few days prior. Hail and Farewells are casual, no-uniform functions, usually held in dives like the one we were in, or trendy breweries so the booze and conversation flows freely. Sometimes a senior officer will invite everyone to their backyard and cook for the whole wardroom. Gag gifts are exchanged along with raunchy stories and inside jokes from underway. While two officers were leaving the command, this particular night, Doug was the only new officer at his Hail, making me the only new wife.

I was unbearably fidgety and self-conscious. The black blouse and jeans I'd ransacked the closet to find felt all wrong. I couldn't stop fidgeting with the buttons on my cardigan, and my lipstick—a deep berry shade I'd hardly ever worn—was too vibrant, too done-up for the crowd we were with. I'd put it on because I remembered reading somewhere that wearing lipstick increases self-confidence, but I must have applied it too thickly, or my lips were too dry because it started to flake off as soon as we arrived and I chewed at the skin compulsively. The opposite effect, at best.

"Oh, I like your lipstick. It looks nice," said a friendly, short-haired woman who'd come our way. In a wave of courage, I opened my mouth to ask which sailor she was married to, but she continued, "I never get to wear fun lip stuff anyone. Can't with the uniform, you know?"

She was another sailor, not a spouse. My courage sank, and I wanted to slip away to wipe off the lipstick entirely, but every time I tried, another member of the command team or a department head would walk over, clap Doug hard on the shoulder, and tell him he was *in for it*, and laugh. To a wife and a worrier, it was disheartening at best.

Beside me, with a foamy beer in his left hand, Doug kept trying to loop his right arm behind my back in a gesture of comfort, a recognition of my uneasiness, but we were so mobbed by his new shipmates, and he was repeatedly being pulled away to shake hands and then shake hands again. Some of the sailors came back for second conversations about his time at submarine school, or to ask how the check-in process was going. Sailor talk—things outside my scope.

A few of the better conversationalists included me and asked if I'd be working in Jacksonville while the boat was gone. Earlier that week, I'd accepted a position teaching middle school reading at a Title I public school on the outer edge of Duval County. I'd never taught before, wasn't certified outside of the three-year temporary license the State of Florida granted me for having a BA in English, but I was quietly thrilled to be able to attach my identity to something other than my husband. I was a teacher, not just a Navy wife—the uncomfortable moniker that hung around my neck like dog tags, labeling me, I felt, as an accessory, an observer, or, worst of all, one to be pitied. The one about to be left behind to wallow and pine—that was a Navy wife. A *teacher*, though, had students, a classroom, grades, and curriculums to occupy her. She could survive independently without worrying about the Navy and where it took her husband.

I'd hoped this Hail and Farewell would be a chance to meet more spouses with careers to see if my impressions were on track but, from my limited vantage point, tucked up against a wall, it looked like there were only a few other spouses in attendance.

The second wife to come our way introduced herself as the Ombudsman—a term I'd never heard before and was too reluctant to sound *new* asking what it meant. She was loud, bright, and sounded genuinely happy to meet me, but I was most intrigued by the fact that she had a wriggling infant cradled in one arm. She was still breastfeeding, the wife explained without my asking. Their sitter canceled last-minute and she wasn't about to lose a night where she could use her husband as a designated driver. "You'll miss that when the guys go out. Trust me. Download Uber. It's not free like the hubby, but it's better than going dry." She slapped her husband on the arm, grinning as she talked. By the time she walked away I'd already forgotten her name as well. I was going to suck at this.

There was one other wife there, but we never got to talk. She waved at me from a corner where was she was trapped behind another group's conversation, and I waved back, leaning behind Doug while she motioned at me, mouthing the words, "see you next time." I still had no idea what or when *next time* was, except that it was in "a few weeks" as the first wife had said but then, the Captain called everyone to his attention and started off the evening's speeches by wishing us all Happy Holidays, passing out bottles of champagne, toasting to "the Good Ship *Georgia*," as he called her, and reminding us that deployment was less than two months away. "So, start getting ready." Everyone around us looked so, so happy.

I sobbed in the car on the way home, completely overwhelmed by all the new faces, the commotion, and, mostly, by hearing deployment spoken about aloud as an inevitable absolute for the first time. It was the thing I'd dreaded more than anything, and now it was practically kicking down the door.

Teaching job or not, I wasn't ready to be left behind.

For eight years, I'd been by Doug's side as he prepared, achieved, then worked his way through training for this dream: to serve as an active duty member of the United States Navy. I'd been his high school sweetheart as he applied for the NROTC scholarship, his steady college girlfriend as he got up early before class for physical training and drills, his fiancé standing beside him as he commissioned, his bride a few weeks before moving cross-country, and now his wife of just over a year and a half who'd supported him through the nuclear training pipeline that brought him here to the doorstep of deployment.

I'd wanted nothing more than to be all those things, to fill all those roles, to a point. Being a girlfriend, fiancé, and wife to Doug felt right. I knew how to love Doug the civilian. Being a *Navy* any of those things threw it all off-balance. How do I love the active duty sailor? I couldn't figure out what type of wife he needed me to be now, or what I was supposed to do for him while being quickly dwarfed by the upcoming underway, by the Navy itself. How does one learn to be a spouse to the world's most powerful maritime force?

On top of it all, I still had no idea what this mysterious upcoming wife-event was.

The morning following the Hail and Farewell, I got an email from the XO's wife, apologizing for not attending—her son was in a biting phase, they couldn't risk a sitter—and inviting me to her home in a few weeks' time for a dinner and craft night with the other wives. *So this,* I thought, *is the next time.*

"The guys," she explained, "will be doing certifications all night, so we like to get together, have dinner, and make them placemats and halfway boxes for the deployment."

I liked that she called them "the guys." It was comforting to hear someone talk about Doug as a person again, a *guy*, not as a *sailor*, or *shipmate*. But as for everything else, I had no idea what she was talking about. Who on deployment eats off a placemat? "And what the hell is a halfway box?" I remember asking Doug, still half-asleep beside me in bed as I read the email. He had no idea, nor did he seem to care. He was new too, and this was clearly *wife stuff.* He rolled over, pulling the quilt with him, stirring up that sweaty morning smell I hated, but would woefully miss in a month or so.

I wanted to be more excited for the get-together, but I was still so deeply put-off by the idea of being a military spouse, it seemed impossible. Every day I felt further pushed into the role of *waiting woman.* The wife who, in the old movies, sits by the window, longing for her uniformed husband to saunter back down the sunny lane, returning home after years apart. In those war movies, the waiting woman is the one whose photograph stays tucked in the doomed soldier or sailor's helmet or breast pocket. Sometimes she gets a flashback montage or speaks clandestinely across time and space to the hero as he gets shot full of holes and fades out on the battlefield, or as the hull of the ship is breached and the hero is trapped in rising water. If she's lucky, she gets to collapse weeping in the fresh dirt over his grave. I say "lucky" because very few submariners who die onboard their vessels will get an earthen grave. Their final resting places are watery and far out of reach. While I knew Doug's chances of being shot, fading out, drowning, or even wearing a Kevlar helmet were low, it wasn't how I wanted to see myself or our future—one-dimensional and defined by Doug's absence. Could I not just be a teacher, and, he, a sailor?

Waiting, for me, held such a powerful stigma I couldn't see beyond it. A modern woman made her own decisions and steered her own future. Her goals came first and she only accepted a partner who felt likewise and supported her in every possible way. She put herself before all others. So therefore, waiting for a man, following him, even as he went off to war, was a choice of weakness. No matter how objectively happy I was to be married to Doug, no matter how excited I was to have made that choice, I felt like I'd done it at the expense of who I wanted to be and now, my only role was to wait.

I wanted us to be husband and wife, *Sam-and-Doug*, equal partners. Even more, I wanted our marriage, our relationship, our little family of two and a dog, to be the guiding force of our lives and what we poured our energy into. I wanted to give equal space to each of our goals so that we could help each other climb and celebrate along the way. But of course, Doug was the one going out to sea; he was the one fighting, therefore, the one in need of attention.

Everything in those last few weeks together revolved around him and getting him prepared to go underway for the first time. There was not a day the deployment didn't insert itself between us: we shopped for it, packed for it, signed papers for it, and, even when we went out on our last few date nights, or to see friends, it was all we could talk about. Once or twice, we'd talk for a minute about our dog or my new students; sometimes he'd mention a fellow junior officer's wife, whom he wanted me to meet, but mostly we talked about the logistics of his leaving: what type of towels he should bring, the cheap terry cloth kind or the expensive but absorbent microfiber? What number of undershirts and pairs of socks? Should he bring bungee cords, like some of his fellow officers suggested, or bunker netting to rig up extra storage above his rack? How many little tubes of toothpaste would get him through the projected four months at sea? What if they got extended and he ran out? Unfamiliar as these conversations were, they were essential to ensuring a successful underway. Whatever that meant.

There I was for all of it. Up close and unable to back away from the deepening sadness that closed in over our home in the weeks before his departure, always rising faster than I could kick to the surface, no matter how much I needed a gulp of air. But he was the one for whom the air was meant, it seemed, not me. I needed to learn to go without. Sub wife—always second to duty, always just below. There was a love triangle between me, him, and the Navy, but it was completely lopsided. I was the other woman getting in the way of their rightful union.

If the Navy wanted him to have a wife, they would have issued him one. That's how the saying goes. By the time he checked into the *Georgia* in November, 2016, I'd read every article, every etiquette book from every era, every memoir, every Pinterest post, and every single Navy wife blog I could click. Doug could talk to me all day about his job, about his boat, about the crew, but he couldn't tell me a single thing about being married to a sailor. That was something I needed to learn on my own, so, like I'd been assigned a research paper, I cracked the books, desperate for some idea of what I was getting into, or of how to be what Doug needed. All my reading assured me that I knew the general "types" of wives I could expect to meet when Doug joined a sea command.

The Answer Book on Naval Social Customs from 1956 and the *Navy Spouse's Guide* from 2002, which, for all the decades between them make equally valid and timeless points about the importance of having quality pantyhose and a good sense of humor, are generally vague when it comes to "defining" spouses. They both say what a Navy wife should be (patient, supportive, resilient) and what she shouldn't be (spiteful, needy, easily disappointed). While they mention certain mild *faux pas* that I had already committed (going to the commissary in gym clothes, wearing flip flops places other than the pool, calling a commanding officer *sir* instead of his first name after he invites you to do so) the biggest spousal offense they caution against is confusing your husband's rank for your own. You are a wife. You have no rank. A captain's wife, for example, while etiquette dictates that she merit a certain amount of respect, does not have the authority to boss around more junior spouses or act as if she "ranks" above them. I, as the spouse of an O-2, a Lieutenant Junior Grade at the time, was not "above" any of the enlisted wives or Ensigns' wives. As a spouse, you are just a spouse. The job is the job, and it is not *your* job, no matter how much it affects your daily life. Doug used the term "Collar Flipper" to describe sailors who pulled the rank card on other sailors—describing the way they'd conspicuously flap the rank insignia on the collar of their uniform to remind their intended audience who was above whom. He had another name for them: assholes. "Even if sometimes, you do need to pull rank to keep your division on track," he said, "you don't need to be a jerk about it." Collar Flipper wives, I conjectured, were the ones who would ask your husband's rank before your name. Without ever having met one, I was sure Collar

Flippers existed in no small number if they merited a note in spouse guides from two different centuries.

After the books, I tackled the blogs I'd found through Pinterest or simple Google searches. Almost every single military wife or mom blog had their own version of a list of types of wives a new spouse was "sure to encounter"—*encounter*, like an animal in the wild. Was I on a spouse safari?

There would be the Super Moms who organized boat-wide playdates and created dozens of diversions to fill the days for their little ones. Everyone likes Super Moms, they're fun to be around, especially if you've got a kid as well, but it's hard to emulate them which can leave any "non-super" feeling inadequate and dull (and a lot of them are probably secret drinkers, I'd guess.) The Workaholics would be the ones buried in their careers or their education. They'd show up to boat events after working hours in skirt-suits or slacks just to make sure you knew they were employed and they were fiercely proud to have a life outside the Navy—supposedly, they'd talk about it often to anyone who'd listen. Then there'd be the Winos who drank to cope, the Worriers who tried to drag other people into their spiral of panic, and the Helicopter Wives who hovered around their husbands, trying to defend them from criticism or singing sugary praises to the command team, constantly sticking their noses in where they weren't welcome or qualified to be.

I laughed reading about the *Hoo-ya* wives—Doug called them *moto*, short for *motivated* which, in the military, is not often a compliment. *Moto* wives went to every FRG meeting, baked cookies for every event, completed every look with patriotic "Navy Wife" tees, and decorated their cars with stick figure families, the stick-husband always dressed in boots and camo. They were explicitly described as intense and over-involved. There would of course be the unflappable veteran spouses with ten or more years under their belts, and the dreaded *depend-opotomuses*: the ones who marry in to glom off their sailor's paycheck, often depicted in online comics as corpulent and nagging with dozens of unattended babies crawling around them like flies on a dung heap. More dependents, more money, it seemed. But it was always made clear, in all the spouses, that no matter what type of wife you were, you were, above all else, a *Navy* wife. These mothers, employees, cheerleaders, cookie-bakers, and naggers were only second identities, subcategorical to their paramount role as the dutiful wives of sailors.

You are there to prepare for his return. You are there to encourage the sailor and run his household in the meantime. Your worth is measured in how long and through what you're willing to wait.

I'd met only a handful of wives before Doug attached to the USS *Georgia*: two of his NROTC commanding officers' wives during college, and maybe three junior officers' spouses in Charleston, at Doug's Power School functions. The CO spouses were kind, but rarely present—training commands like ROTCs are incomparable to sea commands in terms of spousal involvement, I'd learn. The junior officers' spouses in Charleston were cordial but not particularly conversational. I can't blame them, blame *us*—it's hard to get a word in edgewise when all the majority of the room, the sailors, can talk about is nuclear propulsion systems and developments in the Tomahawk missile. The sailors' conversations sounded, sometimes, like a high school cafeteria filled with gossip about which overinstruct was the best to have for which checkouts they had to get signed on their qualification cards. However we wives didn't go to that high school, couldn't participate, so we'd hang back only half-listening, rarely taking that extra step to form our own conversation about whatever we may or may not have had in common. Beyond that, married couples were extremely outnumbered. Charleston was a training command full of young, single, newly-minted sailors. There weren't many wives to be met or categorized.

I often wondered what type of wife I would be, or rather, what type I would be seen as. Would there be a difference between the two perceptions, my own and the outside world's? The more I read and the closer we got to deployment, the more I could see myself becoming each type of wife. I didn't have a child, so I couldn't be a Super Mom, but I did have a very beloved dog, our gangly mutt, Louie, so I could easily become a Super *Dog* Mom. I am not a big wine drinker, but I enjoy anything on draught. Would I—could I be a *Beer-o?* It seemed unavoidable that I'd be a Worrier. Anxiety is my natural state. I'm just as natural a Workaholic though, and I was very proud to be teaching. It felt better to introduce myself as a middle school teacher than as a spouse. It was an identity both military and civilian people easily understood and respected. However, I attribute my Workaholic slant not to my role as a military wife or a desire to escape that role, but to, quite simply, my personality. I've always been an all-or-nothing kind of person. That far predated Doug and the Navy. "Go Big or Go Home" was the title of at least three of my college admissions essays and a supervisor once kindly described me as a "glutton for over commitment." She wasn't wrong.

Sometimes, when Doug did poorly on an evaluation or received criticism that seemed unfounded or undue, I'd have nasty Helicopter Wife impulses. If Doug came home a little down and told me what happened, I'd grumble about how stupid the instructor must have been to think or say what he had or hadn't. *You're an idiot. Don't take your bad day out on my husband*—things I'd say in my head, intending to say them to his face, if I ever got the chance. Of course, I never did. I have guts, but not a death wish.

On good days, I could feel how easy it would be to wear my bubbling pride in Doug on a *Love My Sailor* t-shirt or trade in my old water bottle for a shiny pink *Navy Wife* bottle from the spirit store on base. I once baked an assortment of cookies and Rice Krispy treats for Doug's Power School section the week they holed up in their windowless classroom, studying for their comprehensive exam. Did that make me *moto?* I was only trying to be thoughtful. While my paycheck went to our joint account and I pulled my weight around the house, I could still nag him like the best of the cartoon *depend-opotomuses*.

In all the lists of all the identities, I could never find one that fully described me, or defined that odd spot where I stood in relation to Doug and the Navy—reluctant but willing, unprepared but trying hard to be ready.

About the only thing I could assure myself of was that there was one type of wife I'd never be: a Collar Flipper. I understood that I had no rank, nor did I want one. I did not want to boss around any Ensigns' spouses or snub the enlisted sailors' wives. There was no joy in that, no satisfaction in some false sense of control. There's nothing like living under the thumb of the Navy to remind you that you have no power.

Hail and Farewell was a faraway blur. All I could remember about the *Georgia* wives was that they were tall, gorgeous, talked fast, and seemed to have themselves completely pulled together.

On the other hand, I had hardly been sleeping. If I thought too much about Doug leaving; I'd get dizzy and lightheaded. Sometimes I vomited after meals if he talked about deployment while we ate. My skin was blotchy and paler than normal, and my hands trembled if they weren't occupied. They got worse if I thought about making a bad impression on these fellow spouses, no matter what type of spouses they might be. The other wives had done this before, many times, and survived. I wanted to as well—desperately. They were the only military connection I'd have once the crew left. My immediate family, my friends, and coworkers were all civilian. I didn't want to come across to the seasoned wives as the fearful, doe-eyed, newlywed, in need of guidance and support, but of course that's exactly what I was.

CHAPTER 3

Waiting for Magic

When I met Doug Brown, he wasn't yet a sailor. He was a middle schooler, like me.

I'd known his name since sixth grade camp, when his cabin won the award for biggest bonfire. He was one of the Boy Scout, outdoorsy types with braces and buzz cuts, none of whom talked much to girls—definitely not as dreamy as the popular boys with their frosted tips and Hollister tees. I was the shy, bookish type, remarkable to no one. Doug and I had a few classes together each year, usually math or science. We were friendly, but not friends. On the weekends, he umpired at one of the local baseball complexes where my brother played. I would always point Doug out to my mom. "I go to school with him, Mom. That's Doug Brown." I mostly just remember knowing his name, *Doug Brown*. Short, sweet, and uncomplicated. Fun to say. It rolled quickly off the tongue. Doug Brown.

Back then, I wanted nothing more than to be a Sea World trainer. I wanted to be in the water, swimming with whales and dolphins every single day, performing in their shows, and educating visitors about marine mammals. That was the dream. In my journal, I'd write pages-long stories about being a trainer and saving Killer Whales, not quite realizing yet that writing was what would become my focus in the years to come, more than swimming with dolphins.

Most of my desire to be a trainer stemmed from my early childhood obsession with mermaids. I grew up watching and re-watching *The Little Mermaid* and *Splash* on VHS. So much so, that I used to spend every day of my summer pretending to be a mermaid like Ariel and Madison in my grandmother's subdivision pool, the main part of it, lap lanes with a diving well off the far side. The shallow end had long steps where toddlers played and a tanning ledge with just a few inches of water to cool its slowly baking loungers. Adjacent to the main pool was a large, rectangular kiddie pool, its corners always peppered with dead ants and drowning bees pushed there by the gentle movement of the water. Both pools were always that perfect, inviting shade of turquoise.

My mother would bring me to this pool almost every day of the season when I was a child while my baby brother napped at my grandparents' house just up the road. I'd hop around impatiently, breathing in the tang of chlorine while my mother slathered me with sunscreen before we left, so I was free to play while she lay out.

With goggles sucked tight to my face and legs pressed together like a tail, I would sink below the surface and turn into a mermaid. The pool was my ocean, my Atlantis.

For hours, I'd swim around, undulating along the bottom, which I imagined was full of bright coral and schools of talking fish. The deep end was a cave full of hungry sharks and sinister eels, or it was a sea witch's lair. The only way to escape was to swim down, touch the drain with both hands, where the water was coldest, then spring back to the surface, making it just in time before the shark's jaws closed on my magnificent fins. Sharks and eels couldn't be touched by sunlight in my ocean.

Breathing was for the ordinary. I'd toss rings far across the pool and see how many I could get in one breath, always forcing my lungs to hold off longer, to be less human. In time, I was able to go back and forth down the entire length of the pool without once coming up for air.

I loved the way there was no sound underwater except the muffled thumping of my pulse.

I'd hum songs and watch the bubbles rise or blow bubble rings. I could somersault forwards and backwards and twist about. Underwater, I was graceful and strong. I knew the currents and ripple of my little ocean as if I'd been born right there in the foam of the waves.

For a time, I was so committed to the idea that I was a mermaid that I imagined if my feet were touched by salt water, by the waves of a *real* ocean, they'd actually transform into a mermaid's tail and I could swim out to sea where I truly belonged.

As I got a little older and grew out of my days playing pretend, around when I met Doug, I read books about working at Sea World and would use my hours at the pool to "train" for the job. I'd practice my strokes, time how long I could hold my breath, and retrieve weights off the bottom and swim with them down the lanes like a trainer would a bucket of fish or piece of equipment.

It was the best feeling in the world, being underwater. Completely weightless, the air escaping from my hair as I sank to the bottom, erasing the things that made me heavy. By holding my breath, it was like I switched off a part of my brain that I understood from a very early age, was not right. Misfiring. It clung to bad news and swirled it around and around until I would obsess over things like a missing library book or, years later, my dad flying for work after the Towers fell in New York when I was nine. My heart would race all day and I wouldn't be able to sleep, no matter how exhausted I was. I'd cry when John Denver played on the radio because in his song where he left on a jet plane, he didn't know when he'd be back again. The lyrics would burn right through my chest. I was so afraid of losing people I loved. In those days, my parents traveled often, and when they did, my brother and I stayed with the same grandparents whose house was just up the road from the subdivision pool. They'd cook our favorite foods, play games with us, take us on weekend excursions, and read endless bedtime stories every night when we stayed with them. For more years than I can count, despite all the love, attention, and bedtime stories I received from my doting grandparents, I would end each night sniffling and sobbing big, fat tears, missing my parents. It did not matter how safe I knew I was, nor how loved they made me feel, everything was *wrong* until my whole family was home, together, like I thought it should have been all along. I was so afraid of being left behind.

My parents, back then, described me to friends and family as a *worrier* when they thought I couldn't hear them. They said it ran in the family. Just like my mother, just like my grandmother. But I looked at my mother and grandmother and saw two normal women, if anything, I saw easygoingness and calm so I assumed the static in my head would fade as I got older. It would all be ok one day.

Instead, the fear of being left behind grew with me, through high school and college, and I learned to live with it, never seeking treatment. In time, the rhythm of it became a part of me, just as a tide is part of an ocean. It stopped feeling like something I needed to be ashamed of or avoid. It was just the way I was. I fought to make myself the best of the best, un-leavable. Often, I wonder if seeking help or treatment in my youth and adolescence would have made the Navy days any easier.

There were waves. The highs were times of stress and hyper-energy— when I'd work the hardest and be the most accomplished student, teammate, daughter, sister, friend, girlfriend, and whatever else I could be. The best anything. I'd say *yes* to everything: volunteer projects, leadership positions, study groups, committee meetings, writing contests, internships, and swim meets. I'd put myself in charge of massive efforts to start and direct a children's choir for a low income community or solicit, illustrate, and print books of students' poetry for a local hospital. I was especially dedicated to my writing projects because, by high school, I'd realized that I *loved* to write. My English teachers would save my essays to use as examples and introduced me to the idea of publishing by helping me enter contests and submit to student journals. One of my favorite teachers suggested I become a writer or a professor—I rejected the idea at first, but as my involvement in creative writing deepened, the thought began to percolate.

I'd usually have a craft project or two going at the same time under the guise that painting or needlepointing would be therapeutic and relaxing when, in reality, it just added more weight to my heavy load. In one year of high school alone, I swam for two teams, played water polo for two other teams, sang and danced in my school's competing show choir, and had a soprano spot in the all-female a cappella group. I was in nine honors societies and held leadership positions in two of them. Water sports remained my favorite because the water still had enough power to put my horrible, swirling thoughts temporarily at bay. Nothing could stop me from overcommitting, even when I started to drag. My parents never seemed to worry because my GPA remained above 4.0 and, with every passing semester, as my children's choir, writing projects, and myriad of other ventures came to successful fruition, my résumé grew more and more impressive. I was praised, awarded, and lauded. The highs were so high.

Eventually though, I'd run out of steam, drained of all my energy, and let the exhaustion close in over me. During the lows, I struggled to get out of bed. I'd forget to eat or eat too much and spend long hours crying into my pillow when I should have been sleeping, completely overwhelmed and immobilized. I'd go to school the next day running on empty, barely able to function. Worst of all was that I'd never see it coming. There was no clear pattern or obvious trigger anymore as I'd had in childhood when my parents traveled, and I knew their leaving would cause me pain. Sadness would just arrive like a swell in the dark and wash over everything. A lot of the time it felt like I was caught in an undertow that was impossible to kick free of. Not once did I ask for help or think that what was happening to me wasn't healthy or right. Everyone said highs and lows were a normal part of life, so I let the lows in. That habit, that inability to see the problem right in front of me, sank me often. It sank me deep.

Sometimes, it felt like the only way out of all my obligations, all my commitments, and all the stress of keeping up the impression that I was, without failure, part and parcel of all these accomplishments was to dissolve away like sea foam.

The shallow part of my childhood swimming pool was where I went to save the sailors from the sinking ship in the storm. Swimming hard against the imaginary swells, I'd rescue the captain, recover the first mate, bring back all the members of the crew, dragging them ashore to the stairs, one by one saving their lives. But most importantly, I'd rescue the prince—a humble sailor himself—with whom I'd fall in love almost instantly because we were both of the water. I'd lie on the tanning ledge when no one else was around and imagine I was on some sandy beach with my shimmering fins in the foam, caressing the face of my handsome sailor, hopelessly in love. Hopelessly.

My mother would shatter the illusion by calling me over for more sunscreen. She'd let me take sips of her warm orange soda while she scolded me for getting burned on my shoulders or face, freckles covering my cheeks. I'd remind her that it was because mermaids weren't supposed to spend too long on the surface, or their scales would dry out and they'd lose their magic.

I did everything I could to keep from losing the magic.

I joined the high school swim team with girls who had also happened to have grown up as mermaids in their own subdivision pools. After freshman year, a few of us signed up for a summer strength training class to help stay fit in the off-season and check off our sophomore gym requirement ahead of schedule. Doug Brown was in the class too, fulfilling his physical education requirement so he could take a second band class during the school year. One of my teammates said he and a friend of ours would make a cute couple. She was right, but, for reasons I could not name, the idea bothered me.

Doug and I talked often on AOL Instant Messenger when we were supposed to be doing homework. He told me about his camping trips, his dog, and his dream of joining the Navy to see the world.

"What parts do you want to see?" I'd ask him.

"All of them. Any of them. I want to see it all."

"Will you enlist?" I asked him once, spinning in my desk chair, waiting for the *ping* of his reply.

"No, my mom would kill me. She says I need a college degree too, so I'm going to apply for the Naval Academy. If that doesn't work out, I'll do ROTC, or something." He was an obedient son.

I never dwelled on his Navy plans long then. That future seemed so far off and nebulous. "Tell me again about the night you camped in Minnesota. Tell me about all the stars." One of my favorite stories of his. He promised to take me to the same spot he'd been with his Scout troop someday, so we could lie under the same stars together. We were quite sappy in those early days.

By then, I'd adopted and embraced my English teacher's suggestion that I become a writer and professor, so I talked to Doug about my dreams of publishing novels and teaching young writers about literature and craft. His desire to be in the Navy didn't frighten me off the way it perhaps should have, or the way it might have if I'd realized that early on how very deeply in love I'd fall with him, how inextricably our futures were bound. I thought the want of a bigger tomorrow made him sound adventurous and brave.

"I'd like to see the world too," I told him. "Write books about it." What writer would balk when offered an adventure? Still, I did not fully grasp the role I'd have to assume for that to be a reality.

Both shy, we'd go to the movies with mutual friends as a buffer, hands resting side by side on the seats, never touching. Sometimes, if he stayed after school and his ride home was late, he'd come to my swim meets and sit in the bleachers. When I was in show choir, he played saxophone in the jazz band that traveled with us. We kept getting thrown together, and I very much enjoyed it. He asked me to be his date to the homecoming dance by typing out "H-O-M-E-C-O-M-I-N-G-?" on a graphing calculator in Pre-Calculus junior year. I said yes and wore a silver dress that shimmered when I moved.

To my friends, I confessed that I liked Doug but I was scared to do anything about it because it might change our friendship and make things between us awkward. I liked how mellow he was and how easily conversation came, how sincere he was. He liked to laugh at himself as much as anything else, wasn't cocky. I resolved not to tell him that I liked him. He was just a friend. It came out like one word: Doug Brown is *justafriend*. More than a little defensive.

My mother, all-knowing as mothers are, suggested I invite my *justafriendDoug* to a casual family gathering at our house with all my aunts, uncles, and cousins to watch a University of Missouri football game. When I'd asked him to come over, I'd forgotten to mention all the people who'd be there so when he rounded the corner from the foyer to the living room, the whole room full of adults turned around, "Doug!" They shouted his name, raising their drinks, and waving enthusiastically from the couches. My mother had briefed them without my knowledge, it seemed. Doug's face went pink, and I was sure I'd lost him, but he waved back, grinning, and shook my father's hand. We watched the football game in the basement with eight or nine of my cousins and played Apples to Apples between quarters. Doug was competitive, but instead of protecting his hand, he helped my youngest cousin, a second grader, read the cards he couldn't sound out and quietly traded when my cousin drew ones he didn't understand like *Jack Nicholson* and *Monica Lewinsky*. After that, I was hopelessly hooked.

On Doug's and my first official date later that fall, after we'd agreed that *yes* we wanted to try and be a "real" couple, we went ice skating. Doug held my hand for most of it, lacing his cold fingers between mine and talking low. About what, I can't remember. Neither of us can. It was so, so long ago. But I do remember saying something that must have made him laugh. He pulled me toward him, pressed his forehead against mine, and the warmth of our skins touching was so stark against the cold of the rink, I almost gasped. For our second date, we met at an away football game against our rival high school, since the marching band didn't have to play. I only remember two things about that date: first, that it was unusually frigid for the end of October and Doug, being chivalrous, offered me his school baseball hoodie to put over my jacket, which I accepted and have never given back, and second, that a good friend commented a while later that it was one of the last times she'd ever think of *Sam* and *Doug* in the singular sense because, after that, we were, to her, inseparably *Sam-and-Doug*.

Back then, we were only allowed to see each other outside of school one day a week because getting good grades was the priority, according to our parents who set all the rules. We watched a lot of movies in my basement and Blues hockey games in the winter, surreptitiously making out on the couch between periods the dead-silent way only rule-bound teenagers do. When he left for the night, my clothes always smelled like his: powdered Tide and Old Spice, with a hint of cigarette smoke from his mother's house. Another favorite haunt in those early days was the expansive park near my house full of walking trails and hidden bridges where we could lock lips without being seen. So similar were our upbringings in strict households, we gravitated toward places where parents wouldn't walk in or strike up a conversation.

The pull toward Doug was otherworldly. It was as if we operated on the same plane, or all the molecules in our bodies were vibrating on the same wavelength. We were each other's opposite: he, the left brain, I, the right. We complemented well and conversations came easily. What made me laugh, he laughed at too.

When I was having what we called then a *bad day*—when the swirling thoughts grew menacing—his voice, or the feel of his hands on my shoulders was enough to ground me for a while and give me focus like the water always had before. He'd talk through my worries logically, propose alternate solutions from other perspectives and it bewildered me sometimes, how easily his mind could cut through the sludge of my anxieties. Doug calmed the waves so that when we were together murky waters turned calm and clear as glass.

I believed in fate and in signs. I believed there was something or someone out there in the universe, perhaps God, perhaps some other powerful force, some magic, telling us we were meant to be together.

But by all logic we never should have made it. Doug and I should have ended our relationship right about the time we hit college because that was when he stopped being just *Doug* and became a *midshipman*—a future Naval officer. We both attended the University of Missouri, Mizzou, in Columbia, Missouri, but he went on a full scholarship through the Naval Reserve Officer Training Corps program to study mechanical engineering and, when he finished, would have to pay back the Navy's investment in him by serving in one of four designations available to midshipmen: aviation, special warfare, surface warfare, or submarines. What got to me wasn't just that he *had* to pay them back, it was that he *wanted* to. More than he wanted to see the world, as he'd once said, he wanted to serve it.

Since he was a child, Doug had dreamed of flying. He wanted to be a pilot. After a childhood trip to the Naval Academy in Annapolis, he wanted to be a *Navy* pilot, an aviator, nothing else. I, on the other hand, had so romanticized the times where my family was all together, not separated by time zones and plane rides, that togetherness was all I'd grown to value in a future. I wanted evenings after work, weekends, vacations, the two of us together. Togetherness was inseparable from my idea of safety, which was, necessary for being *ok*. I wanted to come home after a long day of teaching, sit down, and write novels in the company of my husband. Doug being in the Navy would alter every single facet of that vision, turning times of would-be togetherness into long periods of solitude. I was leavable again.

Doug moved to school before I did, only by about a week, for a super-condensed version of boot camp called NSO: new servicemember orientation. His days were built around physical fitness challenges, dietary restrictions, and concentrated instruction in uniform care, basic drill commands, and the required conduct of a man or woman of the armed forces.

We Skyped near the end of that week, one day before the last of the training because he said he had time. I was so excited to see him. We hardly ever went without talking and it had been six days—what felt like an eternity back then. I was working as a lifeguard and had rushed home from my shift to shower and put on makeup before he saw me. I'd logged on early, carefully setting up my computer, so he'd see me in the best light.

He had his laptop set on the bottom bunk where he could see me from anywhere in the room, but I could only see him in brief blurs as he walked back and forth and all around the dorm, still full of suitcases and boxes from a hurried arrival, getting ready for his uniform inspections the next morning.

His connection was choppy and the sound came in and out. The few times he paused long enough to come into focus on the camera, I could see he looked sunburnt and gaunt. His already short hair had been buzzed down close to the scalp. I think I was recounting some forgettable story about my day lifeguarding when he suddenly let out one huge, speaker-shaking, "*Fuck!*"

I jumped. "Doug?" He hardly ever cursed. "What?" Was he mad at me? Had I said something wrong? Or did he stub his toe? Since the video feed was so pixelated, it was hard to say.

"I can't find my shirt. My yellow PT shirt."

"What?"

"My yellow *fucking* PT shirt!" He shouted, not at me. He was tearing around the room, throwing non-yellow clothes left and right, upending boxes, suitcases, chairs, bumping into things, looking for the uniform shirt the ROTC battalion issued him to wear during physical training. I could hear him panting even through my crackling speakers.

I tried to be helpful, squinting at his blurry room. "Is it here, on the bed?" On the right side of my screen I had the corner of something yellow in view. I pointed, as if it would help.

"No. That's my *other* PT shirt. I need *both* PT shirts."

I never should have asked. I should have let it go, hung up, and had him call back later. But I didn't. "Why? That's weird. What's the difference?"

My quiet, sweet, warm Doug, with whom I'd shared every bit of myself since we'd gone circles on that ice rink years before, turned his back to the camera and shouted even louder than the first time, "*You don't fucking get it, Sam!*"

And he was absolutely right. I didn't fucking get it. For the rest of college and many years into our marriage I wouldn't get it. I didn't understand the importance of not just wearing the uniform but maintaining it as well. I had no idea that the instructors would be dumping out each midshipman's sea bag to make sure they had all their issued pieces and that anyone missing, say, a yellow PT shirt, would be disciplined with push-ups, laps, or any other creative restitution the instructors could dole out. The military is not something made for outsiders to understand or feel kin to, even if their future is bound to it. In the name of camaraderie, morale, pride, and national security, it places a deliberate distance between those who are *in* and those who are, like me, *out*.

We fought after he told me I "didn't fucking get it." We fought hard. I accused the military of changing him already; he accused me of being selfish and naïve. Neither of us was wrong. I don't remember how the conversation ended but I remember bawling so hard afterwards, and for so long that my parents almost didn't let me move into my college dorm two days later for fear I'd do something rash.

When I saw Doug at school for the first time, I met him in the common area of his floor full of buzz-headed midshipmen and cadets from the other branches' ROTC units. Doug sat at a table in the middle of them all, scrubbing furiously at his oxfords with a cotton ball dipped in wet, black shoe polish. For an hour, I sat beside him, trying to make conversation.

"Have you picked up your books yet?"

"No."

"Did you try the donuts from Dobbs yet like you wanted to?"

"Not yet."

"How's your roommate?"

"Haven't met him yet."

It was like talking to a wall. Nothing like the Doug who used to talk for hours and hours about anything I'd like. Between the smell of the shoe polish, sweaty bodies, and the stagnant conversation, it got hard to breathe.

I waited an hour for him to finish polishing his oxfords so we could go on a walk around Mizzou's campus. Once we got out of his dorm, and we were finally able to talk out in the open air, he loosened up and I saw that though the changed had started, so much of him was still the same. He still walked with his feet turned out, still laughed at my stories, and even still smelled faintly of Tide.

"How was moving in? Did your clothes fit in the closet? How many books did you drag from home?" His voice seemed deeper and a little hoarse from all the orientation yelling and cadences. The old mixed with the new.

He was still Doug, but sometimes now, and with ever-increasing frequency, he was going to have to be the Navy's Doug, not mine. He was going to have to march and drill and keep his uniforms in order. And, one day, he was going to have to actively serve: train, deploy, return, train, deploy, return.

I tried for a while to simply accept Doug's new status as a midshipman and move on from there as if it didn't bother me, but it was more difficult than I expected. Because while I could certainly handle his college commitment of a few hours each week, and some weekends away, I struggled with anticipating all the years after college that the Navy now owned. Aviation, his dream career path, would cost him—cost *us*—ten years of our lives together, if we still wanted to be together, which we both agreed, we did.

That meant ten years minimum of moving around frequently to bases all over the world with no promise of university opportunities for me, no stability to build my career on. No guarantee of jobs or proximity to family. All it promised, for me, was at least a decade of waiting. Submarines, however, was only a five-year commitment, and it was statistically safer than flying planes or being stationed on surface ships. Because of the rigorous nuclear training program, going submarines offered Doug the best post-Navy career options as well. It still carried with it the geographic problem of fewer opportunities for me, but, again, the amount of time that would be a problem was cleanly halved. I posed the question to him: would he consider serving in the submarine force instead of flying planes, and making the Navy a career pit-stop, rather than a true, lifelong vocation?

We debated and argued about it for a long time. After many months, he agreed to go subs. But even after that, we still argued because I wasn't at peace with his choice to join the Navy at all. How could he, I wondered, honestly say he loved me if he was going to put me, with all my instability, my fears through multiple rounds of deployment on a sea tour? How could I claim to love him though, if I could not support his life's dream? It was an impasse we butted against for years and years, but one that was never able to eclipse what we both came to understand was the one solid thing we could agree on: despite all logic, and regardless of personal goals and well-being, we loved each other more than anything that might get in the way. We loved each other fiercely, stubbornly, and deeper than any submarine could dive.

I agonized often--probably more than I should have—to close friends about the situation. One friend, the same with whom I'd taken the strength training class all those years ago, told me I'd make a great military wife, saying, "You could write such great letters to him while he's gone." I tried for a long time to make that mean something to me, to turn it into proof of bravery or resolve.

Doug and I agreed, eventually, to no end in tension, that Doug would serve his required sea tour, then one shore tour so he could get his master's in whatever field he settled on, then he would leave the Navy and we could, as I put it, "start our lives." Though Doug would often remind me that the "Navy years" would be part of our lives too, and we would have to live them, one way or another.

"Whether we are together or apart, I'm going to be in the Navy now, I'm going to deploy. I'd really like you to be the one I come home to, Sam, but if you can't do it, I understand." That's what he said to me one night, while we sat on the wide base one of Mizzou's landmark columns in front of Jesse Hall. The air was sticky and smelled of cut grass and beer from the bars just across the street. Not far off, a band was playing. I wanted to bottle the whole of it up and keep it for when he was out to sea.

Hearing Doug say that he wanted me there for him when he got home was all I'd needed to push me over the edge. I still didn't want that lifestyle, not by a long shot. But maybe I could do it, could be strong enough, if I knew how badly he wanted me there. In the same way I'd imagine a doctor grits her teeth before resetting a broken femur, or the way a boxer braces for a punch they couldn't block, I gritted and steadied myself. "If we're going to do this, then let's do it together."

I'd decided I'd rather suffer with him than without him, even though technically I'd have to suffer without him no matter what.

That night, after our talk on the columns when we got back to Doug's dorm, we found that the temperature knob on his air conditioning unit was jammed on high, blasting the room with cold air. I put on his Navy-issued PT sweatshirt and was overwhelmed by the smell of Old Spice and Tide— the smell of him—just like the baseball hoodie I'd had since our second date. Although the PT sweatshirt was a required part of his sea bag, he never asked for it back, only borrowed it sometimes when a sea-bag inspection was scheduled. Eventually, he bought himself a new one, this time with a hood, so we'd never confuse which Navy sweatshirt was his and which was now, forever, mine.

Doug proposed four years later, on an unseasonably warm afternoon in February 2014, sitting on the same column we'd struck our bargain on years before. A month later, he interviewed in Washington DC and was selected for the Navy's Nuclear Training Program, committing to the submarine force. I graduated in May 2014, he, one semester later in December. The next day, he commissioned as an Ensign in the United States Navy. He asked me, along with his mother, to pin on his rank and stand beside him while he took the oath. My parents rented a party bus to drive my entire extended family in from St. Louis for the ceremony, most of the same relatives who had so boisterously greeted Doug when he arrived at our party all those years before. They all wore novelty sailor hats bought from a party store, got tastefully drunk, and made videos of themselves singing along to the Navy's march song, "Anchors Aweigh."

Doug and I were married in the Old Cathedral underneath the Gateway Arch three months after commissioning. We became the third generation of high school sweethearts in my family after my parents and my grandparents. My mother cried when she saw me in my wedding dress, an ivory creation made of scalloped lace and pearls with a veil that floated several feet behind me when I walked down the aisle.

Three weeks later, the Navy movers boxed up our first apartment while we sat on the kitchen counters and watched, clinking stale beers to our first permanent change of station, our first military *PCS*. After all those years of waiting, it was all about to get real, we said because we thought we knew. Doug had orders to the Naval Nuclear Power School in Charleston, South Carolina where he'd begin the year-long Navy nuclear training pipeline.

It took a full day to drive from our family homes in St. Louis to our new apartment in the suburbs of Charleston. It was a small, sunless place, just big enough for the two of us and the gangly puppy we'd adopt from the local shelter a few months later. It wasn't fancy, but it was under budget and only a few minutes from the beach—we couldn't have imagined better.

We didn't bother unpacking too many boxes our first night in Charleston. Instead, we drove to Sullivan's Island and stood with our feet in the sand, watching the orange sunset, turning in circles, in awe of the beautiful place we now felt a part of simply because we lived there. Behind us, Gatsbyesque beach mansions lit up their windows as the sky grew darker. Out in the water, among the paddle boarders, dolphins and their calves surfaced for air. Birds swung low as if suspended by wire, scooping fish out of the foam without making so much as a ripple, then swooping back upwards, gulping down their catch. Massive cargo ships pushed their way from the harbor out toward the smoky horizon.

I remember thinking about how happy my young, mermaid-loving self would have been to know that I lived in a place like Charleston, a place with dolphins and beaches and sunshine all year round. It was the type of place I dreamed of going to most of my life, but now that I was here, I felt jettisoned.

I had believed for so long in fish tales and fate. Would I have found myself here, with my toes in the surf of a place I no longer wanted to be, next to a man whose fate was now tied to the sea, if I hadn't grown up such a dreamer? Surrendering him to the Navy was my anxious mind's nightmare. *My heartbreak and hell*, I wrote in my journal that night. It felt like the beginning of an undoing.

The first time I saw the ocean, I was too young to remember. My parents took me to a beach in Texas when I was just a few months old. There are pictures of me in a ruffled hat and bright swimsuit, plopped on the sand between my father's feet looking generally indifferent to the experience.

I chose to ignore that trip to the beach when I was eight or nine and my family took what I called our first *real* trip to the beach. We went to Myrtle Beach, less than one hundred miles south of Doug's and my future home in Charleston. Because it was a short trip for my dad's work, we only had one afternoon free to swim in the ocean.

But one day was enough. I was resolved. This trip to the beach was going to prove it, I was sure. I was going to march my way down the sand, straight to the edge of the water, and say goodbye to my life as a human because the second the salt water hit my feet, I would be transformed. I would be enveloped in a glowing orb, or a burst of glittering light, and then I wouldn't be human anymore. I'd be a mermaid, just as I'd known I was all those years—I'd just lacked the proper body of water.

My parents made us cover up with oversized t-shirts in addition to our sunscreen to protect our pale, Midwestern skin. I complained, but I knew I wouldn't have to worry about sunburn after being transformed.

Of course, when the first wave lapped at my ankles, not a thing happened beyond my feet getting wet and sandy.

Maybe it was a bad wave, I reasoned, walking a little deeper. But wave after wave hit my legs and they remained just that: legs. On some level I suppose I knew that I wasn't really a mermaid. My skin felt gritty where the salt dried on it. Unremarkable.

I don't know how long I stood there waiting for magic to happen. Eventually I gave up and walked in deeper, letting the ocean move me as it rushed in. When I was deep enough to float, I lifted my feet, closed my eyes, leaned back, and let the salt water fill my ears.

Now it was Doug's turn to head for the water, to be bound for the murky depths. My new titles, slapped on overnight, like bumper stickers: MilSO—military significant other, Navy wife, and the one that rung in my ears like a siren, *sub wife*. The ocean was no longer a place of dreaming and fantasy, but of war, patrolled by things far more powerful and dangerous than sea witches or sharks. Duty was now the center around which we both revolved: his duty to the country, my duties as his wife. Magic wouldn't just happen on its own; magic would have to come from deep within me.

CHAPTER 4

Golden Girls

In December 2017, almost four months into our husbands' deployment, Michelle and I drove home from the wardroom Christmas party with the windows down. The rush of the wind made it so loud we could hardly hear Bing Crosby on the radio, but I didn't mind. Hearing carols at all made me feel guilty. In the very last email I'd gotten from Doug, he'd admitted how sad he was that he'd forgotten to download any Christmas music before he left: *as if things didn't suck enough down here, I don't even have the best part of Christmas.* When I replied, I didn't remind him that carols were only his second-favorite part—he wouldn't have the cookies either.

"That was fun," I shouted. "Tonight was fun!"

Michelle nodded as she swayed back and forth in her seat to Jingle Bells. "So much fun." I was designated driving but could still feel a hint of a warm buzz from my last sips of jalapeño margarita an hour and a half before. It was just enough to make me want to talk about the guys.

"You get any emails at dinner?" I asked.

"Nnnnope." Michelle shook her head and slumped toward the door, buzzing her lips in defeat. "It's bullshit!"

She laughed. Then I laughed. She laughed again. We kept laughing back and forth until we were completely giddy.

"Don't they know," she said, "that we're like dying here? There's literally a sub missing. No one knows where they went. Just *boom*. And ours can't even drop a little '*Hey no worries everything's cool! We're not all dead!*'"

"I know, right? Like, I'm sure the mission is important, but I don't think the world can take my crazy right now. Every day I'm one empty inbox from losing my mind, I swear."

Michelle was taking big gulps of water and messing with the radio. The rush of highway air grew deafening. "No one tells you it's going to be like this."

"Well, they do. But you don't get it until it happens. Then they act like you should've known the whole time."

"Exactly. *Fuck*ing hate it." She threw all her emphasis on the *fuck* of *fucking*. It was divine.

If I hadn't been driving, I would've leaned over and hugged Michelle. There was no relief as powerful as hearing someone else, someone whom you loved and cared about, admitting that this military life was killing them as much as it was killing you.

I wanted to be tough about it, I wanted to be strong but being the waiting woman was so much harder than I'd imagined it would be. The old war movies don't show the hero's sweetheart losing interest in her favorite things; they don't show her ignoring calls from loved ones just to avoid hearing her sailor's name or talking about him. They don't show her crawling into bed at seven o'clock and swallowing sleeping pills to escape her fears for just a few quiet hours. They certainly don't mention what happens when world events suggest your husband's submarine could possibly be wrecked at the bottom of the ocean. They only show what the fighting heroes go through. If this were Doug's movie, I wondered, what would we see?

"We can't live like this, worrying all the time," Michelle declared matter-of-factly, taking another swig from her water bottle. "It's going to kill us."

"Ok, what's the plan then?"

She barely hesitated. "If they're alive, great. We go on as planned." Another sip. "If they're dead? We *Golden Girls* it." Her expression turned deadpan.

"*Golden Girls* it?"

"Yep. We pool our survivors' benefits and go live together on the beach somewhere."

I wanted to laugh, but I couldn't. Somewhere between tipsy Michelle's steely forward gaze out the front windshield and the actual seriousness of the USS *Georgia*'s silence, her plan made perfect sense. Why wouldn't I want to live out my widowed days with the person who'd been for there for me the most?

"Ok, I'm in. What beach?"

Michelle reanimated. "Well, if we wanted it to be a short move, we could definitely take a look at St. Augustine but, personally, I don't want to stay in Florida."

"Definitely not. Too hot. Too many gators."

"North Carolina is a possibility, but maybe too cold?"

"What about South Carolina then? Like Charleston on Shem Creek or Sullivan's Island or something?" I recalled two of my favorite spots from when Doug and I lived there.

"Yes! Yes, I love that!"

"Obviously a place on the water."

"Or like, walking distance?"

"Yes. And with a good porch for sitting on."

"And room for a garden."

"Close to shops and restaurants."

"A nice kitchen, but not too big."

"A yard for the dogs."

"Of course. Paddleboards?"

"We'll definitely need paddleboards."

"And a pool?"

"How about a hot tub?"

"Both."

"Even better."

"It'll be great."

"So great."

I stopped talking when I realized that everything I was spelling out in my *Golden Girls* plan with Michelle was in my *rest-of-our-lives* plan with Doug: a house on the water, paddleboards, gardens, a pool, and big sunny porches. Was that why Michelle had gone quiet too?

Still, I was comforted. For the first time since almost Thanksgiving, I felt at peace. Yes, there was still a chance the world as I knew it would be destroyed. Everything I'd ever wanted and planned for with Doug could disappear with one phone call. But now, if the worst happened, I knew I wouldn't be doing it alone. Even if Michelle's plan was a tequila pipedream, I knew we were in the same place. We were just as committed to one another now as we were to our husbands.

War movies don't give the hero's sweetheart this moment: where she learns that, even if the worst thing happens, it will be ok. It will be ok because, no matter how lonely she is, she is not alone. For just a little while, it didn't feel like the worst thing in the world to be waiting for my husband to come home from war because the waiting wasn't an act of submission, but an act of camaraderie with the other spouses on the homefront.

Michelle stayed the night in my guest room. The next morning, we refreshed our emails over coffee at the kitchen counter, not saying much. We texted Emma to see if she'd gotten home alright the night before. She had. Michelle let her in on our *Golden Girls* plan. She said Charleston sounded perfect.

The rest of that Sunday that I should have spent grading papers, I spent on Zillow and Redfin looking at three-bedroom homes for sale in Charleston. It was the longest I'd gone without checking my email in days but, by the time I went to bed that night, the *Georgia* remained dead silent.

Before I slept, I wrote Doug an email about the day, as I always did. Every day I went without a reply from him I struggled more to make my mundane existence feel worthy of another message. I chose not to tell him that I'd spent my day looking for the house I'd live in if he died. I said I'd thought a lot about Charleston and missed biking to Sullivan's Island. I told him the Christmas party had been fun, and that I hoped he got to celebrate a little down there, even though I had no idea how far deep "down there" really was.

CHAPTER 5

Fallout

On September 12, 2001 my mother went into my playhouse and took down all my photographs of New York City.

She and I had been on a trip there just before New Year's Eve in 1999, before the turn of the century—a phrase I'm sure to use in my old age and want to demand some type of reverence from my grandchildren. The tickets were a Christmas gift from my father who'd planned a whole weekend of activities for us. She and I saw *The Lion King* on Broadway, walked through Times Square (where I marveled not at the bright lights, but at pigeons), and rode to the top of the Empire State Building where I took photo after blurry photo of the foggy cityscape on my disposable Fujifilm camera, clicking the shutter then quickly winding the wheel to advance the film and capture another nearly identical shot from a few feet further along the roofline. The Twin Towers appeared in almost all of my pictures. After the trip, when we'd returned to St. Louis and gotten the roll developed, I Scotch-taped each glossy print to the interior walls of my playhouse, trying to arrange them in balanced groups like my mother did when she hung pictures in our house, but there were so many the final result more resembled wallpaper.

When I was in fourth grade, and the North Tower was hit while I was getting ready for school, and the South while I was eating breakfast in the kitchen, I knew what buildings were being talked about on every broadcast station, radio program, and, not long after, printed in full color across pages in newspapers and magazines lining every grocery store checkout lane. The Pentagon took me longer to conceptualize, and I didn't know anything about the plane intended for the White House that went down instead in Shanksville, Pennsylvania until a while later. But I knew enough, however, of New York and the Towers to understand that the world had changed forever.

My parents did not shelter me from the broadcasts nor did they deny me answers to any of my questions, although I sometimes wonder if they had, would my worries have been any more manageable? They allowed me to read whatever I wanted and watch story after story on television. I was already a somewhat anxious child by nature and I sometimes wonder if my fixation on the attacks stoked my anxiety into an early forte, especially since my dad's job at the time require frequent travel by airplane and work in office buildings. For months after the attacks, I had vivid nightmares of jumbo jets slamming into my father's eight-story building in the suburbs of St. Louis. I dreamt I was standing across the highway, unable to tell if my father was inside the fireball or safely on the outside. I struggled to sleep and was eventually allowed to play a radio at night because my parents thought soft music would help me relax. Instead, I'd listen to the *Delilah* show, where callers from New York described their lost loved ones, pleaded for help, or recounted their harrowing escapes from the collapse.

When my mother went into my playhouse and took down my pictures, she collected them all in a manila envelope labeled *Samantha—NYC, December 1999, Twin Towers* and stored them in the basement safe. She apologized for baring the playhouse walls, but told me I'd want the pictures someday, to show my own children when I was older. I told her I understood because I believed I did.

There is a picture of me in Times Square from the second time I went to New York that my father often says is one of the best he's ever taken of me. I am fifteen years old in the photo, smiling at the camera, lit up all over by the flashing ads, pressing a cell phone against my cheek. My hair is short, just a few inches poking out from under my hat, because I'd broken up with a bad boyfriend earlier that year and had marked the end of the relationship with an impulsive trip to Great Clips. I'd cycle through one more bad boyfriend and bad haircut before my first date with Doug, my future husband, about a year after taking the photo in Times Square.

I was there because my dad flew in from St. Louis monthly and worked in New York City for the weekend. I was starting to look at colleges, so he bought me a plane ticket for a long weekend off school. By then, I'd shifted my career focus from animal training to writing at the encouragement of an English teacher who'd pulled me aside with a copy of my essay on *The Sea Wolf* and encouraged me to pursue scholarship opportunities with my writing, presenting me with contest flyers and brochures. He'd given the class an assignment to write a personal narrative over the long weekend. He told me to look at the assignment as a way to expand my portfolio.

Since my dad had to work on Friday during the day, I had the freedom to explore New York on my own. I wanted to see Ground Zero and, for my class assignment, write about what it was like to visit the site of the event that I felt had defined my childhood—given it a "before" and an "after." Even after eight years, the events of 9/11 still fascinated me. I wanted the chance to take in the actual site of all the horrors I'd now, essentially, grown up with.

Armed with my map, it should have been a short walk from our hotel in the financial district, but I got turned around and thought I was lost. It wasn't because I didn't know how to read the map, or because I got nervous and overwhelmed by all the tall businessmen in long, black overcoats flooding the streets, but because Ground Zero didn't look at all like the Ground Zero

I'd seen on TV. I'd pictured flowers, candles, cards, and signs drawn by children, American flags everywhere. But instead, it looked like any old construction site—one of countless in New York City. Of course, that was logical but, regardless, I missed it. It had been six years. Foundations were being laid for a new skyscraper and museum, a rebirth-esque testament to the strength and spirit of New York and, by extension, the country entire. I kept walking past it, looking down at the map, then up at the fence, wondering how I was supposed to get around this massive crater and find Ground Zero. For almost an hour, I circled the blocks around the footprints, not realizing where I was.

What eventually clued me in was a group of people, other tourists, gathered around a small sign with a computer-generated illustration of the future Freedom Tower. I didn't take any pictures there, but I spent hours outside nearby Trinity Church photographing its silhouetted spires, headstones, and the reaching fingers of trees against the skyscrapers.

Instead of writing about what it was like to see Ground Zero, I wrote my narrative about getting lost in Lower Manhattan and, with it, earned my first college scholarship.

Doug and I met up in New York City in September of 2016, about a year and a half after we got married, for a short weekend getaway while he was off attending Submarine school in Groton, Connecticut, and I was still living in Charleston, South Carolina, in our first apartment. He'd never been to New York, so we packed our schedule with activities. We crossed the Brooklyn Bridge, watched the boats in Central Park, and squeezed our way through packed Times Square, where I recreated the picture my dad had taken of me the last time I visited, phone up to my ear, grinning. We went up and down Wall Street and circled Trinity Church, which was closed for renovations. I pointed out all the things I'd photographed and written about as a teenager. Some of those photos still hung around my desk in our Charleston apartment, as did the scholarship certificate from the homework narrative about getting lost. We were tired from walking, but most of our exhaustion was emotional. We'd spent nearly six hours that day in the 9/11 Memorial & Museum.

Inside the museum, beneath the reflecting pools where crowds gathered reverently as the sun came up, the space was huge, the ceiling stretching higher than I imagined possible, as if to make room for all the heaviness down at eye level. My husband and I started off being pulled in different directions by what grabbed our attention, like we were caught in our own currents.

Doug was captivated by the colossal bars of steel, folded in half by the heat of the fire, and twisted like soft clay during the Towers' collapse. Bolted above the museum floor for viewing, from below they looked suspended by invisible thread or God Himself. I found myself riveted in the darkened memorial room, listening to clips recorded by loved ones, speaking about the lives and final days of their dead. The structure and the stories—Doug, the engineer; and me, the writer—our paths seemed laid out before us.

As spouses, Doug and I often complement each other in this way: he likes to know how things work or fail, whereas I like to know about the people who make those things work or fail. Sometimes, it makes it hard for us to agree on things because no matter what we're looking at, our perceptions are so different.

It took me a long time to leave the darkened room and search for my husband again among the photographs and exhibits—I didn't want to drift away from him anymore. My legs felt limp and wobbly, my head like it was floating inches above my shoulders, tossing and spinning around. It would be inaccurate to say that, over the years, I'd forgotten about 9/11. I never would. Who could? But this was the first time I'd seen 9/11 not through the eyes of a distant bystander, or a child, but those of an adult, a twenty-four-year-old military wife. Previous memories seemed distant now, like the thoughts of some other person who I barely knew.

In all the museum's photographs the rubble still looked like rubble, the dust cloud still looked like dust, but the faces were different. As a child, when it happened, it was possible that I saw them all like characters in a movie. Real, but not-real at the same time. I knew they felt pain, and it was deeper than any pain I'd ever felt, than most have felt, but I was separated from it, as if by a fence. But now, the pain, as it appeared photographed and displayed all over the museum's walls looked different, almost undefinable. I wanted to believe I understood each face, but of course, I never could. All I could genuinely take away was that these were real people, just like me, just like Doug, just like everyone around us in the museum, who were and still are in need of protection. Doug now had the opportunity to serve them, as did I, by extension—albeit in a very different way. All the photographed faces, though they were of the past, to me now, looked like the future. Doug's overarching role as a service member was to prevent this type of tragedy from ever happening again, prevent these types of faces from needing a museum and memorial at all.

I've asked Doug many times over the thirteen years we've been together why he chooses to serve and been wholly disappointed by the simplicity of his answers: *because I've always wanted to, because I just have to, Sam.* Though he's never said it outright, I always wonder if Doug was one of many who decided what they wanted to be when they grew up on that bright September morning. I thought about asking him when I found him again, nearly running into him in my daze, but all I could manage was, "Stay by me, ok?" He nodded.

In an open foyer between two rooms sat a fire engine, bathed in spotlights. The back half was sheared off by a falling beam during the towers' collapse, all the insides hanging out like veins from a severed limb. Doug bee-lined to the tangle of pipes and wires, examining them with squinted eyes. I circled slowly, more transfixed by the other visitors than by the engine. There was no face untouched by emotion. Some sobbed freely and without abandon—men and women alike. Others dabbed gently at the corners of their eyes. I had a few tears dried on my face, ones I hadn't even realized I'd shed. Doug's face was drawn tight, his jaw twitching. It'd been too long since he'd gotten his standard Navy-buzz haircut but, the way he was clenching his face, he looked as chiseled and military as ever. Even the tendons in his forearms were jumping when he folded them. He looked strong. A man next to him dug into his wife's purse for a tissue and scrubbed at his eyes. She didn't seem to notice. Where were they when it happened? How did the towers crash down into their lives? It felt a little like standing around the casket at a wake. Though we grieved as a group, we allowed each other the space, the compassion, to mourn in our own ways.

When we were there, standing before the fire engine, the museum had been open only an hour and already attendants were refilling the tissue stands that stood like sentinels around the broad space.

In an adjoining exhibit, set up as a minute-by-minute timeline of the day and all the events that precipitated, a small video screen played a three-minute segment of the Today show on loop: Matt Lauer interrupting his interviewee, cutting to commercial, and then reappearing beside Katie Couric at a news desk, just as bewildered as the parents and their children watching miles away still getting ready for work and school, just as I had been at my mother's kitchen table.

All around it was as silent as church—the space too reverent for speaking. The only sounds I could pick out with regularity were sniffling noses and the *swish-swish* of tissues being pulled out two at a time from the newly-filled stands. I tried to let my feet roll gently across the cold stone floor, heel to arch to ball, not shuffle or squeak, lest they make any noise that took away from the awe around us. The whole place felt like a vacuum.

Doug stayed near me in the timeline exhibit. He put his arm through mine and let me dab my eyes on his jacket sleeve, something he usually hated, when I learned for the first time that there had been children on the plane flown into the Pentagon—they got a small mention on a wall placard. In one corner, veiled away by a partition for those who might find it too hard to look at, was a photographic vignette of those who jumped. Here I lingered, recalling writer Brian Doyle's words of reflection on an unknown couple who leapt from the South Tower, hand in hand, choosing death by falling over fire. Their photo was featured behind the curtained display: "extraordinary ordinary succinct ancient naked stunning perfect simple ferocious love…love is why we are here." Doug held his hand on my back, just between my shoulder blades.

One of the last rooms of the timeline exhibit had passport photos of the terrorists printed on the wall, the men who'd flown the planes into the towers and the ones who'd planned it. A short blurb beneath them explained how the hijackers slipped through surveillance cracks for years and years to board the planes that day and pilot them into infamy. Seeing their faces in such huge relief was unsettling and sparked in me a muted anger that sat uncomfortably on top of all the heavy melancholy we'd accumulated in the rooms before. I hated it. I didn't want to waste space meant for grief on hatred.

Doug placed his arm around my shoulder and squeezed it.

"Just think, in a few months, when you hear about an ISIS leader being killed in an airstrike, it could've been me sending up the missile," he whispered like he was excited, or proud. He kept his arm squeezed around my shoulder—it felt funny. We aren't usually overtly affectionate with one another, especially Doug and especially in public. What was it about this room in particular that made him want to hold me tighter?

His comment about the missile was as true as it was unsettling though. Doug's future sub, the USS *Georgia*, could carry up to one hundred fifty-four Tomahawk land-attack cruise missiles—TLAMs or just Tomahawks—in addition to a sizable payload of torpedoes for underwater assaults. I'd seen plenty of videos of the Tomahawks being launched vertically from submerged submarines. Despite all the violent reverberation below as the boat initiates the launch, the surface of the water never appears unusual until, in less than a second, a missile rockets upward, impossibly fast, trailing flames and thick white smoke, up to where the nearest ship or carrier can take over control and deliver the payload to its intended target. Although I knew it wasn't how sequences worked, and although I know launching a strike takes more than just one person, I imagined Doug and Doug alone before a control panel slamming his hand down on a big red button, firing Tomahawk after Tomahawk up from the depths.

That image unsettled me even more, and I couldn't stop thinking about it as we walked, shoulder to shoulder through the exhibit full of the signs, crosses, photos, and makeshift memorials that adorned the rubble and streets surrounding for months before cleanup began. If you were to take all the colors out of context—the red, white, and blue—they could have been from a Fourth of July parade. These were the images I remembered most: prayers for the city Sharpied on poster boards, silk flowers in bright bundles tied to the streetlights left standing. I wanted badly to reach out and touch something, feel the brush of an artificial rose on my fingers.

I support the need for national and international action to prevent future acts of terror both in the United States and around the world. No parents should lose children, no children, parents, to this brand of violence. Having an actively deploying military in support of this mission should always be, in my mind, a national priority. Selfishly, however, I wish almost every day that Doug wasn't a part of it. Anyone *but* him—my self-interested but persistent desire. As an American, I want to feel our country is protected, as a submariner's wife, I support the mission and understand its purpose but, as solely a wife, I am nauseated by the danger it puts him in.

How do you feel about what your husband does? I've often meditated on this question, trying to find some concrete answer, an answer I feel I should have on hand as the wife of a service member. Some days, I'm all for it: *I'm proud that Doug's out there, fighting for us and keeping us safe.* Other days, it feels as if our sacrifices mean and accomplish nothing: *It's all bullshit and I just want him home.* As a military spouse, it's hard to balance or separate national interests from personal ones. It's conflicting, confusing, and often painful to continually set aside what's best for our family for what someone up the chain of command deems best for the boat (or for the nation.) For a dozen years I've tried but have never been able put my thoughts together the way I'd like to. Instead, every day is a kaleidoscope. The colors change, the picture changes, my "answers" from days before that seemed so right, sound misguided and wrong.

All this to say, I don't think there are any easy answers for me.

I am not anti-war; I am anti-spousal-risk. But, in the military, war cannot exist without people risking their lives, and I fear the danger to society as a whole would be far, far greater without his mission.

I am not allowed to know what Doug does while he's underway, nor am I allowed to know where the *Georgia's* specific missions take him. All I am allowed to know is that he and the rest of the boat are, as the *Georgia's* captain once put it, "giving the bad guys a reason not to sleep at night."

Whatever it is he does, Doug is a part of the 9/11 story now, part of the endless fallout.

Stepping into the sunlight when we left the museum was almost as disorienting as the journey below. The air was lighter, easier to breathe, but only by so much. We kept walking around, stopping for me to photograph landmarks: The Statue of Liberty, the Washington Square Arch, the Flatiron Building, which we almost walked right past because we were so distracted by a group of street artists dancing with their dogs. We watched them, leaning against the cool concrete façade of a skyscraper. I relished walking on the uneven streets, using every little jut and bump in the sidewalk to massage my aching arches. Doug teased me for zipping up my jacket as high as it would go—living in the South for as long as I had, it'd been a while since I'd walked against cool breezes.

"Ah! I should have brought you with me to Groton. You've gotten weak." I nodded in agreement, my teeth chattering behind my lips.

By the time we got to the restaurant where we were supposed to be meeting a friend, my phone was completely dead, and Doug's had only enough battery left to receive my friend's message that the subway was delayed, before it died too. We ordered drinks and people-watched in the window to pass the time, the way we always have in restaurants. No more touching or shoulder squeezing, we were back to *us*, back to *Sam-and-Doug*. Nothing out of the ordinary, we sipped and waited.

It would be dishonest of me to pretend to understand all the reasons why, this many years after 9/11, people oppose the US's seemingly endless involvement in the Middle East. Do I understand some of them? Absolutely. However there are as many opinions as there are people and I often feel I do considerable disservice in conveying my own vacillating day-by-day feelings about war, seeing it not from the most inner circle, but near it.

For all the times I've heard service members, my husband included, hailed as heroes, exemplars, and even saviors, I've heard them called criminals, rednecks, rapists, and, as an acquaintance in college once put it, "invading, ignoramus, baby-killers." That was the only time I've been offended enough to get up and walk away. (That same acquaintance tried to ask me out for drinks a few days after I gave up my seat at his soapbox. I told him to go fuck himself.) I support and encourage people to use the Freedoms of Speech and Press that Doug and all our military work to defend. If no one uses it, then why keep up the fight at all? But I also strive for mutual compassion.

Despite how young I was when 9/11 occurred, I remember the national unity just as well as I remembered the chaos. I remember bows hugging trees, ribbons on lapels, and "I Love NY" t-shirts all the way out in the Midwest. On the radio, "Proud to be an American" was an hourly encore. While I'm sure those disgusted by the outpourings of patriotism were present, they were hardly audible. When the US went to war, the outcry against it was still small compared to the resolve that we needed to "get" the people responsible for the attacks. I sometimes miss the unity of those days. At least then the answers seemed clear and simple; compassion was doled out freely and without condition.

As time and the Global War on Terror—the *GWOT*, as its fighters call it—have gone on, those who oppose it have gained more platforms from which to speak. That is their right. What I struggle to tolerate are those who demean and degrade the individual men and women of the armed forces because they disagree with the military's overarching mission. Despite combat operations in Afghanistan ceasing in 2015 and likewise in Iraq shortly thereafter, that means very little for most of the armed forces, especially submariners. Subs like Doug's, the GNs, are forward deployed boats, always out there, executing their missions, ready for further action when orders are given. Submarines like Doug's *Georgia*, an SSGN, remain overseas for long periods of time, sometimes years regardless of wartime status. They have two complete crews that operate them, gold crew and blue crew, who swap ownership of the boat after a period of months at forward ports, only bringing the boat back to her homeport every three years or so for major maintenance; everything else is completed overseas. It doesn't matter who's elected or which party has the majority in Congress. No political opinion or policy will ever change the fact that Doug, along with the spouses of so many more, not just submarine sailors, but those on surface ships too, will have to deploy and deploy and deploy again to be at the ready for whatever the next battle is, the next war, because there will always be another. War-work doesn't stop just because one conflict is declared over. It's hard on sailors, hard on families, and hard on young marriages like ours. There's always a battle at home to try and hold together what gets neglected while "the men" are out fighting (though, of course, now, many women make up the ranks as well.)

Knowing relatively little about what Doug does out in the world, about his mission, I do know that he and his fellow submariners are well trained, well intentioned, and have saved many thousands more lives than they have taken, both on foreign and domestic soil.

As a spouse, all I ever want and all I'll ever ask for, for my husband and myself, is compassion. It is hard to be trapped in the revolving door of deployments. As soon as one is finished, the process of preparing for the next one begins. And with each deployment comes a new set of possibilities, new dangers, and all the unaccountables of days that start off seeming perfectly normal, but end in terror.

Though the gulf between military reality and civilian understanding is a wide one, I feel particularly fortunate to have a circle of friends who, though their politics and opinions differ greatly from my own, never fail to offer their understanding when the military lifestyle makes things hard for Doug and me, even in the time before he started to deploy.

When we were in New York, the evening after we'd visited the 9/11 Memorial & Museum, we had dinner with one such opinionated friend. I both love and fear for her views so different from my own, and her uncanny ability to debate and argue without mercy. Yet she's never once spoken ill of Doug for the implications of his job, though she's had plenty of chances to do so, even that night as the three of us debated the need for the terrorists' exhibit at the 9/11 museum. She knows and recognizes the difference between supporting the military's global mission versus the people sent to carry it out—ordinary people who've made an extraordinary choice—and even those of us who go on to marry them. Compassion in the flesh.

After dinner, Doug and I walked the thirty-two blocks back to our hotel, leaning against each other for warmth. Our phones were dead, so our pockets didn't buzz. We were at peace and alone, save for a few passers-by, which felt funny in a city as big as New York. Even the streets were quiet, reflecting the fuzzy glow of stoplights Not only could I see my breath, but I could *hear* it as I tried to keep up with Doug, always a fast walker. I remember how we kissed on a street corner while waiting for the crosswalk signal to change and were nearly clipped by a cab that hopped the curb. We laughed, "Phew, close call."

I remember telling him that I loved him, for no reason, except that I wanted to say it then.

Extraordinary ordinary succinct ancient naked stunning perfect simple ferocious love.

Neither of us heard anything nor felt unusual movement in the city. We didn't hear people screaming or see them running. It was late; the streets were quiet, even for New York. The hotel doorman said nothing, nor did the staff in the lobby, or the guests we rode the elevator with. It was all rather unremarkable. When we keyed into our room, we didn't turn on the TV. Doug hopped in the shower and I kneeled over a chair at the window to watch cars pass by below. It wasn't until I'd plugged in our dead phones and they'd had a few minutes to charge that we received the dozen text messages and voicemails from my father and grandfather, his sister, neighbors:

Where are you guys? Are you alright? I saw the news.

Please call me ASAP.

You're not in New York are you?

My friend from dinner: *You got back safe, right?*

Doug turned on the TV, and we learned that as we'd headed south, a religious extremist, a terrorist, had set off a pressure cooker bomb by the Flatiron district in Chelsea. The explosion launched a nearby dumpster over one hundred feet in the air and caused structural damage to nearby buildings. Thirty-one civilians were injured by shrapnel—flying glass shards and metal shavings—but no one had been killed. We'd been on the corner he'd chosen just before dinner, watching the street performers and their dogs. We guessed the attacker hadn't planted the bomb before we got there, but shortly after sunset, when we were just getting to the restaurant. He had planted numerous other bombs in driving distance of Manhattan before he was apprehended, taken alive for trial.

Just as Doug's upcoming deployments would soon swing him in and out of war zones, now and again, the war appears at home. Sometimes, it feels like a losing battle, but I don't know if that's truly for me to say. I'm a wife, not a strategist nor a fighter. What I know is that if we live in a world of risks like these, then compassion is our only weapon against it. If we can't unite in our views, we can unite in *simple ferocious love* of one another.

Doug and I and answered the messages. We are safe in our hotel, we are ok. We were close but fine. Close but fine. For now.

CHAPTER 6

White Pants

By my count, Doug owns seven different uniforms: camos, coveralls, khakis, PT gear, dress blues, choker whites, and summer whites. It doesn't seem like a lot until you take into account that every uniform has at least three pieces to it, not including a hat (or a *cover* as they're called in the military.) All the uniforms must display the proper insignias—pinned or embroidered, depending on the wearer—and correctly arranged ribbons or medals, depending on the formality of the occasion. Doug owns two pairs of combat boots, two pairs of black oxfords in two different leather finishes, traditional and patent, and one pair of white oxfords. The uniforms rotate by the season and by the command and must fit a certain way to be *in regs*—within regulations. Almost all of them have a cold-weather or rain variation that requires a certain type of overcoat, fleece, sweater, or parka.

If it's a uniform he wears more than once a week, like camos, khakis, and coveralls, he has two or three sets; those get folded or hung in the closet with his civilian clothes, usually, and are far less of a hassle to keep up. But every place we've lived, we've had to designate one closet as "the uniform closet" to keep the more formal uniforms separate and pristine for important ceremonies, balls, graduations, weddings, and even the occasional funeral or memorial service. I thought we'd be attending one such memorial in

Charleston when Doug graduated from Prototype in August 2016. A young enlisted sailor at Doug's training command had committed suicide a few weeks before graduation.

The uniform for Prototype graduation was one of my favorites: summer whites. They're not as formal as the high-necked choker whites but are short-sleeved and suited for hot weather, and it felt every bit of southern summer on Doug's graduation day. I'd been to a few Navy graduations by now, but never a Navy memorial service. I assumed there'd be something done at the graduation to commemorate the lost sailor since it had only been a few weeks since his passing. White, a historically traditional color of mourning, didn't seem like a bad choice.

Before Doug wears his summer whites, he washes and irons them days in advance, pressing in each crease and seam into the snow-white polyester until they're so sharp, they could have been chiseled. He hangs the slacks and blouse off our bedroom door and, with a tiny pair of scissors, snips off any stray threads. He covers the uniform in plastic. Even after he's finished, and the uniform looks immaculate, he'll still throw the plastic sheath back and find another thread or two to clip whenever he walks by.

With a small lint remover, he rolls over the dark shoulder boards to remove any errant fuzz before fastening them to the blouse. The gold belt buckle gets removed from its velvet box, fogged up with hot breath and polished with a soft cloth, like a pair of glasses, then threaded onto the white webbed belt to be lined up precisely with the *gigline*—the perfectly vertical line from the top of a sailor's collar, down the buttons of the blouse, past the rightmost edge of the buckle, down through the zipper of the pants.

He uses a specialized ruler—a *measuring device*, as he calls it—to pin his ribbons on, measuring over and over to make sure they are properly spaced in relation to the breast seam, his nameplate, and exactly one-quarter inch from the top seam of the pocket.

The night before wearing them, Doug will spend hours polishing his white Oxfords one at a time with an oiled rag and a stiff horsehair brush, pausing every so often to hold it up to the light, inspecting the shoe meticulously as he goes. By bedtime, everything else he needs is laid out beneath the hanging pieces like an assembly line: underwear, undershirt, inner socks, outer socks, shirt stays, dress watch, and hat—combination cover—in its black zippered case, protecting it from the light or our dog's curious nose.

The boxers Doug wears with his whites are the only time I ever see him break regulations. The Navy issues sailors three pairs of white boxer shorts to be worn under white pants. However, they tend to show through the slacks under even the slightest illumination so, as he learned from older midshipmen back in college, he wears light gray briefs instead.

While Doug showers and shaves the morning of, I always remove the combination cover from its case, set it on my lap, and buff its dark, shiny brim to remove the dust and fingerprints. If I see lint, I blow across the white top, and, when he's ready for it, I carry it to him the way he showed me: upright, between my wrists, so the oils from my hands don't smudge the brim or yellow the white fabric.

All dressed, Doug immediately seems taller and broader. His jaw looks squarer, his shoulders, prouder. His bright eyes turn from cerulean to deep sapphire, and I could swear his voice grows deeper and more commanding. In his summer whites, my husband looks less like a man and more like a column on an ancient temple—as if he was pulled straight out of antiquity and given life. Already possessing a squarish look about him, there's something about the uniform that takes him from rough marble to chiseled masterpiece. But I'm just being sentimental.

He walks so quickly I have to do a few hop-skips to keep up. When he notices me trotting behind, he apologizes. There is no way to keep up with or compare to my sailor in his whites.

The Prototype graduation ceremony—where I expected a memorial— was held in the hangar of the USS *Yorktown*, an old aircraft carrier now moored as a museum in the Charleston Harbor; it commemorated Doug and a few hundred of his crew mates' completion of the second phase of the Nuclear Training Pipeline: six months of shift work onboard a refitted training submarine, where they simulated various casualties and were observed and tested by instructors in control rooms overhead. Finishing Prototype marked the end of the brutal trainings it takes to complete the pipeline. Next for the officers would be Sub School in Groton, Connecticut, spending a few hours a day in the classroom, and the rest of the time on liberty.

The affair was marked with an overwhelming amount of pomp and circumstance. Music, balloons, streamers, and a stage lined with bunting, and backed by a thirty-foot American Flag. Upon our arrival, Doug left me almost immediately to muster and line up with the other sailors.

I wandered, looking for some sort of commemoration of the sailor who'd died. I expected there would be a photograph propped somewhere, a poster on an easel, or a chair left empty in his honor. Suicides are a problem that plagues both the nuclear training pipeline and qualified Nukes alike. Numbers are near impossible to find, but one anonymous contributor to a Charleston newspaper a few months prior estimated that Nukes specifically kill themselves at a rate three times higher than that of civilians.

The hangar was buzzing with families there to watch the graduation. The museum portion wasn't yet open to tourists, but our party of hundreds flooded throughout the main deck making it as crowded as any time I'd ever seen it. Everyone was decked out in red, white, and blue—the unofficial civilian dress code of many Navy functions—in varying levels of formality. There were tall men in suits with American Flag ties and women in church dresses with rhinestone flag pins on their jackets congregating beside those in denim cutoffs and Old Navy flag tees with the sleeves ripped off. I was sweating through my sundress and cardigan as I roamed through the crowd. All of us still looked sub-par compared to the mustering graduates. They gleamed.

I walked for at least half an hour looking for something, anything memorializing the sailor who'd died, but found nothing. I tried to remember if Doug had said anything more about him but there wasn't much information to begin with. No one in his section knew how he'd done it, or if he'd left a note. All anyone talked about was how he'd been struggling with stress in the pipeline.

Upon learning the news, Doug and I argued in the car on the way home from a bar about the pressure the training command puts on sailors, whether or not it was necessary or avoidable. I remember being a little drunk, and a little weepy.

He held that the fleet needs sailors who can handle working under constant pressure. "If they can't handle the training then they shouldn't be Nukes in the fleet because nothing is easier out at sea." I scoffed at him because he himself hadn't been out to sea yet.

He and the other sailors attended monthly briefings about mental health and suicide prevention; they wore mental health hotline numbers on laminated cards hung around their neck, right next to their IDs. Posters lined the hallways of every command building and admirals often made video speeches encouraging those struggling to reach out for help. What more could the Navy do?

"Sam, they aren't our moms, they're our bosses. We *work* for them. It's a high-stress environment. Nothing's gonna change that."

I couldn't fault him. The Navy was trying. They try. It's hard for me to accept that not everyone can be or wants to be saved. But still I argued that limits of exhaustion and exertion were being pushed—I saw it already in the training tempo, and he hadn't even joined the fleet yet where, as Doug said, nothing is easier or less-stressful. We didn't even broach the topic of toxic chains of command, where sailors are too often abused by those tasked with leadership—an experience Doug would have a brush with his first year on the *Georgia*. That night, I told him I thought the Navy glorified him—all the sailors—too much, to the point of peril.

"How are you going to ask for help if you're already supposed to be Superman?"

"I don't know, Sam. Can you just drink some more water? Please?"

At his graduation, I circled the hangar twice more looking for a memorial before I gave up and took a seat in the third row, close to the aisle, between two middle-aged couples in their red-white-and-blue Sunday best.

The ceremony began with bright spotlights beaming up the flag and the National Anthem, the marching in of the sailors, introductions of the platform party, and rousing, patriotic speeches. We applauded the huge number of veteran and active duty family members in attendance who all stood for recognition. The Master of Ceremonies heralded the graduates as the future of the Nuclear Navy and the pride of the nation. One speaker called them "forces of change" and the other, "the enemy's worst nightmare." They were *academics fighters, warriors,* and, at least a dozen times, *heroes.* Over and over, the chorus repeated, *These are the best of our best. These are our heroes.*

And the crowd embraced it wholeheartedly. Women dabbed at their eyes with tissues and men swelled with pride, growing visibly taller in their chairs as their sons and daughters were lauded so highly. I handed a tissue from deep in my purse to a woman two seats down from me, a mother, I assumed, who blubbered almost the entire time. At first, she sniffled so much I thought she had a cold, so I leaned away to avoid the germs.

When it came time to present certificates to each graduate, the Master of Ceremonies invited families, as they do at all Navy graduations I've attended, to get in the aisles or come close to the stage for pictures, but to hold applause until the end. But the audience was too riled. Everyone cheered and clapped and hollered for their sailors, their sailor's friends, anybody. Flags waved and one mother in the row in front of me thrust out metallic pompoms and shook them high in the air when her son crossed the stage. *That's my baby, right there!*

It was the largest and most enthusiastic show of support for the military I'd ever seen—and it made me more than a little uncomfortable.

With every clap, every cheer, every *that's my boy*, the idea of the battle proof military man, the chiseled statue, the *übermensch*, was thrown into sharper relief. It was as if these men and women, brilliant, brave, and accomplished as they were, weren't allowed weakness anymore. They were heroes, after all, and heroes are supposed to save, not be saved. The uniforms alone do so much to erase their individual humanity. The graduates stretched far back into the hangar as each sailor waited their turn to climb the stage and accept his or her achievement in one long, immaculate white line.

But the spotlights were bright—too bright for the white uniforms. When the sailors took the stage, one by one, the same lights that illuminated them and made them look so flawless, beamed straight through their white pants and showed off their underwear to the adoring crowd. I noticed it shortly before Doug was due to cross the stage. Most of the men were safe—they'd worn the Navy-issue white boxers. They still lit up like flashlights in the dark, but they were far better off than their peers in polka dots, stripes, plaid, or, in one case, what looked like Snoopy boxers. Doug and most of the other officers had on the illicit, non-Navy issue gray briefs; they'd been in the service just long enough to know the tricks. For many of the younger enlisted sailors, this was their first time putting on their whites for a ceremony. They would learn someday but hadn't yet.

Their uniform blunder kept me from going crazy while the crowd lost its collective mind. Of course, I was proud of Doug—I popped into the aisle, snapped a few pictures on my phone, and grinned excitedly when he shook hands with the commanding officer—but I was planted in the reality that, after the graduation and following luncheon, I'd have to wash the uniform with stain-fighters because *my sailor, my hero,* is a very messy eater. Talented, smart, brave, and capable as he may be—as so many of them are—he isn't perfect.

I have no idea what happened to the young sailor who ended his own life. I don't know his history, his pains, or anything about him other than the fact that he is no longer alive. Wrong as I know it was to speculate on things I know nothing about, I couldn't help but wonder if he *hadn't* been trying to achieve the Navy's Superman ideal, would he have had a chance of surviving?

After the ceremony, Doug and I went home and he shucked off his uniform for a nap, still catching up from the months of working the watch bill. He left the whites in a crumpled pile on the bedroom floor.

A few months later, after he'd finished Submarine school, and we'd both moved to Jacksonville, Doug deployed for the first time. We emailed as often as we could. I tried to entertain him with stories about my students or our dog. He wasn't allowed to tell me much, but when something funny happened in the officer's mess or with his division, I'd hear a little about it. For the most part though, all he talked about was being tired. Exhaustion permeated every message: *Just got off watch. Did six hours of paperwork. Ran drills so I didn't get to sleep.* When his division came under intense scrutiny before an inspection for things that occurred years before he even joined the crew, his emails became so bleak I ended up speaking to the Ombudsman about it, half-desperate for a way to help him breathe under all the stress. I can only imagine the way it bottles up underwater.

The captain, whom I had experienced to be a genuinely good man with his crew's best intentions at heart, implemented certain "morale practices" during the deployment that were supposed to break up the week and provide respite from the breakneck operations onboard. "JO Retention Nights" is the one I remember hearing about the most: the department heads all stood watch while the junior officers gathered to discuss issues on the boat, then watch a movie for morale. Doug said they often disbanded about twenty minutes into the movie because too many were nodding off in their chairs, or busy with paperwork for their divisions. Sometimes, the captain would step in and enforce their enjoyment and, on at least one occasion, things got heated when he ordered an older junior officer to sit and watch the movie when the officer was trying to finish a stack of paperwork in time for an audit, per the captain's orders from just a few hours before.

Doug came home from the deployment and slept almost continuously for three days. When he was just starting to act like himself again after his prolonged sleep, the USS *Fitzgerald* collided with a cargo ship off the coast of Japan. The preliminary inquiries cited fatigue, paired with lack of training. Two months later, the USS *John S. McCain* caused a near-identical incident near Singapore. Seventeen sailors were lost in total. While these were the two most publicized incidents, they were actually the third and fourth disasters of the year in the Pacific Fleet. The Navy ordered a one-day, fleet-wide operational pause—a *safety stand-down*—to give commanders a chance to reexamine their watch-standing, training, and operational practices. As far as I know, nothing changed drastically on the *Georgia*. But Doug's sub was reportedly running well and making gains—including winning the Battle Efficiency Ribbon—while other boats faltered and fell behind schedule. The captain was tough but fair and, that alone seemed reason enough to thank our lucky stars.

A friend's husband went out to sea for three weeks for his boat's sea trials in preparation for leaving Kings Bay, the base where both he and

Doug worked, after the sub spent nearly two years in dry dock for maintenance. His command had them working through Hurricane Irma to get the boat ready. For weeks, he couldn't come home, even though the boat was moored to a pier. When I spoke to his wife, she told me how they were both looking forward to deployment, just so he'd have a reliable schedule again, and could get more than a couple hours of sleep each day. The crew of the sub had been making dozens of costly mistakes the last few weeks, many of them because they were simply too tired to stay alert. She breathed a sigh of relief when the boat pulled out for sea trials. "This will be good for him."

However, in her own words a few weeks later, "he came home broken."

He stayed in bed for two days, sobbing at intervals. In his journal, he'd written about being berated by his superiors during meals, or being followed to his rack by shouting department heads. His division's Chief was put on suicide watch, and when the boat returned to Kings Bay, at least five sailors "sadded out"—they reported suicidal thoughts or ideation and were put under review for release from sea duty.

His wife, my friend, was distraught. "How are we supposed to watch this happen? How am I supposed to let him go?" Indeed, her husband was scheduled to go on an even longer underway in a handful of weeks to deliver the boat to her overseas port. I didn't know what to say. Trauma, we often forget, is not just found in combat, but in the fast-paced intensity of war zones, in the overworked chains of command, in the silence of waiting.

Even in our short time in the periphery of it all, we've seen how the Navy has repeatedly upped its mental health awareness and suicide prevention programs. They drill into sailors' heads the importance of a full night's sleep, balanced nutrition, and regular exercise. But what good is that on a submarine where you have no time to sleep, no choice in meals, and one treadmill for the entire crew?

By September 2017, Doug had already deployed again, and was having a hellish time. Many of the junior officers above him were leaving after this deployment so the captain was preparing them to take their places when the boat came home to port for a maintenance period, much like the one their sister ship was exiting. But the *Georgia* was so run down at that point, they couldn't leave their forward port for more than a few days at a time before having to return and repair the latest breakdown. At the same time, one of the *Georgia*'s department heads started singling out Doug and another JO, preventing them from sleeping and scrutinizing their every action to the point where others in the wardroom began to express concern. The emails from Doug in those months were the hardest to read because he couldn't explain what exactly was going on. All he could say was, *It's bad, Sam. Things are really bad here.* Doug wasn't the type of person to get low. I had no idea what to expect or how he was coping onboard. A few times I worried I'd never hear from him again.

The JO spouses got together often during that deployment, worried sick for our sailors, but covering it up with parties, drinks, and, sometimes, softly whispered prayers:

Please keep them safe; please make them strong. They are only human, only men. Please bring them home alive and in one piece. Please protect the protectors.

When Doug deploys, he doesn't usually have to bring any of his formal uniforms, which is not the norm in the sub community. Since submariners only get spruced up to bring the boat into her home port, and his boat remains overseas for years at a time, his dress uniforms, blues, khakis, and whites all stay waiting in the closet, pristine and untouched.

CHAPTER 7

Red and Black

I've listened to Beatles music for as many years as I can remember, first with my dad, either in his car or sitting in his woodshop while he built tables or turned bowls. When I was seven or eight, he burned copies of all the albums for me, and I would listen on my stereo during the day, and sometimes on a portable CD player hidden under the covers at night when I was supposed to be sleeping. I listened while I wrote stories. I liked the sad tale of spinster "Eleanor Rigby" and the heavy piano riff of "Hey Bulldog." The repetitive *na na nas* of "Hey Jude" were mesmerizing, but nothing resonated as much as "Yellow Submarine."

I was fascinated by the way Ringo sang *submarine*, pronouncing it distinctly so you could hear the *b* in *sub*. *Sub-marine*. Under-sea. Not *summerine*, like fast-talking Midwesterners say it, or *summer-bean* as a friend's nine-year-old daughter did once, stumbling with it, having never said the word out loud before being asked if she knew what one was. "Yellow Submarine" had a lilt to it, lightness. Simple like a bedtime story. I'd close my eyes and picture a bright yellow sub against a cerulean sea, like a sun in summer. Equally attractive was the idea that this singer and all his submarining neighbors had all they needed underwater. It wasn't about a one-person sub, it was *we*, it was *every one of us*. There was togetherness. They had their friends, they had their music, the sky and the sea; everything was simple and fine—a feeling I struggled to find in the years before I understood what anxiety was and how it affected me.

In school, I wasn't the only Beatles aficionado. One of my best friends was also raised on the band and we commiserated with smug, elementary school superiority over our sophisticated musical tastes that went far beyond the Backstreet Boys and Smash Mouth of our peers (though we knew, and still know, every word to "All Star.") When we had sleepovers together, we'd forgo Blockbuster's newest releases to rewatch the trippy 1968 animated movie about the band taking the magical submarine out on a mission to save Pepperland from the Blue Meanies, oblivious to the 60s drug culture references, totally along for the ride.

The Beatles were a way of life. Later, in high school when I had just started talking to Doug regularly, just started to see him as more than a friend, he mentioned that he could play "When I'm Sixty-Four" on his saxophone, and I thought that was really cool.

In college, when my elementary school best friend and I found ourselves studying abroad in England at the same time with our respective universities, we met up for a weekend in Liverpool. We called it our "Magical Mystery Tour." and spent a night drinking beer and singing along with a cover band in the Cavern Club, where the Beatles were "discovered." By then, I'd given up on choosing a definitive number one Beatles song but paid homage to my childhood favorite by snapping a few pictures of myself beside a barge in the harbor painted to look like the yellow submarine itself. If memory serves, I think one of those pictures made the family Christmas card that year.

And while my friend and I sang and drank the weekend away in Liverpool, Doug was on a midshipman training cruise somewhere between Guam and Pearl Harbor, beneath the Pacific on a real submarine, shadowing members of the crew, learning how things operate in the belly of a beast.

The next time I found myself contemplating the colors of submarines, I was deep in planning for Doug's and my wedding—a task taken on with gusto mainly by my side of the family. My aunts threw a beautiful shower and my grandmother unboxed all the traditional heirlooms and recounted their stories. My closest cousin, who has always been more like a sister, acted as a documentarian, thoughtfully photographing each item, as well as each moment leading up to the big day, creating an album of memories that I cherish. At the helm of the wedding preparations, my mother and I spent our days picking everything from invitations to invocations to match our shared vision. I made the final call to have a civilian ceremony rather than a Navy one.

Doug's biggest request was that he be allowed to help choose the cake, which he did, but it was my mother's idea to have the baker create a fondant submarine rising from the top of it, complete with a breeze-blown American flag and miniature soda cans tied off the stern, making the sugar sub our honeymoon getaway car.

Following my mother's lead, my dad, who was already building us a large wooden bench for guests to sign in lieu of a guestbook, came up with the idea to make a card box shaped like the top of a sub—the *tower*.

I called it the *tower*, at least, assuming that was short for *periscope tower*—a label I unknowingly invented to describe the tall, vertical part of a submarine whose primary function, I assumed, was to house the periscope. On the Beatles' sub, the tower had two yellow and two orange periscopes, four in total, all facing different directions. The tower my dad built—a *conning tower*, he called it—had two antennae at the top, one periscope, facing forward, an American flag, and a slot—a *hatch*—down which guests could drop their cards. He gave it fairwater planes—which Doug teased me for calling *wings*—and presented it to me, unpainted, sitting on a tarp in the basement, ready for my mom to finish with color and our wedding date "hull number:" 032115. We called it the USS *Brown*.

"So, what color do you want it?" my dad asked.

I *ummed* for a few seconds before I realized I couldn't name what color real submarines were. The only sub I'd ever paid attention to was yellow. "I don't know, gray?"

"Gray?" My dad raised his eyebrows.

"Gray. Gray?"

It seemed like a logical guess. All the ships I'd seen in museums or harbors growing up were the same "battleship gray", or "haze gray" used across the fleet to make surface ships harder to spot by eye.

"You know they're black, right?"

I suddenly felt very stupid. Not all that long ago, a few years back maybe, Doug had shown me pictures he'd taken from the top of one sub's *tower* when he pulled into Pearl Harbor at the end of one of his midshipman cruises. In them, the bow of the boat was, of course, black. I pulled out my phone and Googled *submarine*. The top results were black as coal. When a sub is near the surface, black keeps it camouflaged against the dark of the water.

In the end, despite the inaccuracy, we went with gray instead of black for both the cake and the card box because gray didn't seem as bold against the soft spring palette of our wedding. We wanted to honor the Navy, not make it the centerpiece. My mother bought a few yards of sea-blue tulle and arranged it around the base of the card box to make it look like the wake of a sub rising from the deep.

On the wedding day, the card box held up well but the submarine atop our cake suffered pitifully from the effects of gravity. The conning tower leaned forward at an angle and one fairwater plane had to be propped up with wooden skewers because it kept falling off and landing in the blue icing ocean. We laughed about it with our guests in the receiving line—some of whom pointed out that, on the tier of cake below the sub, the baker had placed the blue fondant *B* of our monogram upside down as well.

Doug informed me sometime after the wedding, when he was starting in the Nuclear Training Pipeline, that *conning tower* wasn't the correct term either. The conning tower was a watertight compartment housed within the tall, vertical part of the boat where periscope operators used to control and read their equipment. And technically, he told me, conning towers hadn't existed since the end of World War II, after which advancements in technology allowed for longer periscopes and antennae that could be controlled from the forward command rooms of the boat. The "tower" I'd spent months talking about was called the *sail* and, above that was the *bridge* because the very top of the sail is where the crew drives the boat from when it's surfaced.

When Doug told me, I tried not to feel as ignorant as I had when I learned that submarines are black, not gray. One of the lingering after-effects of us being a pair of high school sweethearts who spent years enrolled in many of the same honors and AP classes was that we'd developed a sort of intellectual competitiveness between us. We always wanted to be the more knowledgeable about a subject. After exams, we'd compare scores and try to outdo one another during presentations with more elaborate PowerPoint effects and visuals. In college, we took a few overlapping general education courses, albeit in different semesters, and would help each other when the assignments diverged from our areas of expertise. I edited his essays; he coached me in statistics. Even now, we can't watch Jeopardy together without turning it into a staked competition. *Loser empties the dishwasher. Loser folds laundry. Loser vacuums the dog hair off the couch.* We keep score on the back of unopened junk mail.

So Power School—at the beginning of both our marriage and his nuclear training days in Charleston—was extremely new for us. He launched into a rigorous classroom program where sailors likened the daily flow of information to "putting your mouth on a fire hose and turning it on full blast." I couldn't have kept up with him if I tried. I knew it was pointless for me to ask him about the equations or the math, but I still held onto my textbook knowledge of nuclear reactors. For a little while, he could come home talking about coolant or feedback loops and I'd understand, but the gaps in knowledge grew quickly until he was officially, in my mind, speaking a foreign language. It wasn't all one-sided. When I started applying to MFA programs, I'd try to bring him into my deliberations about the workshop model versus the tutorial model or, after I'd been accepted to Queens University of Charlotte, tell him about a book I was reading for a class and try to talk about the way one writer had personified New York, versus the way another brought life to the desert, only to be met with similar blank stares, polite smiles, and *uhh yeah*s. Additionally, the further he got into his nuclear program, the less he could tell me, not just because I wouldn't understand, but because I did not share his Top Secret security clearance. We tried to laugh about it, but that didn't make it any easier, nor did it erase my small but growing fear that we would one day be so immersed in our two separate worlds that we would no longer know one another.

I'm not a submariner, not a sailor, just the wife of one. It isn't my job to know the boat, but I was trying hard to conceptualize the submarine, the ship I'd likely never see, that was supposed to house and protect my husband for months and months on end. Although I had no practical need to know the names and functions of the engine components and reactor workings, I wanted to, for reasons more than to compete with my husband in terms of volume of knowledge. It was bizarre to me, nearly incomprehensible, that I was supposed to willingly give Doug up to some machine I barely understood. The submarine, while his arrival on it was still over a year away, was an inevitability and, while the physical distance was a given, I hadn't been as prepared to deal with the growing intellectual distance. How far, I wondered, could that gulf span? As someone who's spent a fair amount of her life dedicated to learning and acquiring knowledge, this was highly disorienting. Beyond that, there was emotional distance too. For the first time in our lives, Doug and I had something we couldn't share with one another. We'd never tested our relationship in this way before. Would we be strong enough?

I listened and gradually learned. During Power School and subsequent Prototype, where he spent long shifts onboard a moored, decommissioned sub whose reactor remained live for training, Doug often came home talking about turbines, evolutions, nucleonics, and steam pipes, trying to memorize systems and immediate actions by working through them aloud while I washed dishes. When we went out for beers with other sailors in the program, and they talked about their qualifications—*quals*—for hours that dragged on like years. Here and there, when they weren't talking solely about nuclear power, I picked up tidbits about the boats they trained to man. I learned about ballast tanks and what could happen if they failed to blow or flood, and about the crucial difference between *flooding* and *leaking*. Leaks on a submarine were normal; floods could be fatal events if they occurred in the wrong places. I learned that the visible black hull of a submarine is just the outer layer; beneath it is a steel shell that flexes with the varying pressure of water to protect the inner hull and her crew of two hundred or more, in the case of Doug's future boat.

I developed a fascination with the massive cargo ships that plowed beneath the Ravenel Bridge, into and out of Charleston Harbor, not far from our house. I watched them from the park under the highway and on the beach of Sullivan's Island, trying to fit their hugeness into my idea of how big or small Doug's boat would be. Some subs are small and stealthy like the Los Angeles and Virginia class *fast attacks*. Others, like the Ohio class he ended up on, are nearly two football fields long and four stories high, not including the sail. How could something so enormous move through the ocean unnoticed like a shadow?

Not knowing bothered me. During all six months of Nuclear Power School, six more of shifts at Prototype, and two more months after that spent away at Submarine school, Doug tried his best to explain what he felt I'd want to know, or what would make me feel better about his future deployments. So great was the gap between his knowledge and my understanding, I couldn't even formulate coherent questions to ask him, so he'd just toss out information if something related came up, or if he thought of a fun factoid offhand. *Did you know we have a bunch of glowsticks on board to indicate emergency lighting and air? Did you know the wardroom can become an operating room if someone needs surgery underway?* While I never said anything outright, I think Doug had a sense of how much it bothered me to be unfamiliar with what was now his entire life's focus. He tried so hard to help, and I loved him even more for it.

Some things saddened me to learn for reasons I could not articulate. The periscopes I imagined, for instance, with eye pieces to be peered into—optic scopes—were highly outdated, he told me. While there was one periscope onboard his boat, it was a distant second to the digital scope and photonics mast. Images came through on video screens that could be viewed almost anywhere onboard: control, missile control, CO and XO staterooms, officers' study, the wardroom, and even in the crew's mess. The screens, Doug said, can be tuned to any number of displays, but are usually set to cycle through the periscope view, sonar, and mapping displays—safety displays, because there is more out there to endanger a sub than only that which could threaten it from the surface. Doug tells me now that the periscope's usefulness is largely dependent on the mission. A lot of times though, he says, the periscope and photonics views are their only visual connection to the surface at all. "You're totally cut off down there. There's literally nothing else."

I knew by then there were no windows—no *portholes*— on the submarine, but it didn't stop me from wishing there were so that Doug and his shipmates could see sunlight, get a glimpse of the outside world. But on a sub, I learned, it's less about seeing sunlight and more about not being seen in it.

In late January 2017, a couple of weeks before Doug's first deployment, in the waiting room of the Defense Enrollment Eligibility Reporting Systems Office—the *DEERS* office—in Kings Bay, Georgia, I spotted a framed illustration of a submarine. Doug and I had been sitting around for some time already, waiting with half a dozen others to be called to the window so Doug could sign the papers confirming that, yes, I was his lawfully wedded spouse of almost two years, and yes, I was eligible to renew my military ID. We'd looked at the calendar earlier in the week and realized today, an unassuming Thursday, was one of the last days we'd be able to meet up to take care of this and a few other paperwork-centric items on our pre-deployment to-do list before I started teaching and lost my daytime availability. Although he was overdue to return to the off-crew building where he worked, I implored him to wait around.

"I know you've got to go, but let's try, *please,* to get this one thing over with. Just so we accomplish *something* today." I was very concerned by how quickly the calendar pages seemed to be flying off the wall.

The framed illustration leaned against the back of a cheap glass trophy case on the wall opposite our seats. The display also held a few engraved plaques and formal portraits of the base's commanding officers in their dress blues. The sub in the picture was long, very long, in proportion to its sail, and the bottom half of the hull was not black, but bright, crimson red.

"Doug," I whispered, tapping his arm and nodding toward the case. "Is that one yours? Is that the *Georgia?*"

He squinted and leaned forward a little bit. "Yeah. Think so."

"Why is it red on the bottom?"

"What?"

"Why is the top of the hull black and the bottom red?"

He frowned a little. "Hm. Don't know."

I believed him, mostly. It seemed reasonable that I would be the only one of us considering the visual aspects, the color of it. He was only supposed to know how it all worked within. But this seemed too important not to be something he'd learned in all his training. In my mind, already frayed and exhausted, his avoidance meant he was trying not to talk about the danger, about leaks, or flooding, or ballast tanks. To me, if black was meant to hide the boat, to make it invisible, then red must be to make it easier to spot against dark water.

A great steel submarine in distress, gone belly up like a fish. Red-side up toward the sky so someone might be able to save them, or at least bring them home. The sailors on board, *my husband* on board, maybe alive, maybe dead.

Perhaps bleeding from a head wound from some unexpected collision. Maybe starved of oxygen.

Crushed by collapsing bulkheads. Burned on a steam pipe. Torpedoed and trapped in fast rising water.

Broken bones. Angry, bleeding lacerations. Internal trauma. Severed limbs and roughly torn muscles. Gushing arteries. A lung punctured by debris or filled with cold sea.

In the engine room, in maneuvering, on the bridge, in the wardroom, in his rack while he was sleeping. Drowned.

Killed instantly. Killed slowly.

Killed. Dead. Belly up.

I was consumed.

How could Doug have known that the contrast of colors, of red and of black, looked like so much more than paint to me? The sharp line between them was the difference between life and death. I didn't say anything to him, just kept studying the far-off frame, until the office closed, and we left without any new IDs.

I know that that's not how subs go down. Or, at least, not the only way. Floating belly-up like I imagined would be an anomaly. Most subs that go down implode first, then sink and settle where they may. The knowledge of how submarines go down is something I acquired before the disappearance of the ARA *San Juan* during Doug's second deployment. During his silence I became intimate with it.

Doug tells me now that around the time we sat in the waiting room before his first deployment, he started to police what he said to me, keeping things to himself entirely, or breaking them up into bits of information he'd tell me over days, trying not to overwhelm me. He'd tell me what week the boat *might* leave, then a range of *possible* days, then, from those days a range of hours, then finally the exact date and time I was to drop him off when really, he'd had that information for a week. He may not have known how, in the waiting room, just the sight of the red hull paint made me imagine dozens of ways he could die underway, but we'd been together too long for him not to intuit that something wasn't right, and he reacted the best way he could think of. I'm still unsure of my feelings about the way he doled out information. At first, I was insulted. In my head, I should have been capable of handling any amount of information at once especially since no amount of time I sat with it would change how long he was gone or what day and time he was to depart. On the other hand, there was a good deal of wisdom and care in the way Doug gradually told me what I needed to know in the dwindling days before he left. I still wasn't ready by any means, but at least, when all the emotional waves of deployment hit me at once, the logistical ones weren't there among them adding to the storm.

A few months after we visited the DEERS office, I remembered the illustration from the waiting room and, I suppose, because enough time had passed, got more curious than fearful. Doug was deployed, so I couldn't ask him if he'd ever learned why the bottom of his hull was red. I Googled "submarine red hull," instead, and clicked a few of the top results, mostly military Q&A forums.

They called it "red lead" because the lower halves of submarines used to be painted with anti-corrosive lead paint, since they are the parts of the boat that remain in the water whether or not the boat is surfaced. The lead oxide made the paint turn nearly crimson. Now that the Navy has recognized the toxic effects of the lead paint on its sailors and marine environments, all ships have since been scraped and repainted, however many subs have retained a band of bright color on the hulls as a nod to their collective history.

On that first deployment, Doug sent emails often, telling me as much as he was allowed to about his day—which wasn't much. Almost everything he did in his waking hours was classified so, it only took him a line or two to say the crew "ran drills" or that he "stood watch." He talked instead about life underway, about meals, about the rare moments of downtime, or he'd update me on his qualification process. Sometimes though, without meaning to, he'd drop in a detail or two about the boat that I hadn't known before.

The racks were small, that I knew, but I learned from an email that the bunkrooms didn't have doors, just heavy curtains. Barely anything separating them from the watch bill, the mission, the orders—all of which never *ever* stop. I didn't know that loud, hissing pipes snaked beside their heads while they slept, nor did I know how the boat resupplied before running out of food, when possible. Perhaps I should have known that they'd run out of fresh fruits and vegetables within a week of leaving port, but it still shocked me when I read an email from Doug, celebrating a small shipment of iceberg lettuce and melons brought onboard during a BSP—a *brief stop for personnel*—months later. I didn't know the walkway between the boat and the pier was called a *brow*, nor did I know that the computer systems keeping the entire boat running were older than most members of the crew.

I tried comparing the image of the sub in my mind to the inside of an airplane: things stored in compartments on walls, everything made to fold up and lock away. But cabins and cockpits were still too bright, too inviting, roomy, and clean. In a cockpit there are no exposed pipes or wiring, no oxygen masks hanging in plain sight, in arm's reach, because danger is always one sprung bolt away. On a submarine, nothing looks like what it is, or would be, on the surface. Not computers, not chairs, not showers, or beds, or even hallways. Not a single solid reminder of land and home save for the few photos and mementos each man or woman keeps tucked away by their pillows. Inside a submarine is the root of isolation, the epicenter of alone.

After Doug came home from his first tour, as he talked more and more openly and readily about the underway and saw that, outwardly, I could handle it, he'd describe things in more depth that I hadn't even considered. There are few stairs, just ladders. The wardroom has a formal set of silver-embossed china for serving on special occasions like holidays, halfway nights, or the presence of inspectors. They eat their meals in two shifts, formal, family-style, and no one can eat until the captain has started eating, no matter how soon they must all be back on watch. Because of the low oxygen levels onboard, wounds heal slowly, so a sunburn or scrape gotten on a final day in port can easily last a sailor through the first month or more underway. Doug has a profound triangular scar on his scalp, just behind his hairline, from clipping his head on the corner of an open locker while climbing a ladder in a hurry. After almost six months, when I finally saw it, it was still a thick scab. I maintain he should have gotten stitches, but he disagrees, saying that it wouldn't have helped. Boat wounds just don't heal, he says. Certain sections of the boat, especially the engine room, are painted seafoam green because someone decided it made sailors feel less claustrophobic.

Each new revelation of life onboard the sub, or the sub itself, brought a new wave of unsettlement. It didn't matter if I lived one hundred years, I would never know enough about the sub to make me trust it, or to understand what my husband's life was like when he was away—and I was desperate to know, desperate to create an image I could understand, an image that would last so that I could continue to feel connected to him like I used to. I wasn't satisfied to live in a state of not-knowing. The physical distance the Navy puts between us was enough, and I could not stop myself from probing for as much as I was allowed to know.

The décor in our house is deliberately sparse and devoid of reminders of the Navy. There's a rolled-up wool surplus blanket and an anchor-shaped pillow on the wedding guest-bench in the foyer. My desk faces it. When he's home, sometimes Doug sits on the bench while I'm working and tells me to Google things like *maneuvering* and *control* to pull up images from the insides of subs so he can tell me more about what his days are like when he's out. I'll laugh at how outdated the panels look until he starts to name each switch, each gauge, each throttle. The *Georgia* is an old lady, he reminds me; her keel was laid in 1979 and the technology that she runs on is much older, museum-grade stuff. Newer classes of subs like the Virginia and Columbia classes are made up of sleek tablets and screens, not unlike an iPad.

Our Christmas tree has a small collection of submarine ornaments. We have a dish towel that reads *Home is Where the Anchor Drops*. As far as Navy homes go, our home is tame when it comes to nautical-themed décor. The more obvious *submarine-y* things we own act more as homages to my love of the Beatles than to Doug's job. A fully-assembled Yellow Submarine Lego kit, complete with Lego John, Paul, George, Ringo, and Jeremy Hilary Boob, PhD. —the "Nowhere Man"—sits beside our TV. Sometimes, its periscopes annoyingly block the tiny receiver that reads signals from the remote, so someone has to get up and scoot the Yellow Submarine a little to the left, or a little to the right in order to change the channel. In my office, a shelf above my books, I have a metal Yellow Submarine-shaped lunchbox on display.

Admittedly, I'm a bit of a minimalist, so my decision to limit the number of Navy-related things in the house isn't solely a statement against their presence as much as it is me trying to limit the amount of unnecessary clutter in our lives to a minimum before the next inevitable move. What we do have though, is an overabundance of picture frames. I chose only the ones we received as wedding gifts to hang on the walls when we moved into our house. Most were easy to place: wedding portraits in the bedroom, family and friends in the hallway. I hung a matching set of three silver frames in a vertical column to the left of the bookshelves in the living room but, the problem was, the frames had nothing in them.

For a while, I thought about printing photographs from landmarks near our previous three homes—The St. Louis Arch, Columbia's columns, and the Pineapple Fountain in Charleston—but none of the pictures I had were any good. Subconsciously, I think I realized how little our home reflected Doug. We were overrun with books and greenery, but there was nothing that really spoke to Doug's half of our lives.

Instead of buying anything frameable or printing photographs, I sketched out three cartoonish submarines on plain paper and inked over them with Sharpie. The sub in the top frame is long and as menacing as a line-drawn-sub can be. The lower part of its hull is shaded to look like red lead paint and the periscope is just a straight antenna. The bottom sub is made up of riveted panels. It's a little more steampunk-looking than the others. Then there's the middle one, which looks the most like the Beatles' Yellow Submarine. It has three large portholes so those inside can get a glimpse of the sea and the periscope on top is big and round like an eyeball.

When I hung the subs, I never intended for them to stay up for as long as they have, but I've grown to enjoy the look of them and the balance they add to the wall. When I'm home alone, sitting in the living room, I study them without realizing I'm doing it, analyzing the thickness of the hull lines or the angle of the sail. If I can stare at their flatness, their two-dimensions enough, perhaps I will one day convince myself I know enough of submarines to trust them with his life.

CHAPTER 8

Unplugged

After fifteen fruitless days, the Argentine government called off the search and rescue operation for the ARA *San Juan*. The search would continue, but no longer would they be looking for survivors.

Now, three weeks later, families of the missing sailors were still marching in the streets. They congregated at the port of Mar del Plata holding homemade posters and huge Argentine flags, messages of hope, anger, and grief scrawled across them. They called for the president to come speak to them personally, complaining that they were given no advance warning of the rescue efforts ending. Many found out at the same time as their friends and neighbors. They were furious; they were shattered.

I was furious and shattered too. Marching, pacing back and forth across my bedroom from the dresser to the bathroom door, then back again, bathed in the blue glow of the television screen.

Still not a word from Doug on the *Georgia*.

Since the wardroom Christmas party, I'd been doing a little better: crying less, focusing on work more. It was easier to survive moment to moment knowing the other wives were just as uninformed as I was.

Tonight, I'd self-sabotaged. When it was time to settle in for the evening, I got too ballsy, too confident in my ability to cope. Instead of turning on a movie, South Park, or Food Network to fall asleep to, I turned on CNN. What the hell had I been thinking?

The coverage flashed back and forth between images of the protesting families and photographs of the sailors. The latter were young and smiling, the former, exhausted and gaunt. I tried to pull the quilt higher, like a barrier, but my sleeping dog was dead weight on top of it. He grunted in protest, and then resumed snoring. I wanted to be pressed against the screen and both a million miles away all at once, so I got up and started to pace.

Step. Step. Step. Step. Step. Step. Step. Turn. The room isn't large. My thoughts bounce around it like a rubber ball.

There are forty-four lost submariners out there—not just missing but *lost*. Lost souls. The eternal patrol.

Doug, where are you?

On the screen, mothers are screaming.

Why won't you answer?

Fathers are weeping, bowled over like mountains.

Are you there, are you there?

Children stand with their signs and shuffle. One is playing with his sandal, taking it on and off, kicking at the rocks and dirt in the road.

Doug, I'm dying. Please write to me, send something now. Anything.

One young woman with a long brown ponytail sits as if to catch her breath, then bends forward, head hanging limp between her knees.

How much longer can this silence last? I can't do it. I can't take another minute, I thought.

The *San Juan* families walked slowly, out of step, looking down, looking around. Some held signs, a few, candles. The news anchor's voiceover started narrating the submarine's likely implosion.

At the words *crush depth*, I dove behind the dresser and tore the television plug out of the wall. The screen went black.

"No more," I said to no one but the dog. "No more."

I sat on the floor at the foot of the bed and reached up with my hand to scratch under his collar. He was warm, soft, and smelled like oatmeal shampoo from his bath the day before. I closed my eyes and focused on that memory, cold water from the hose, sudsy bubbles on slick black fur, high pitched whining, shake after shake, three fluffy beach towels to dry the both of us. Afterwards, I let him run wild in the backyard, throwing his tennis ball so it knocked against the back fence. The sun was high and hot. I hadn't checked my email for almost an hour—a tiny respite.

The *San Juan* families had no such option.

I thought about being underwater. It used to be my sanctuary, my Atlantis, a place with no sound but the thumping of my own pulse. Now I strained across oceans, waiting to hear again.

CHAPTER 9

Beard

If I ever tell Doug that I said I loved him first, he's always quick to jump in and correct my mistake: "No, you said you *thought* you loved me."

And he's right. I said I thought I loved him, and then he said he loved me too. It was right around Christmas of our junior year in high school. We'd only been dating two or three months.

"Hey, Doug? I think I love you." I said it so quietly, I wondered if I'd said it out loud, or just in my head.

I said I *thought* because not too long before, in the spring, I'd been in a relationship with another guy, an older guy, whom I'd met lifeguarding. He was twenty-one to my fifteen, I'd known, deep down, he wasn't a great guy, or even a good one, but I liked the attention he paid me. When he could have been looking at all the older, prettier girls, he'd looked at me. I thought he saw something special in me, but what he saw, was vulnerability—an opportunity.

When the older guy said *Sam, say I love you*, I said *I love you*. When he said *come with me*, I followed him to his Camry in the school parking lot. It was dark out. My swim meet had run late. He hugged me, then gripped me, groped me, and tried to push me down into the back seat. His beard was coarse against the skin of my neck. I only got away because my friend, my ride home, was just a few cars away, looking for me. She called my name twice. He stopped. I ducked under his arm and ran towards the sound of her voice. Three days later he dumped me. Despite the logic that said the breakup was a good thing because he was so clearly a terrible person, I was devastated. I had my long hair cut off into a bob; it was my way of mourning and ridding myself of the last part of me he'd touched—his fingers tangling up at the back of my neck, yanking hard.

I understood after the fact, after a month of despondence, depression, and wondering why he'd attacked me, that I hadn't loved the older guy; I'd been infatuated and manipulated. But that was the only other brush with the *L* word I'd ever had. My hair was still short when I started dating Doug, just barely touching my shoulders. So, I told Doug I *thought* I loved him because I did. Falling in love with Doug felt different, much different, than it had with the guy before: easier, more natural, like standing in a house you've never been inside, but knowing its every creak and corner like you've lived there your entire life.

I wanted to be sure that I loved him before I said it. I wasn't yet, but would be as we grew closer over time, as my hair grew back little by little, until it was long again, the way it had been before. By the time I could French braid it again, sometime later that spring, I was absolutely sure that I loved him—no thought required.

I was Doug's first and only girlfriend. For years, however, my old boyfriend felt like a third person in our relationship. Certain things—walking alone, dark parking lots—made me remember almost being pulled into the Camry. The feel of a sweaty hand on my arm or the scratch of a wiry beard across my cheek was enough to catapult me back into heartbreak and panic. Just the sound of a man scratching at his chin-stubble was enough to make me want to back away.

Doug couldn't grow much of a beard when we first got together in high school, even if he tried to let it go, just a few whiskers appeared on his upper lip and chin. We usually only got to see one another once a week outside of school then. Despite his sparse and soft facial hair, he always came to pick me up newly shaven, smelling like Old Spice, powdered Tide, and his mother's cigarette smoke. Fresh-faced and cleaned up just to impress me. I loved it and told him often, so he'd do it even more.

By the time he joined the Navy ROTC in college, about two years later, Doug had to shave almost every day to stay within regulations. His whiskers reappeared quickly in uneven patches against his pasty, Irish complexion. We saw each other almost every day then, and I grew as familiar with his routines as I did my own.

Doug shaved at night with an electric razor, buzzing away short stubble from the night before. For all his physical strength and mental toughness, his skin was painfully sensitive and soft. The razor—no matter how sharp and clean the blade was—left itchy, red bumps and faint claw lines all over his neck and jaw. Many nights, I lay in his bed and watched him wince his way through it in front of the bathroom mirror, dabbing away blood with a towel or a tissue.

Fridays after three, he was freed from the Navy's grooming standards and didn't have to touch a razor again until Sunday night. I knew how much he wanted to let his beard grow out, if even for just those few days. But if he kissed me, if his face brushed my skin, so would the prickly hairs that reminded me of my old boyfriend and the parking lot.

It didn't happen often, but sometimes we'd spend a few days apart and he'd forget to shave before I saw him. Or he'd come home from a weekend in the woods with the battalion, drive straight to my apartment and kiss me when I swung the door open, his many days' worth of whiskers scratching my face by surprise, shocking me, when he only meant to be sweet and romantic.

I had an animalistic response the first few times it happened. I'd push him away—hard—with every muscle in my body, taking huge steps backward. I'd start to cry, we'd go inside, retreat to a quiet room, so I could sob my way out of the back of the old, gold Camry in the parking lot. Doug knew all about it, he'd known for years but, in his excitement to see me, he'd forget, and I'd fall apart.

For a while I feared—we both feared—that my old boyfriend would never leave. That, for the rest of our lives, we'd be sharing our home with the ghost of what he'd almost done, letting it control us, down to the last hair on Doug's head. I spoke to a counselor through the university once. She suggested I take up jogging, so I did. Regular exercise, she said, would help regulate the strong emotions that came with a traumatic experience. Something about the exertion, the endorphins, and the rhythmic pounding of my feet helped me regain a sense of control over myself and my surroundings that I hadn't felt since the close call in the parking lot. If I'd been a more responsible patient, I would've made another appointment, but I wasn't and I didn't. I just kept running and that seemed to do the trick.

About a year and a half after we got married, the Navy sent Doug to Groton, Connecticut, for two months to finish his submarine training. After graduating, he took a few days to drive from up north down to our new house in Jacksonville, Florida, that I'd moved into while he was gone.

I'd been awake since four that morning. To pass the time, I jogged again and again around our block. When he finally pulled into our driveway later that afternoon, I was exhausted waiting at the door. I was so happy to see him, to welcome him into our home for the first time that, when we kissed, when I collapsed into him, I didn't notice the several days' worth of stubble that'd accumulated since he'd checked out of his hotel almost a week before. I didn't notice it even when we lay close in bed and I could hear it scratching against the pillowcase. The fear response had been replaced by the warmth of love returned, of a home that felt whole again.

With the leave he had to use before reporting to his first submarine, the USS *Georgia,* we decided to spend a week in Washington DC. While it wasn't the tropical getaway I'd been longing for, or the European vacation he wanted, we were both surprised by how much we enjoyed exploring the Capitol together. I teased him a little because he still hadn't shaved. In the pictures I took his jawline looked blurry with fuzz.

We visited every Smithsonian, every monument, every memorial we could—all on foot. Air and Space for him, Natural History for me. He walked me around Crystal City and recapped his last trip to DC for the Nuke Interview, now almost three years ago, with then-Admiral John Richardson, who soon after became the Chief of Naval Operations. The day after the 2016 Presidential election, we did laps around the White House to watch those who gathered in support and in protest of the new Commander in Chief. In Arlington, where we spent almost an entire day wandering through endless rows of the fallen, we paused at the grave of Admiral Rickover—the Father of the Nuclear Navy—and his wives.

They also serve who only stand and wait. Rickover's second wife had those words, the poet Milton's words, spoken at her husband's funeral, according to one of the brochures I'd been reading from. For that, I either wanted to high five her in solidarity or cry—I wasn't exactly sure. *Waiting* was suffocating—it flooded me with confusion. After spending the day with all those dead servicemembers, I held Doug a little tighter on the train ride back to the city. We ended up at the National Portrait Gallery, wandering through the Hall of Presidents, as it was the only museum open past five o'clock.

We'd drifted apart somewhere back at the beginning of the exhibit, he veered left and I went right. I knew he was somewhere a few alcoves behind me, reading slower, taking more time. I "museum" too fast, he always tells me.

I slowed down though at the portrait of Lyndon B. Johnson, captivated by all the colors in it. From afar, his face was pallid and somber, but up close, blues, oranges, peaches, lavenders, and pinks streaked through him, making him almost the same colors as the sunset over the capitol building.

I must have lingered in the portrait longer than I realized, when, sequestered deep in the corner, I felt warmth behind me, a person standing close. Smelling Old Spice, I knew it was Doug trying to startle me. If I didn't move, he was going to clamp his hands down fast on my sides to make me jump and gasp like he always does, so I turned, facing his stubble, just inches from my startled eyes.

From afar, Doug's beard was the same dull brown as the always-receding hair on top of his head, but up close it was a tapestry of dark espresso, sand, chestnut, and amber. All sorts of browns, blonds, and a shocking amount of red. It was rust, it was beer poured from the tap. With the auburn, it looked more like my hair than his. But the bright gallery lights overhead illuminated him in a blurry halo of untrimmed fuzz. I loved the way his whiskers still grew in patchy and uneven, in an endearing sort of way that belied his fading youth and made him look weathered—much more so than he actually is. Thick under his chin and on his neck; sparse in the mustache. Nothing at all grew beneath the corners of his mouth, but a soul patch grew in a perfect inverted triangle in the center of his chin. The hairs on his cheeks and jaw had a gentle curl to them, but everywhere else they came in poker straight. I realized right there, in the museum, that I'd grown fond of running my fingertips down the edge of his jawbone to feel the different textures.

Doug leaned down to kiss my forehead at the same time I popped up on my tip-toes to reach his lips. We met clumsily with his nose in the corner of my eye, my lips squished against his stubbly chin. It was soft; the hairs didn't prick and I did not recoil or feel panic. I was so thankful to still have a few more weeks together before he joined his boat, the USS *Georgia*, SSGN-729.

The sailors, I'd soon learn, called her by many names: *the boat, the sub, the seven-two-nine, The Good Ship Georgia.* None of the names irked me though, as much as when they simply called her *Georgia.* We'd go out with Doug's friends from work, to a bar or a baseball game, and all they'd do was talk about *Georgia.*

They'd talk about the meals they ate and the movies they watched on board. They'd talk about her parts, her controls, and her dilapidating engine room. Over beers, they'd walk through her maneuvers and feats or recount stories from past underways. Like skyscrapers in the dark, the sailors light up from head to toe. Even when he's being sarcastic or gets a little drunk, Doug is rarely more vibrant and alive than when he talks about his *Georgia.*

Over time, after he joined the *Georgia* and I got to know the older, more veteran wives, I'd learn how to cover up my annoyance with their boat-love—how to take a long drink and politely step away, or lock eyes with another spouse and join her conversation instead. The "ultimate poker face," one could call it. We are the wives. We wait on the shore for the men to return filled with more and more stories of their *Georgia.* Their beloved *Georgia.* Her name rolls easy off their lips and sounds like poison.

At home, Doug and I talk about her all the time. We talk about normal *tell-me-about-your-day* things: trainings, drills, schedules. In emails when he's gone, he tells me all about what *cool* new things he got to do with her that day: dive her, drive her, bring her up to periscope depth, lead her in and out of port as lookout. On bad days, he complains of her small spaces, cold showers, and outdated systems. There are always stacks of paperwork to be done, drills to be run, and no sleep to be had. Though the injuries Doug's sustained onboard are minor, they take months to heal, and every time he emails me about them he classifies them by what part of the *Georgia* ailed him: *the sunburn I got on the bridge, the cuts from maneuvering, the spot on my head where I clipped the locker in the engine room.*

"Yeah, there's no way this won't scar. Damn *Georgia.*"

The whole walk back to our hotel that night from the National Portrait

Gallery, I watched the streetlights play off Doug's beard, enraptured, watching the hairs turn from green, to yellow, to red with the traffic signals.

In the room, I stretched out on the bed while he brushed his teeth and laid out his clothes for the next day, carefully refolding whatever he pulled out of his suitcase. I watched him go back and forth between the dresser and the bathroom sink, enjoying the way every movement, every step was so calculated, so efficient and precise. I savored the soft sound of his footfalls on the carpet as if they were sips of fine wine. *This is my partner, my husband,* I thought to myself. *How cool is this? How lucky am I?*

"Hey," I said, smiling at him from the downy mountain of pillows I'd built. "I kind of like your beard."

He stopped and looked sideways at me, "You do?"

"Yeah, it's really...*red!*"

He walked back into the bathroom, rubbing his hand across his chin as if he were blending the colors all together like oil pastels. "Yep. My *Patrick* is showing." Patrick being the middle name he inherited from his father's Irish side of the family.

"Well, I like your Patrick."

He poked his head out from the bathroom and saw me grinning at him so he stepped out and struck a pose like a model, hands on his hips, jutting his chin out and up toward the ceiling. Catching his reflection another mirror, he turned again and stroked his stubble, gazing into his own reflection, as if deep in thought.

"It's so *bad,* so patchy," he laughed, sounding embarrassed.

"No, no. Don't kid yourself," I told him. "It's so thick, if I didn't know you, I'd say you were a...a lumberjack."

"It's a shame," he said, yawning and stretching his arms up, walking toward the bed. "You'll never see how majestic it'll get."

"What do you mean?"

"We don't have to shave during deployments. Keeps morale up and saves water."

I didn't know what to say, but I felt suddenly sick. He continued, unaware.

"It's gonna get *sooo* long and crazy and you'll never know!"

I'll never know.

That night, after he fell asleep, I sobbed quietly in the bathroom.

It wasn't enough that the *Georgia* would soon take up his every waking moment, sap his energy, or convey him across oceans far, far away from home and into zones of imminent danger. It wasn't enough for her to call all the shots: where we lived and for how long, what we talked about, and when we got to see one another, got to hold one another—all things at the mercy of the boat. She was ravenous, always taking. Along with the big things, like the time and the energy, she was taking little things now too, the things about Doug I loved the most: his smile, his laugh, the radio jingles he sings while he shaves, his mirror poses. My newfound love for his beard. Nothing was enough for *Georgia*; she had to have the best of him.

After our trip, the countdown of weeks until his first deployment began. They flew. We fought often and hard over his commitment to the *Georgia*, the Navy, and his fellow sailors, who all seemed to come before me and our still-sapling marriage. We spoke about the *Georgia* as if she were, again, a person right there in the room. *What does that boat care about you? She doesn't need you. I do.* The fights were worse than the ones we had in college over my old boyfriend because the *Georgia* had far more power over us, over me, than the boyfriend ever had.

Doug always argued that it wasn't true, that I came first, but he wasn't the one being left behind. What did he know about feeling second place? His protests made it seem like he wanted to fight for the boat instead of for me.

Just before Valentine's Day, Doug left, bound for the waiting *Georgia* on the other side of the world. There, he and the others would relieve their opposite crew and take the boat out for a four-month mission, doing things I wasn't allowed to know.

In the middle of that first deployment, there were violent attacks and unrest in regions where I knew the *Georgia* might be. I was both glued to the news and repelled by it for fear her name would get brought up. Each time I tuned in for more than a few minutes or CNN sent an update though my phone, I was overcome by nausea and my heart would palpitate wildly. Tomahawks were being fired from the sea. After a month, I had to mute updates from my news apps and consciously keep the TV off the news channels—always one story away from signaling disaster or doom for my husband.

I prayed for the *Georgia* in those days. She was all I had, all that would keep Doug safe. Her hull was the only thing between him and the ocean outside, and, since submarines are largely defenseless, her missiles were the entire offensive the crew would have for whatever danger came her way. I had no choice but to love the *Georgia* then. And I had no idea how often, how violently, the cycle of close disasters would repeat in each of his times underway.

Whenever Doug comes home after a long time away, he always shows me selfies he took of his beard. He never lets it get too long because it gets itchy, he says. Plus, the patchiness persists and makes him a bit of a lightning rod for beard jokes amongst the other sailors. The pictures are poorly lit. The bottom half of his face looks pixelated against the bulkheads around him but is really only blurred by all the hairs on his jaw. There are little white hairs in those pictures now, in the hair above his ears and around his chin.

There is no love letter I could write that would explain how terrible it is to see that beard and not once reach out to feel it. This man of mine, this sailor, he's not a prince, he's not made of marble. He's all I have, he's more.

He's so, so far away.

CHAPTER 10

Louie

The Saturday before my twenty-third birthday, June of 2015, Doug and I were absolutely not going to adopt a dog. We were going to go to the local shelter's weekly event up the street from our place in Charleston to *"just look"* and get an idea about what breed, age, or size dog we'd be looking to bring home in the future. Soon, but not today.

We'd been married about three months and had no interest in having kids yet, but we'd been talking about a dog for years. He'd grown up with a Boston Terrier and I'd grown up wishing for a dog of my own that, for many reasons, never materialized. Our foggy, unofficial plan as newlyweds was to adopt some sort of dog before Doug started deploying as a companion for me. Through Doug's long days at Power School, I'd begun to get a glimpse of how quiet the house would be when it was just me. Adopting a dog was the way, we'd heard, that many spouses cope with the domestic solitude of repeated deployments and long duty days. It seemed the clear solution to our two very glaring problems: loneliness and doglessness.

A couple in line before us pointed to a long-legged, brindle, hound-looking puppy and a shelter volunteer lifted him out of the crate where his equally long-legged black and white brother had been sitting, observing. When the black and white brother realized he was alone, he groaned audibly and flopped over on his side, causing the whole cage to rattle.

A volunteer asked us which dog we'd like to see.

"That one." I didn't confer with Doug at all. I nodded at the black and white puppy who'd groaned. Doug laughed though, and I saw that my arms were already half extended, waiting to receive the hound.

He was deceptively heavy for the six pounds the volunteer said he weighed, and his legs were so long it didn't matter how carefully I cradled him, his paws kept springing free and dangling past my elbows. His long tail wagged loosely down by my hip. The puppy yawned, looked between Doug and I for about three seconds, sniffing at our chins, and then nestled into the bend of my elbow, groaned again, and fell asleep. He started to hiccup and, just as he'd rattled his crate, each *hic* shook my entire upper body. One of his ears draped over my forearm. It was as big as a cocktail napkin and I was smitten as hell.

We asked the volunteer a few questions: What breed is he? How big will he get? He was only seven or eight weeks old; his fur, mostly black with white markings on his paws, nose, and the back of his neck and his belly, where it wasn't pink from newness, was flecked with gray freckles, like someone had splattered him with paint.

"Beagledor. Forty pounds," said the volunteer. I knew plenty of Beagles and Labradors who made good dogs, so the combination would likely be the best of both worlds, I thought. Forty pounds seemed like a good size too: not too big, not too small. It was all the logic I needed.

"Sam?" Doug was scratching the puppy's entire head with just two of his fingers. "Are we—is this…are we actually doing this?"

"This is Louie," I grinned. Louie was the name of the St. Louis Blues' hockey mascot, and the name of our hometown.

"Louie," Doug repeated. "Ok. Hi, Louie. Hey, boy." The puppy hiccupped again, barely stirring.

We were hurried before the shelter director who signed our papers, then spirited away by a pet store employee with a shopping cart who filled it with half a dozen bones, chews, and toys we didn't know we needed. In the checkout line, the shelter's resident trainer, James—a heavily-tattooed older man with a black bandana around his head and a Claus-esque white beard—ran us through his *Puppy 101* spiel like a flight attendant before takeoff: "Just remember: he's an alien. He's not your baby; he's an alien living in your house. He doesn't know your language, so you have to teach him." He handed us his business card and we stepped out of the pet store, blinking in the sunlight, looking back and forth between one another and the still-sleeping dog we'd adopted even though we'd been *just looking*, and asked one another without saying a word, *how the hell did that just happen?*

"He's going to be the best dog."

"I know."

"We'll take him on walks…"

"Teach him tricks!"

"The dog park!"

"The beach!"

It was our foolproof plan to raise the mellowest, sweetest dog ever born. The perfect furry companion for when Doug deployed.

Our small, sleepy beagledor remained that for about nineteen more hours.

Louie put on a good show for our families, whom we Skyped that evening from our apartment floor to announce our "big news." He sniffed at the phone camera, yawned a lot, and, most endearingly, scratched so furiously at his new collar that he toppled over backwards with a loud squeal and then another one of the groans that seemed to be his thing. The next morning, my birthday, after taking him out for a walk around the parking lot, I lay on the carpet facing the ceiling; he climbed on top of me, stretched out on my chest and fell asleep in the space between my boobs. Careful not to disturb him, I raised my arms and took a picture on my phone, then texted it to my mom. She responded with a few niceties: "What a sweetheart, look at those big paws." Then, quite prophetically: "That ain't no beagledor."

After the nap on my chest the morning I turned twenty-three, Louie went from a soft, sleepy lump of puppy into what James the trainer would later describe as "a mouth with legs."

Doug stepped out of the bedroom and Louie bounded off my chest, lolloping toward him. He pounced and sunk his teeth into Doug's big toe causing Doug to leap back and shout, "*Shit*—Louie!" That would be his name for a while: *Shit-Louie*, as would *Ow, Stop, No Biting, Good God,* and *Jesus Christ*.

In so many ways Louie was just a normal, mouthy puppy. Everything that moved was a new friend, a new toy, and puppies do all their greeting, learning, and exploring with their mouths. And, as anyone who has ever played with an eight-week-old puppy knows, there is nothing on Earth sharper than eight-week-old puppy teeth. To his credit, he was not destructive. He knew what his toys were but didn't care. All he liked to bite was Doug and me. He was sweet to strangers: the property manager, our neighbors, and friends who came to meet him but, with us, he was carnivorous.

And it wasn't just that his teeth were sharp; he was stronger than should have been possible for a thing his size. Even at just a few months old, he had visible muscles that rippled when he trotted around outside, hunting for June bugs and fallen sticks which were only temporary diversions until he remembered that June bugs and sticks didn't yelp when you clamped down on them like we did.

Doug and I reached out to anyone and everyone we knew who had ever owned a dog for advice on how to curb the behavior. We posted calls for help on Facebook and committed to trying every bit of advice that filtered back our way. In my spare time, I read page after page on dog training websites and forums for excessive puppy biting.

We started off by ignoring Louie when he bit. If he laid teeth on us, we dropped whatever toy we'd been playing with and turned our back to him to signal that play stopped when he nipped. That was how I got my ponytail pulled, and how Doug got scores of puncture holes in the back of his shirts. Then we tried "time outs." When Louie bit, we'd scoop him up in one hand and put him in his crate for a minute or two which, allegedly, would calm him down. However, crate time outs seemed to rev him up even more and he'd greet whomever came to release him with a wagging tail, a pounce, and full-mouthed chomp on the forearm like a paperclip to a magnet. I took him to the vet to see if the biting was his way of telling us that he was in some sort of pain. The vet determined that it wasn't and recommended a set of expensive teething toys that we'd already bought and Louie habitually ignored.

We called James the trainer from the shelter and he recommended a spray bottle and sent links to videos demonstrating how a quick shot of water to the face could deter unwanted puppy behavior. But Louie loved the water—*loved* it. Somehow, it was better than the water we put out in his bowl and he figured out quickly that if he bit one of us, he'd get a spritz and lap it up off his face greedily, long tail thwacking this way and that. At the recommendation of a friend, I bought a cheap playpen on Amazon to corral him which worked for all of six minutes before our fast-growing dog realized he could easily bound up and over the side to come bite my ankles while I was cooking in the kitchen. We read many places that the key to solving biting was exercise, so every day I leashed him up and tried to take him for a jog or a walk but he was so stubborn and so strong he'd put on the brakes and we'd barely get a mile. In frustration and out of ideas, I sometimes Googled *what the fuck is wrong with my dog* just to see if anything relevant popped up. Nothing did.

For weeks, Doug and I went to work looking like we'd been mauled by small bears in our off-hours. At Power School where he was spending the majority of his time, the sailors wore short-sleeved khakis four days a week or rolled up their camo sleeves on Fridays, which meant baring new bloody scrapes and punctures every day, never mind the cuts on his face that he didn't cover up with makeup like I did. At the time, I worked at a jewelry store. It was protocol there to push up one's sleeves before reaching into a case, lest the fibers of your clothing snag on the jewelry or leave threads and fuzz in the diamond displays. Whenever I did so, my customers would see Louie's bite marks, gasp, and ask what happened, or if I was alright. I sold my first engagement ring to a religious couple who promised to pray that I be lifted out of whatever "darkness" I was going through.

I kept returning to my mother's comment that Louie was "no beagledor" because, as the weeks went on, it became obvious that she was absolutely right. The older and more alert he got, his droopy cocktail-napkin ears perked up and flipped backwards which erased any semblance of beagle and made it clear he was at least part pit bull. Being as ignorant as we were, and partially buying into all the negative press, we supposed his breed to be the reason for his biting problem. Doubled with that was the anxiety that we were living the military life, so more moving and more rentals were in our future and very few properties allow pits. We held out hope when people we met on our leash-dragging "walks" asked what type of hound he was, or when we saw him beside our neighbor's Great Dane puppy and noted the remarkable similarities—even now fully grown, Louie looks like a shrunken Great Dane. But there was no denying his pit-blood and it stressed me out.

But everything stressed me out then. Doug was hardly home anymore. He spent over eighty hours a week studying in Power School on base. Because the material was classified and couldn't be brought home, this meant I was usually alone with Louie, overwhelmed by more than just his biting. Though it would still be a while until Doug was attached to a boat, with every passing day, he was closer to deploying. I'd dreaded the loneliness, the separation, for years with intensity that was reaching its peak. Louie was supposed to be my comforter, but I couldn't get near him without bracing for pain. I'd never truly been able to keep it together when I thought about Doug leaving, but it was even harder now that I was living most of my newlywed days alone because the Navy demanded all of his attention, and I was doing it while cohabitating with an alien that would rather mangle than snuggle.

Many nights, Doug would come home around midnight to find me sobbing on the carpet in front of Louie's crate so upset by the biting that I couldn't even talk and, when I finally could, I'd speak the unspeakable: "We have to give him back."

"Sam," he'd plead, not saying much else. He didn't have to remind me that if we gave up on Louie, or on a dog in general, it would ensure my aloneness in the not-so-distant future. We both knew it was better that I wrestle our canine-shark crossbreed every day than be by myself during a deployment. We *had* to figure this out, we agreed.

Though our budget was tight, we hired James from the shelter to work with us and teach us how to be dog-parents, though he repeated often that Louie was *not* our baby, but an alien. James, for all his grizzled, tattooed toughness admitted that, yes, we had one hell of a biter, a "mouth with legs"—which made me feel a little better to have it acknowledged by a professional. He fitted Louie with a martingale collar that cinched when we pulled it and showed us how to use the cinching not only to deter biting but teach Louie his boundaries. We'd walk him around the apartment on the leash and give a sharp, quick jerk anytime he sniffed something he wasn't supposed to like the trash can or toilet water. James gave us a list of commands to use and rules Louie needed to follow to be a part of our "pack," including never sleeping in our bed and getting "permission to come aboard" before hopping up on the couch. James taught us the best ways to grip the leash for walks, and our dog who'd been previously un-walkable, barely draggable, did three easy miles with his tongue out panting and tail wagging all the way. During one session, we confessed to James that Louie had figured out when to whine to wake me up, versus when to whine to wake Doug up on the weekends and had thus conned his way into getting two breakfasts several Saturdays in a row. James applauded this delinquency and encouraged us to harness Louie's so-called intelligence and teach him tricks to engage his mind so he would be less and less inclined to engage with his teeth.

For Christmas that year, Doug gifted me a Wisdom Panel DNA kit to test Louie's breed and I wasn't scared to learn the results. By then, Louie's biting had stopped, and he'd discovered the deafening joy of squeaky toys. Of the two of us, Doug was the one Louie most liked to play with because he'd play rough and never tire. At eight months old, Lou weighed in at fifty-five pounds—a full fifteen over the shelter's original estimate—and still had many months of growing left to do. I'd become, and remain, Louie's favorite one to snuggle with, which makes Doug jealous. Louie used to join me in an armchair meant for one small person, so I'd read to him out loud as he stood over me, and he'd never make it more than a page or two before circling twice and plopping down, happily crushing me with his bulk.

The DNA test showed that he was mostly Labrador and American Bulldog (one of the many breeds that fall under the pit bull "umbrella," followed by smaller parts Boxer, English bulldog, and Treeing Walker Coonhound. A mutt if there ever was one, but he was my mutt, *our* mutt. By then, he'd even earned his name back and we called him by it with ever-increasing affection.

In the dwindling days before deployment, Doug and I find ourselves talking a lot about the *shit-Louie* days. We reminisce about the hiccups that got him adopted, and the teeth that very nearly got him un-adopted. James comes up often in conversation, especially his rules we eventually, deliberately broke, or the ones we never could quite enforce, like making Louie get permission before hopping up on the couch. Doug gives me trouble for breaking the strict "no dog on the bed" rule when he started shift work at Prototype and his side of the bed was too empty for me to handle, so it became Louie's whenever Doug worked nights. Louie then took full ownership of Doug's spot after our move from Charleston down to Jacksonville because it was just that, *our* move—mine and Louie's. I bought a throw pillow for the bed that read *reserved for the dog*, and it wasn't really a joke.

During the move, Doug was away at submarine school in Groton, Connecticut, so Louie and I were the ones who did the final walk-through in the Charleston apartment and made the drive down to Florida that same day. Louie was the one to bark at the movers from outside as he ran laps around his new, fenced backyard and the one to sniff every nail, screw, and washer that came with the Ikea bookshelves I assembled in the living room. When Doug graduated from sub school and came down to live with us a couple months later, Louie tried to nudge him out of the master bed at night by butting him with his large, square head, and when that didn't work, he went back to groaning loudly.

Doug and I talk about how strong he is, how quickly he grew or how, though he's nearing three years old, still seems to be growing.

We talk so much about Louie, in part, because he remains our *baby*, no matter what James said about him being an alien, but also because talking about Louie is one of the only things that makes us both smile in the dwindling days before deployment.

We've spent days going over packing lists, hours out shopping for more socks and undershirts to make sure he has enough, and long nights fighting about what his leaving means. To him, it's just the job; to me, it's evidence that that he cares more about the Navy than he does about me. We're both a little bit right, and a little bit wrong.

We've sat down in restaurants, intending to have "deployment-free" date nights, but end up talking through all the what-ifs we need to cover before the boat leaves and we lose the ability to communicate freely without censors reading our emails: *what do you want me to do if something happens to your family, my family, the car, the house? What if something happens to Louie or me? What if something happens on the sub; what if you get hurt?* Although I am statistically more likely to die or be injured in a car accident than he is on the submarine, we hinge on the boat, the thing so familiar to him, but so foreign to me, as the source of danger. It's true, in part, that his commission in the Navy precludes him from certain situations, like infantry combat, but it does not, as so many seem to believe, exempt him from danger altogether. I always think about my high school choir teacher, an Army reservist, who laughed when finding out Doug was going to be a submariner: "isn't your battle cry like *Aloha* or something?"

People still die, still get maimed, electrocuted, and burned on submarines. The submarine is made of machinery; it's a delicate task not to get caught in any of it while moving about. One *Georgia* sailor on the opposite crew had his hand sliced off in the trash compactor and had to be medevaced and flown to Spain for reattachment. Doug's crew was unique in the fact that the only medical evacuation they had to do was for a pre-existing condition, rather than an accident: a sailor's stress-induced stomach ulcers flared up and caused him to collapse in the shower just three days out of port. The year before Doug arrived on the *Georgia* was the year she ran aground entering Kings Bay. The way I've heard it told was the captain, who'd only ever commanded a smaller, more maneuverable fast attack boat, took the channel too quickly, making turns at angles the slower, larger *Georgia* wasn't meant for. The sub struck a buoy and then scraped into the shallow shoreline, damaging the bow. Thanks to the Weapons officer who ordered the boat to reverse direction—*back emergency*—the hull never breached. But hulls can breach; they do breach.

Over dinner before deployment, though we always say we won't, Doug and I review what he'd like me to do if he returns injured or if, for whatever reason, he doesn't return home at all. Where should I bury him, or rather, where should I place his headstone, since his body would likely be somewhere at the bottom of the ocean? It is around then, when we are in some dimly lit restaurant or bar, that we realize I am choking up and he is squeezing his glass so hard it may break if he doesn't let go. Our attempts to forget about deployment for a little while have failed. One of us tries to return to talking about Louie:

What do you want me to do if you get hurt and they keep you overseas?

Remember how Louie used to pick up Spanish moss like a beard?

Have you thought about funeral preferences? Do you want cremation? Burial? Does it matter?

Remember how he'd sneak woodchips in his jowls so he could crunch them up inside on the carpet?

What would I tell Louie if you didn't come home?

Tell him I say he's a good boy, even when he's a total shit.

Difficult as it is, these are important conversations to have before his departure, especially in the post—USS *John S. McCain* and USS *Fitzgerald* collision era, but it's unbelievably draining. We are never more relieved than when we pull into the garage, get out of the car (where I've often cried most of the way home), and rush to be the first to let Louie out of his crate.

The final day before deployment, I always let Doug win while I keep careful tabs on all the *lasts*.

Last shower; last shave. Last time he'll have to stop talking in the middle of a sentence, holding up one finger, waiting for a sneeze. Last sex on the bed. Last sex on the couch. Last change of clothes. Last dirty laundry he'll throw in the hamper that I will have to wash, fold, and put away later, weeping because it will be many months before he sees it again, before I see it on him.

Last walk around the neighborhood with Louie trotting between us, veering off to sniff every utility box and streetlight. Last time we will be sitting side by side, leaning into one another on the couch, watching TV, and have Louie stand in front of us, whining until we scooch apart and give him the spot between us so he can circle twice, then plop down with his head on me and his back end on Doug, hitting him with his tail as it wags. Last time making him roll over for a *t-r-e-a-t*. Last time he will interrupt us packing the sea bags by jumping up on the bed with his squeaky alligator, chomping it and growling low, waiting for one of us to take his bait. Last time Doug will wrestle away the alligator and lay on top of it, forcing Louie to jam his paws and nose beneath Doug to try and reach it, frantically barking at me as if to say, *oh my God, help, will you?*

Last laps through the house, checking once, then again, to make sure everything that's supposed to be packed is packed while Louie follows along unaware, nails clicking on the tile, tags jingling like loose change. Last-minute reminders scribbled on Post-its and stuck to my steering wheel so neither of us forgets them when it's time to go, time to drop Doug off for deployment.

Travel card. Phone charger. Put on watch.

I can never watch Doug and Louie say goodbye because only Doug knows it's goodbye.

On his knees, Doug rubs Louie behind the ears, under the chin, and tries his hardest to hug Louie to his chest. Louie usually seems confused by the heaping on of affection from Doug, who's the one to roughhouse with, not hug. He'll lick Doug's face politely then wriggle away, hopping backwards, trying to figure out if this unusual ritual is the start of some new game. His tail wags; his ears twitch. Doug tells him to be a good boy and to take care of Momma—me—until he gets home. I put Louie in his crate while Doug loads his bags into the trunk. Before his second deployment, on the drive up to base, Doug told me that he has a harder time saying goodbye to Louie than he does to me because he can't email with the dog while he's underway.

We aren't sure if Louie is allowed on base for the drop-off. It's not that the information is secret, or impossible to find out, we just never think about looking into it until it's too late, and we can't risk putting him in the car and driving the whole forty minutes to base only to be turned away by the gate guard for having a dog, a *pit bull*, without a pass, (if the supposed passes even exist.) But there are always a few dogs in the training facility parking lot, the predesignated drop-off point, in those early hours of the morning when Doug's deployments invariably begin. My guess is that they're dogs from base housing who would already be approved to come on base, since they live there, but we never ask. It's not the time.

We've sat, on day-zero of deployment, in the dark, in the car with the engine off, both wondering aloud why we didn't think to check into the hypothetical dog-pass so Louie could come with us, and perhaps make goodbye a little easier.

Nothing we've brought makes it easier.

I babble, around and around, reminding Doug where we packed his extra socks, spare shampoo, and his slippers, the words spilling out of me like a pot boiling over as we run out of time. I've never been able to resist bringing up his slippers—a Christmas gift I gave him years ago. And although it's a stale laugh by now, there's something endlessly entertaining about going off to war with sheepskin moccasins from L.L. Bean. What imminent dangers could one possibly face in fuzzy loafers? It's funny until he reminds me how cold it gets onboard when the sub dives and crawls through the deep, how they all bundle up in their racks just to sleep without shivering themselves onto the floor. Then it's serious again. He brings slippers because he's in a metal tube, underwater, leagues away from the warmth of the sun and it's very, very cold down there.

I can't ever bear to look at the assembled caravan: old school buses painted white and a semi-truck for the gear that some members of the crew are already starting to load with the big, black, locked Pelican cases full of mission documents and materials, a case or two of care packages from families, and mountains of sea bags. The sound of sailors' huffing and shouting as they load the truck carries for what seems like miles.

"If Louie were here," I've told Doug, "he'd be in the truck sniffing."

Doug usually drops his bags off right after we arrive, then jogs back to the car to hold my hand while we watch the lot fill with the rest of his crew. Some of the single sailors break out footballs and soccer balls and turn the grassy medians into playing fields to stretch their legs before spending days on the plane. Sailors walk their dogs around, letting them sniff at the asphalt, just as unaware as Louie about what's about to happen. Friend groups congregate on dropped tailgates or open trunks, talking, stretching, yawning. Most though, couples and families with children, wait in their cars, like us. Some are our friends, fellow officers and their spouses, and it's hard to resist the urge to wave or go say hi, as we would in any other situation. If their cab lights are on, you can peer inside nearby cars and watch each little family unit go through their motions of goodbye. In the drop-off lot, I've watched fathers read bedtime stories from the front seat, turned around toward the back to show the pictures to their little ones in car seats. I've watched little babies be rocked and fed bottles by fathers who know they're about to miss first words, first steps. I've watched all-out sobbing as often as restrained weeping, dabbing at the eyes with tissues.

For some reason, I don't cry immediately. There's a surge of adrenaline right there at the end of our time together that keeps me from doing anything but staring at Doug as the minutes, then the seconds, tick away. I squeeze his hand until mine shakes, as if holding it harder will keep him from walking away.

When the all-call comes, it's shouted from the buses as the luggage truck's door slams shut. Children old enough to know, but not old enough to bottle it up, wail openly.

Load up!

Then it all happens quickly. We get out of the car. Stand at the trunk. A hug. A kiss, another kiss. When I breathe, the air burns.

"Sam," he says, whispering low in my ear. "I love you. It's going to be OK."

I shake my head, breathing even harder, but trying to keep it in check. It does not feel like it is going to be ok.

"You have to drive home safely, Sam."

I shake my head again. I don't want to drive home. Not without Doug.

"You have to get home safe for Louie."

Louie. He's right. I do.

I promise him I will be safe. That's usually when I lose it and cry, hiding my face into his chest, leaving a damp spot on his jacket that remains, he'll tell me later, until they've boarded the plane.

Another hug. I get in the car. Doug walks away. Then he's knocking on my window for one last hug, one last kiss. He tells me one last time to be safe. Then it's the last, *last*.

Doug walks away for the last time and disappears into the sea of shuffling bodies and thumping backpacks. I don't see him board the bus. Like I've been plunged into icy water, everything hurts, and it's suddenly like my lungs are filling up with ocean. I could exhale and watch my last breath rise to the surface.

I defy any member of law enforcement to pull over a military spouse as she speeds away from deployment drop-off.

The fastest and most recklessly I ever drive is the drive home from base after surrendering Doug to the boat. I launch myself down I-95 going at least fifteen, sometimes twenty, over the speed limit so the crew's buses, who take the same highway down to the air station, cannot overtake me. Everything is blurry. Everything seems turned upside down.

I can't hear the radio. I'm lightheaded and unable to think rationally. *What exit is mine? Do I go northbound or south?* The car feels like it's steering itself, even though I know I'm behind the wheel, I'm somewhere lost in a world that isn't mine. Over and over I wonder, in a panic, if I know, or still remember how to do this alone. Was that goodbye for now or goodbye forever?

Louie and I have lived alone, just the two of us, before. After Doug graduated from Power School and Prototype, he went to Submarine Officer Basic Course—SOBC—in Groton, Connecticut for just over two months while Louie and I stayed back in Charleston. During that time, I was just starting graduate school and working odd hours as a swim instructor for a nearby school.

Louie and I did everything together those months. He'd wake me up in the morning and we'd go out jogging, then we'd eat breakfast together: him from his bowl and me, standing at the counter. When I had work to do for grad school, I'd sit on the couch with my laptop and he'd hop up and settle down beside me, usually placing his head across my wrists on the keyboard for added closeness. At night, while I read in bed, Louie would chew on a bone until he felt it was time to sleep, then he'd drop the bone off the bed, walk up to my left side—always my left—circle twice, and fall asleep with his body tucked in the bend of my waist and his head resting on my hip. During Hurricane Matthew, we evacuated together and slept this way in a motel outside of Atlanta.

When it was time to move to Jacksonville, Doug was still at sub school, so Louie and I did the move together. Louie was big by then, almost as big as he is now: seventy pounds of long legs and broad muscly chest, still speckled with gray like it was the day we brought him home, his ears still just a hair too large for his head. Standing beside me, the top of his head hits right at my hip.

I chose our Jacksonville house for its big, fenced backyard and its long living room that gave Louie plenty of room to gallop around with his toys. In the weeks before Doug joined us, we'd go on walks through the neighborhood or I'd take him to the dog park and let him run, always taking pictures and videos to text to Doug who, for all the miles between us, was still just a phone call away—a convenience we both took for granted.

I tell myself often, at the beginning of deployments, that *I can do this*. I remind myself that I enjoyed those days of just Louie and me more than I thought I would. I got to be independent, didn't have to share Louie's affection, but still had someone to call every night and Facetime about the new trails we'd walked, or the cool coffee shop I'd found. When Louie would hear Doug's voice, his still-big ears would perk up and twitch around. He'd sniff his way up to the hand where I held the phone and cock his head to the side when Doug greeted him: *Hey Louie! Hi boy! Hi buddy! You being good?* Louie's tail would thwack hard against whatever was nearest. Our family, though separated by miles, never felt closer.

Deployment begins, Doug could not be farther away, and I can hardly bear to look at Louie. The first deployment, I collapsed in the doorway from the garage into the laundry room because I walked in and smelled our detergent and it smelled like Doug. I don't remember if I walked or crawled all the way back to our bedroom, to Louie's crate, but I let him loose and he bounded away, into the other room for his stuffed gator. He had no idea that our world had been upended.

All deployments, in my experience, start on the couch. The first deployment drop-off was at two in the morning on a Friday, the second, at three AM on a Saturday so, while the Friday-starting deployment was briefly punctuated by a day of teaching that I remember nothing of, most of the first few days of Doug's absence I spend wrapped in a quilt, practically comatose with grief.

It's too quiet in the house, so I turn on the TV for sound, but whatever is on, be it the evening news or *Real Housewives*, reminds me of Doug, which is too much to handle, so I switch over to Netflix (a feat that requires me to turn on and access it through the Xbox—another painful reminder of Doug). On Netflix I find the dirtiest, raunchiest stand-up comedy available and turn the volume way, way up. I don't care about the jokes; I'm listening to the audience's laughter, hoping that their raucous joy will somehow dilute my misery. Humor by osmosis, or something. Sobbing comes on and off in rounds without warning. I cling to my phone, watching obsessively for the last texts from Doug during layovers in foreign airports, our last communication before he reaches the boat in a few days' time.

Sometimes a fellow wife will send out an e-vite for a get-together in the coming days—something to look forward to—to get us all out of the slump. Even then though, it often feels like you're suffering alone.

My mom will text to say I can call her if I want.

I don't want to, but after a little while I do anyway. Talking to her is the first time I try to speak after Doug leaves. My voice is raspy from crying, and I continue choking up for the few minutes she's on the line. She understands; she tells me it's ok to wallow for a day or so, which I will, whether I want to or not.

I understand that my wallowing is a privilege I enjoy because I do not have children. The Navy moms I know must jump right into single parenting the second the sailors depart, feeding infants, making lunches, and wiping away their own children's tears if they are old enough to know. However, it is a misconception that I have no one to take care of beside myself.

For those first few days, Louie is the only thing in the house that moves and it breaks my heart. He trots around, sniffing at doors, especially the laundry room, where the garage door lets into the house. I know he is looking for Doug. Doug is the one who plays, so he stuffs a toy in his mouth, like the alligator, and paces around with it, squeaking it, as if to call Doug home. Even weeks into the deployment, I've tripped over the toys Louie scatters by the laundry room door, leaving them there, waiting for Doug to walk in and play, just as I am, but only I understand he won't be back anytime soon. After a while, anytime he pads near it, Louie groans at the garage door Doug left through.

Louie whining by the other door, the slider into the backyard, is about the only thing that gets me upright those first few days. The only thing I want to do less than sob over Doug's departure is sob while cleaning dog pee off the carpet. Taking Louie out into the backyard is the first time I will feel fresh air, or smell rain; it's the first time I will recognize that something pleasant still exists outside my personal disaster. And Louie has never been one to miss a meal, so when it nears his normal breakfast or dinner time, if I'm horizontal on the sofa, he will sit very close to my face and press his nose against my cheek, sniffing until I get up to fill his bowl. In his excitement, Louie performs all the tricks I taught him when we lived without Doug—*roll over, high five, shake, heel*—and I can almost smile, remembering how much fun it was to train him, then Skype Doug to show him Louie's new trick. While he's eating, I start to look at my phone not in hopes of a text or an email from Doug, but for new tricks to teach our dog. I ask Louie if he'd like to learn play dead, and he whips his head up from the water bowl, flinging slobber all over the tile. Louie gives me a new goal, and a kitchen floor to mop.

I work in Jacksonville as a middle school teacher. When it's time for me to go back to work, I wake up at four-thirty in the morning, even though school doesn't start until seven. I always walk Louie before getting ready, whether Doug is home or not. The return to routine is comforting and while, for those first few weeks, I know I will still weep in the car and drug myself to sleep early to avoid accumulating more conscious, miserable hours missing him, I will also try to play with Louie like Doug does. We will roughhouse on the carpet or out in the yard, and I will make him growl like he does when Doug wrestles the alligator out of his mouth and holds it high in the air before chucking it as far as he can for Louie to chase and retrieve. The first time I laugh after the start of a deployment is usually because of something Louie does, like barking at a lawn ornament, or crashing into the fence while chasing a moth. It feels good to laugh again, even if it takes a while.

When it comes to receiving his due affection, Louie does not care that Doug is gone, he never changes his habits. If I am sitting down, he'll walk up to me and push my hand around with his nose until I scratch underneath his chin, or he'll sit next to me and nudge at my arm until I raise it so he can turn twice and flop down, half beside me, half on top of me. Louie still gets the hiccups almost as much as he did as a puppy, but now that he's bigger, they're many times as jarring if you're the one he's chosen to lay against. And in those first hours, when I can't stand up from all my crying, Louie worms his way up onto the couch with me, stretched out to his full length which is almost as long as mine, and lays on his back next to me, in the sliver of space between my body and the back of the couch, with his head tucked under my armpit. My *pit* bull, I call him then. We both lose a big part of our lives when Doug deploys, and our little family of three feels harshly fractioned when it's just us two.

I try to do laundry as soon as I can after Doug leaves just to get those last few pieces of his clothing out of the way, so I don't have to endure the sight or smell of them any longer than I have to. I don't shed my last tears of the deployment over his t-shirts or socks as I move them from the washer to the dryer, but they're the last of the hard tears, the parking lot tears, that began at the last of the last goodbyes. I can place the last of his laundry neatly in the drawers without cramming or stuffing because most of his shirts and shorts and socks and boxers are with him now, under the ocean.

Louie sits on the end of our bed when I put away laundry, no matter who is or isn't home. He tips his head to one side if I talk to him and jumps if I drop a hanger or shut a drawer too loud but, for the most part, he simply stays there, just looking, just watching me try to go on.

CHAPTER 11

Chopped

F ood Network is a safe place.

Bravo's got entertainment value. I love binge-watching *Southern Charm*, looking for our old Charleston haunts in the background. After a few episodes, though, I get exhausted by the fighting and drama. Sometimes, I watch it on mute for the style and scenery. I love watching *South Park* on Comedy Central but again, the crudeness wears me out. Worse, sometimes I'll see a favorite episode Doug and I used to watch together (There's something timeless about Kanye West, the gay fish, is there not?) HGTV is great, especially *House Hunters International* and *Fixer Upper* but, when I'm missing Doug, the parade of happy couples building beautiful dream homes waxes garish. Movie marathons are a great escape, but do you realize how many of them involve lovers' separation or tragic death? Game shows are a little intense—hosts are corny, the audience is wild, and sometimes contestants lose everything at the last possible second. Of course, the news is worst of all. Every night, every hour someone loses everything.

But not on Food Network—nothing bad ever happens there. Chicken under-bakes, soufflés fall, vegetables burn, and sometimes a chef slices their finger with a knife, requiring the studio's medical team to swoop in with disinfectant and bandages. That's the worst of it. Most days, The Pioneer Woman sweet talks her way through soups and roasts, Bobby Flay beats everyone at everything, and Guy Fieri in his convertible cruises to *Flavortown*. It's predictable, therapeutic even. A lot of times, it makes me wish TVs transmitted smells.

I adopted Food Network as my safe space halfway through Doug's first deployment when my grandmother died in March 2017. Home from the funeral, missing her, I stopped my channel surfing on one of her old favorite shows: *Chopped*. We used to watch it together when I stayed at her house. Four chefs compete through three timed rounds by cooking gourmet appetizers, entrees, and desserts featuring seemingly incompatible ingredients from their "mystery baskets." After each course, one chef is "chopped" from the competition until only one winner remains. Hosted by the affable Ted Allen, each episode is both thrilling and inane. After my grandmother's passing, it was the perfect audiovisual morphine I needed to dull the grief and, just like morphine proper, *Chopped* was addictive as hell. The competing chefs whisk, boil, blanche, season, sear, and plate with intense passion, sweat rolling down their brows. It's like watching a soul in rapture. My life on the other side of the screen felt a little more hopeful, a little brighter, whenever I watched them finesse fennel pollen, banana bread, leeks, and squid ink into something edible and, dare I say, appetizing.

Like so many things, *Chopped* made me think about Doug. Difficult as it was sometimes, I preferred to miss him through the lens of food and cooking than all the other ways I'd missed him already.

For all the ways Doug and I are compatible, culinarily is not one of them. He could live contently on cheeseburgers, chicken parmesan, and canned corn. I, on the other hand, most love seafood and brunch. Doug's three least favorite vegetables—Brussels sprouts, asparagus, and spinach—are what I prepare for myself nearly every day. When we were first living together, the majority of our shared meals were grilled chicken, roasted broccoli, and sautéed mushrooms simply because we "agreed" on them. No complaints, but also no excitement.

Knowing how much he missed his late mother's cooking, I tried again and again to recreate the spaghetti Bolognese she used to make on his birthday every year: a stick of butter, a pound of onions, ground beef, no salt, no pepper, no seasonings, and many spoonfuls of acrid, gluey tomato paste. It always came out smelling like old shoe, nothing like the warm, comforting sauce I'd had at her house dozens of times. After my fourth failed attempt, Doug kindly asked me to stop.

I love the challenge of the Bolognese though, so I used his long nights training and, eventually, his deployments to sharpen my culinary skills. I steamed, marinated, grilled, and sliced to my heart's content. Since he ate most meals at work, I was cooking for myself. I stuck to my favorites: salmon, tilapia, and shrimp with dark, leafy, odorous vegetables. By the time Doug left on his second deployment I was effectively pescatarian and hadn't cooked a meal for him in months. Some parts of deployment begin before you even realize.

Chopped made me think of him though, in gentle ways that I could manage. Anytime a competitor made their basket ingredients into a burger, I thought of Doug pressing beef patties on our George Foreman. One episode had chefs working with cookie ice cream sandwiches—Doug's favorite dessert. Another time, a chef made some sort of loaded cornbread in a cast iron skillet that looked so *Doug*, I backed up the episode and wrote down the steps as best I could. And of course, spaghetti, in any form, was forever a direct, unavoidable path to thinking of my deployed spouse.

Then, the *San Juan* went missing.

Food Network took an immediate, extended backseat to CNN, NBC, and any other outlet covering the sub's disappearance. I spent every waking minute patrolling headlines for good news that never came: *Found: ARA San Juan's Rescue, Miracle: Saving the Crew of ARA San Juan*. I hoped for immediate talks of survivors' book contracts and movie deals, but hope waned so quickly.

When Doug's emails stopped coming shortly after, I knew it was time to switch back to Food Network, to *Chopped*, as often as I could. The more steps back I took from CNN, NBC, and every other outlet covering the *San Juan*, the more likely I was to remain semi-rational. The *Georgia* probably hadn't sunk. Doug probably wasn't dead. They were probably on a mission or the communication networks were probably down. Doug probably just didn't have time to sit down and write. Probably.

Sometimes I'd text other sub wives and try to get them to watch Food Network with me, to discuss the appetizers or desserts. To distract me.

"Turn on *Chopped*! It's the one with that chef from Charlotte you like!"

"Would you believe it? The Italian guy is making bruschetta. Shocking."

"I know, I saw. Water in the risotto instead of broth? Rookie move."

They answered my texts about *Chopped* as often as I answered theirs about *Grey's Anatomy* or reruns of *Friends*. We were all just trying to get by.

The lonelier and more desperate I became, the more conversations with other wives weren't enough. The dog had little to add, so I started talking to God, almost always through *Chopped*. I didn't go to church anymore—hadn't been since my wedding day. I am a rather lapsed Catholic, but talking about *Chopped* with God somehow made perfect sense.

"Looks like this chef's making a pizza. That's creative. Do you know if Doug gets pineapple and black olives on his boat pizza? Is the boat still making pizza?"

"Stir fry chef is gonna win the round. Doug's never liked my stir fry though. I guess it's the shrimp. If he comes home safe, I swear to you I'll make it with chicken or steak, just for him. Every time. I swear."

"If you bring him home safe, I'll make him pure, unadulterated fudge brownies every night. I'll never try using zucchini again."

"If Doug's ok, I'll never complain when he wants barbecue."

"If you keep him alive, I'll learn to make that damn Bolognese."

When you marry into the military, many assume you knew what you were getting yourself into. (Many of those many will tell you as much.) Hand on the Bible, I swear I never thought I'd spend so much time talking to God about *Chopped*. If He was listening, I hope He didn't laugh. I hope He reached his big, omnipotent hand out and guided the *Georgia* out of harm's way, kept her in safe waters. I hope He filled the sailors' heads with thoughts of their loved ones and families, so they remembered for whom they were out fighting for and whom they were to return home safe for.

And I hope He then ignored me and went across the ocean to hold the *San Juan* sailors, the *San Juan* families even closer.

CHAPTER 12

Support and Defend

Our house in Jacksonville, Florida, has a fence around the backyard. It's a privacy fence, made of sinking wooden pickets and bent nails, that stands about six feet high and squares off our little parcel of land: a patch of vine-like St. Augustine grass, flowering weeds, and fire ant mounds. Its gate has been sagging further and further into the mud since Hurricane Matthew and anytime either Doug or I are out in the yard together, we end up discussing what we should do about it since the landlord had all but forsaken us.

We don't want our house to end up looking like our next-door neighbor's, whose fence is missing so many pikes and sections that they essentially have no fence left. It's been like that since we moved in and has only gotten worse with each hurricane its weathered. Because of their lack of fence, when their dogs are outside, they are always tethered to the sapling tree, and always, *always* barking.

My husband and I are born and raised Midwesterners, we cannot always shake the "nice," so we usually say the dogs next door are *talkative* or *chatty* whenever they go ballistic at the sight of our dog, Louie—their female, Nyla, poking her head through a broken picket, snarling and snapping her jaws. The male, Rock, whipping his head around, straining against the collar, barking until he's hoarse. We only know their names because at least once a day, usually in the early evening, someone from inside the house next door will open the slider and shout at them: *Shut up, Rock! Shut up, Nyla!* Lou makes a game of it, bounding around on his back legs like he's on a pogo stick, taunting them with his fenced-in freedom, tearing about the perimeter in wide circles, the whites of his eyes huge with excitement, tongue lolling out sideways like some cartoon dog's.

Nyla and Rock are pit bull mutts just like our Louie, but where he is tall, lanky, and black, they are short, squatty, and fawn-colored, much handsomer and more menacing-looking than Louie. You can see every ripple of muscle in their broad chests when they dig at the base of our fence, all the thick tendons in their legs and shoulders pulling in time. Their snouts are shorter and show more teeth when they pant; I've never seen the whites of their eyes like I do Louie's when he's running, just beady blackness. Both their tails have been cropped short and can't wag, so on the day I was outside, helping Doug kill some fire ants, all I saw when I stepped into the side yard was a rush of light fur, muscle, and teeth coming at me, completely untethered.

Our sagging backyard gate was open because Doug was working in the yard for the first time since he'd returned from deployment and I was out helping him with a fire ant mound when the neighbors' dogs got out. They were fast. I was clomping around in rain boots and only had time to turn around before Nyla and Rock got to me. In the corner of the backyard, from the side of my eye, I could see Doug jumping up and down where he'd dropped the weed whacker, throwing his hands up, shouting my name.

"Sam! *Sam!* The dogs!"

When a sailor takes the oath, the ninth and eleventh words he or she speaks are *support* and *defend*: "I, Douglas Brown, do solemnly swear that I will support and defend the Constitution of the United States..." My husband said those words at the end of college, three months before he became my husband. They are resolute terms, well-chosen and easy to articulate. *I will support and defend.* Doug supports and defends.

I stood beside him on the stage when he raised his right hand and recited the Oath of Commissioning. In the pictures, I am smiling like a First Lady, bright and a little dead inside, as I mulled over the opening phrases.

In the years before we married, I believed that Doug would support and defend anybody but me. When we were dating in high school, I'd let other boys chase me and flirt with me, leading them on, toeing lines just to see if I could provoke any protective instincts in the ineffably steady boy I knew, even then, would one day be my husband. I wanted to see him get riled, tell the others to back off and that I belonged to him and him alone—possessive and grossly immature as it was. To me, his anger would have confirmed that he felt as strongly about me as I did about him. It's so clear now that my desire to provoke Doug, my desire to be guarded, was fallout of the last relationship I'd been in—when I was attacked instead of protected. Would that I could rewind and tell myself that, to undo all of my carelessness. But Doug was unfazed and trusted I knew when to tell the other boys to step down. Because I did. I never wanted to cheat, I just wanted to see one of the nation's future defenders spring to only my defense. Bait he wouldn't take.

In college, only marginally more mature, I goaded him by walking through campus alone at night and jogging on the shoulders of the busy roads that cut through Columbia, Missouri—thrilled by the rush of cars buzzing past, especially on hilly, winding Providence Road where the speed limit topped out at fifty miles per hour, but rarely did anyone go less than sixty-five. Doug never did anything beyond shaking his head and asking if I'd at least brought a flashlight. Sometimes, it made me mad. He'd asked me to marry him by then, so didn't he care about my physical safety? The few times I asked about it, he said he trusted that I would always choose to be safe over reckless, trusted I would be ok. A distant and succinct answer from the future Navy Nuke, the man of plans, patterns, and systems.

And I can't blame him for not getting wrapped up in worrying about me. If he were going to be a successful, effective officer underway someday, he couldn't allow himself to be distracted. Worrying too much about his wife's jogging habits could risk the safety of his crew, or of the boat entire. Doug trusted me to become an independent wife, a military wife, who does the heavy worrying, so he doesn't have to. By never once protesting my recklessness, he supported my transition into a wifehood where I would constantly be policing my own actions: *is this right, is this safe?*

When I did finally marry him, I took the unspoken oath of the military spouse: *I will support and defend my service member.* When he was stateside, I mended uniforms, trimmed hair, rubbed sore shoulders, attended meetings, and always stayed awake enough to kiss him good morning or goodnight, depending on when he returned from shift work or studying. When he readied to leave for trainings or deployments, I was the one packing the sea bags, writing letters for the months we'd be apart, making sure he had enough Icy Hot, protein bars, and pictures of me and Louie to get him through.

That was supporting. But when you're about to be separated by an ocean, supporting is easy compared to defending. Defending doesn't always look like raised fists or strong offense. Sometimes, it's as quiet and unnoticed as whispered prayer.

Before Doug's first deployment, I gave him what I thought was a St. Christopher medal I bought at the Vatican, blessed by Pope Francis—a last line of defense from a Catholic wife to her Presbyterian husband. The chain was cheap and kept falling off his neck, he said, so he kept the medal in his breast pocket the entire time he was gone, saving it twice from being lost in the boat's laundry. It was only a week after his return that we discovered it was actually a medal for *San Rocco*, the patron saint of bachelors, gravediggers, and dogs.

Four days before I was scheduled to move from Charleston, South Carolina to Jacksonville, Florida, I had to flee Hurricane Matthew, my first hurricane. After the evacuation order came, I left a string of pissed-off voicemails on Doug's cell phone. He was living eight-hundred miles away in Groton, Connecticut at the time, attending Submarine school. The officers-only program was colloquially known amongst young officers as a "relaxing break" for future submariners after the rigors of Power School and Prototype. Power School and Prototype were twelve-plus-hour days in the classroom, the former, or, in the latter, lengthy shifts manning a live reactor in a decommissioned sub while over-instructors activated casualty simulations and graded trainees on their response. Submarine School, by contrast, was just a few hours a day in the classroom and trainers honing warfare tactics, leadership skills, and mental math, then the rest of the day off to enjoy the vistas of New England.

Governor Haley ordered Charleston's evacuation while I was at work, giving evening swim lessons at an indoor pool just down the street from the apartment which was already packed up in cardboard boxes for the move. It was less than a mile from the pool to my apartment. I'd driven because it was drizzling and I was tired. If I had realized a mandatory evacuation was in the cards, I would have walked or ridden my bike to avoid the frenzy, but this was my first hurricane. I had no idea what to expect. Instead, I spent an hour trying to get through the single stoplight between the pool and my apartment. It happened to also be in front of what I can only infer was the last operational gas station in Charleston, judging by the gridlock of cars surrounding it. I had plenty of time sitting practically parked on Mathis Ferry Road to call and make sure my husband knew exactly what I thought of his absence at that particular moment as I idled within eyesight of our front door but was still unable to get there. Doug never picked up because he was playing trivia with his friends in a burger bar. It was just me—there were no other wives to lean on in Charleston.

I packed a suitcase for me, a duffel bag of toys, food, and chews for Louie, and a few two-liter bottles of Sprite I'd drained and filled with tap water in case we got stuck in traffic on the way out. Before leaving, I asked the frat guys who lived upstairs to help me lift a few sentimental pieces of furniture up onto the beds in case the apartment flooded. The safe with our passports and a Rubbermaid full of mementos from our wedding, I hid beneath towels in my trunk. Around four in the morning, I leashed Louie into the backseat and we skipped town, bound for a motel just outside Atlanta.

By then, Doug had called back, a little buzzed, and I'd given him another piece of my mind. I needed him to know how shitty it was that I had to do this all on my own while he was off having a blast. He gave some stale apology, asked what he could do, and I admitted there was nothing, that I needed nothing, but I was mad anyway. My mood didn't improve after I arrived at the hotel and was told it would be at least six hours before they could give me a key card and that I couldn't wait in the lobby because of my excitable dog. "His face is too *pit bull-y*. He might scare the other guests."

Unable to go anywhere else with Louie in tow, I posted on a grassy hill across the parking lot and started scrolling through Instagram on my phone, hoping the battery would hold out till the afternoon. Louie orbited around me, still on his leash, sniffing in a circle, picking up sticks and crunching them into slobbery pieces before spitting them back out beside my leg. Gifts for conveying him to safety, I presumed.

After a while, I'm not sure how long, a man about my age, maybe a little older, walked out of the lobby and lit up a cigarette. I wouldn't have noticed him at all if he hadn't shouted across the parking lot and waved.

"Hey, how's it going?"

Louie perked up, more interested in the man than the discarded hot dog buns under a nearby bush he'd been straining for.

"It's good." I didn't want to talk.

"Whatcha doing out here?"

"Just enjoying the sun." There were hardly any clouds.

"Cool." He took a few more drags on his cigarette. "You wanna come up?" He nodded his head back toward the building.

I sat up a little. "No, um…no thanks."

"Alright, have a good one."

"You too." He waved on his way back inside. I went back to my phone, and Louie went back to the enticing hot dog buns.

Doug called not long after, asking how the drive had been. I stood up and started walking the length of the parking lot as I talked, recounting the drive.

"All the gas stations were already closed. Out of gas. People were in line for ice machines and stuff, it was crazy."

"I *can't* believe I'm missing it." He was frustrated.

Doug had been looking forward to experiencing a hurricane to since we moved to the coast. He loves extreme weather, and I knew he was bitter to be missing it, another detail that ticked me off. If he had been home, he probably would have chosen to ride out the storm by himself. One of those crazies you see on the news walking on the beach while the storm rolls in. We got to talking about how, if he'd stayed in Charleston, the National Guard would probably have had to helicopter in and pluck him off a roof.

Then there was a bit of movement from one of the hotel windows. A flash of skin, quick motion. I thought I heard a man calling out. *Hey. Hey, come on up.* It sounded familiar.

When I turned toward the motion Louie circled too, wrapping my legs in his leash. Doug was talking about his trivia team or the bar or something but he stopped when I gasped.

"Oh. Oh *fuck this.*"

"Sam?"

In the open window, I saw again the flash of a man's white palm, moving vigorously up and down his penis—unmistakable.

"You've *got* to be kidding me." I may have been shouting by then.

"What?"

"Doug, I have to go. There's some guy jerking off at me." I hung up on Doug before he could answer.

Inside, the woman at the front desk stood and started to remind me that my dog was not allowed in the small lobby. Indeed, Louie was already rearing up to put his paws on her counter. I stopped her with one finger in the air and informed her that there was a man masturbating and shouting things out a window on the second floor—fourth window from the right—and that I would either be waiting in this lobby with the dog or going immediately to whatever room she had that locked—I didn't care if it was clean or not. In the glass of the picture behind her desk, I could see myself: red-faced and wide-eyed, barely able to catch my breath. Trembling. No trace of nice. I described the man with the cigarette who'd spoken to me earlier, saying I thought his voice was the same as the man's who was shouting.

She took me immediately to a readied room down the hall and told me to phone the front desk if I needed anything. The police were called, but if they showed, no one contacted me. The woman told me later that there was no one staying in the room four windows to the right, which I found hard to believe. The entire East coast south of Myrtle Beach had scurried inland when they saw Matthew gaining strength after it hit Haiti. When I'd arrived that morning, she herself had told me the place was booked solid, and I'd gotten the last room.

I didn't call Doug back until after I'd been to Walmart where, for $17.21, I bought a four-pack of chip-clips, pepper spray, and a black camping knife. The pepper spray, I hooked onto the loop of Louie's leash. The knife, I tucked in the front pocket of my sweatshirt—Doug's old baseball hoodie I've had since high school. When I took Louie out to the grass periodically, I'd keep one hand on the trigger of the pepper spray, while the other flipped the knife open and shut at the hinge, counting the *clicks* like seconds on a clock. Other evacuees outside with their dogs invited themselves over to talk about the storm or about their tribulations getting to where we found ourselves now. I tried to stay at least two leash-lengths away.

When I did talk to Doug again, I called him an asshole because, if he had been here, evacuated, with me instead of hanging out in some burger bar, the man wouldn't even have approached me. I would have been safe.

"Yeah, but he still might have done it without you even knowing. Just because you saw it this time doesn't mean it doesn't happen more often." Doug was right. Safety is a fairy tale.

The curtains in the room were made of stiff fabric, like old couch upholstery, and wouldn't stay shut no matter how I pulled or tugged them, so I chip-clipped them together down the middle and laid awake all night with the knife in my hand, lest I catch any more movement through the panes.

For many years, I've tormented Doug with the way I use knives: improperly, at odd angles, always in slight danger of slipping and hitting a major artery or severing a digit. He is an Eagle Scout and has no patience for my misuse of such a simple tool. Swiss Army knives were problematic for their complexity, and I'd sliced my hand with a butcher's knife on two separate occasions in Charleston while butterflying raw chicken breasts. Both kitchen cuts resulted in me running my bleeding palm under cold water, laughing, and him leaving the room, ticked.

After Hurricane Matthew blew out to sea and I was able to move to Jacksonville where the house still stood, dry, I sank a box-cutter too deep into a wardrobe box and left clean slits across the left sleeves of a half-dozen of his shirts. When he moved down after sub school and discovered my mistake, he calmly told me I was banned from using knives anytime he deployed.

Of course, Doug knew he couldn't actually keep me from using knives just as well as I knew he couldn't shield me from every pervert on the street. It was inevitable that we spend long stretches of time apart while he was out supporting and defending the Constitution and I *held down the homefront*, whatever that meant—the role of the wife. My safety was my own job. He could defend everyone except me, it seemed, except for when I counted as one of the population, one of the whole.

We talked a few times in passing about paying a little extra each month to activate our house's security system or buying me a handgun and practicing with it at the range like the other officers did with their wives, but all our ideas got lost in the rush to prepare him for his first underway.

Louie would alert me to any intruder, I assumed. He'd give me enough time to barricade a door or run. The hurricane knife stayed in the top drawer of my nightstand somewhere amongst the cough drops and bobby pins. Uneasiness is hard to shake. Because of my work schedule, Louie and I normally do our morning jog between four and five, long before the sun or any other dogs are out. Everything is suspicious then; everything is a threat.

I don't have to spend time anymore aligning my fingers on the leash to get the best hold on the pepper spray—the grip is automatic now. Even in the summer, when the mercury creeps into the 80s before sunrise, I wear the fleece jacket Doug gave me with the crest of his boat embroidered on the front, zipped up to the neck. It's cut for a man with broad shoulders and a narrow waist, a triangular man. When I put it on, I grow in size, look taller and stronger—like a five-foot linebacker, a friend once quipped. The jacket is my armor, the pepper spray, my weapon against all the variable, unpredictable danger that could be lurking.

Doug doesn't comment on it, doesn't ask, because he's either gone or still sleeping.

I was outside the day our neighbor's dogs got out, pouring poison on the fire ants Doug had found with the bottom of his shoe. He'd been weed whacking the yard, enjoying the sun, three days free of the sub's recycled air, when he stepped on a mound, hidden by thick dandelion stalks. I'd been in the living room working through an online class when I saw him bounding toward the patio, flinging off his shoes and socks and batting at his ankles. I knew he wouldn't get near enough to the mound again to take care of it. He went back to the weed whacking; I put on my clunky rain boots and was walking around the side of the house to pour mound killer on it when the dogs came running.

"Sam! *Sam!*" I heard him drop the weed whacker. "The dogs! The gate!" His hands were up in the air, then on his head, clutching desperately.

The female, Nyla, got to me first. She barreled in with drool flinging off her jowls and skidded to a stop just a few feet in front of me, tail stump wagging. Rock halted when she did, just a few feet behind her, so I stretched out my hand and let her sniff. For all her barking and snarling, she was extremely sweet, letting me scratch behind her ears and under her chin. She rolled over and presented her white belly for rubbing. Her companion hung back, watching. Doug was still waving his hands around, shouting about the gate, I thought. I could barely hear him now. Our neighbor came quickly to collect his escapees, apologizing, assuring me they were ok, "just lickers."

Maybe it's because it all happened so fast, but I hadn't felt scared at all in the few moments between Doug shouting and the dogs reaching me at the fence. Startled, yes. Now that the dogs were gone, my heart was barely even pounding.

But Doug was still wide-eyed when I got back to him. Panting, it took him a while for him to articulate it, but he said he hadn't been shouting for me to *close* the gate, he'd wanted me to get on the other side of it. He'd been certain, he said, the dogs were going to attack me.

"And what if they did?" I asked him. "It would have been ok. You were here."

I kept myself from reminding him that scarier things happen all the time, whether he's watching or not. His job is to worry about the big picture, mine is to worry about me.

Plus, he couldn't have saved me if the dogs had been vicious. Even though he was in eyesight, he was still too far away. But I felt a small flutter of joy in seeing that yes, the protector wanted to protect me too.

The next week, we vacationed in Mexico. While walking along Playa del Carmen, I stepped onto what I thought was a low, wet sandbar. It turned out to be a weak wall to a tidal pool of watery sand—quicksand, almost. I sank almost immediately up to my hips, ocean rushing around me. If I moved, the sand pulled me in deeper, tide tugging at my waist now.

Doug had taken a higher, dryer path so he looked down on me, laughing, waiting for me to extricate myself from the sucking sand, but I was struggling. I feared whatever current or undertow created the pool and had no idea how far I had to go to escape the soggy, unfounded trap. For some reason, the growing panic made me laugh uncontrollably.

"Doug!" I cackled, "Help!"

"You're fine!" He laughed back, pausing impatiently on the high side of the sand. "You don't need me."

Thankfully, it wasn't far. Ten, maybe twelve feet of careful wading, moving in slow motion to avoid losing my footing, Doug laughing the entire time. He offered me his hand at the last few steps and I took it trembling. When I had my balance, I punched him hard on the arm, and asked him what his problem was. "Why didn't you help me?"

"Oh, come on," he said, as we continued our walk. "I would have if you were in any real danger."

"And that wasn't danger? I was scared! I could've drowned" Never mind that I had actually asked him for a hand.

In Doug's world, in the world of submarines, it's only real danger, it seems, if you need to destroy it with a Tomahawk missile. There's a difference between a tidal pool and terrorism, to be certain but, when you're wading through it waist-deep, danger is danger, plain and simple. Where was the Doug who'd jumped and shouted at the dogs in our backyard? Was there shame now in my asking for help—in asking to be saved?

About two months after our sojourn in Mexico and mere weeks before his second deployment in September 2017, Doug finally got his first hurricane. Hurricane Irma came to town and, in preparation, all of Florida and Georgia squealed to a halt and, as every news outlet in the country phrased it, got "the Hell out of Dodge." My school district called off and Doug's base closed, giving us ten uninterrupted days of what we called *hurrication*. I expected evacuating with Doug to be remarkably easier than when it was just me and the dog, but instead, I found he tended to be in my way—asking what to bring, did we need this, should we bring that too? The only time I was thankful to have him buzzing around was when it came time to lift the sentimental furniture up onto the beds.

Doug, Louie, and I evacuated far past the suggested radius around Atlanta, all the way up to my parents' house in St. Louis, enjoying time with our families and watching the news to see if the flooding had reached our door. When we returned, we were overwhelmed with relief that we'd only lost a few strips of siding and the door of our mailbox. Somehow, the shoddy fence remained upright. While I was squishing around the yard in rain boots, taking pictures of the damage for our landlord, Doug unloaded the car. I stepped back into the garage just in time to see him remove his locked handgun from beneath the passenger seat, where I'd been sitting for the past sixteen hours.

"You brought your *gun?*" I wasn't angry, just surprised.

"Yep."

"Why?"

"Because." He stared at me hard, but only for a second. It was the only answer I'd get. He'd already hurried inside to stow the gun in our safe, hide it out of sight. I was glad he hadn't told me about the gun beneath my seat. If he had, I surely would have lost myself in worrying about all the waifs of concealed carry. *What if we get pulled over and he forgets to tell the cops? What if someone breaks in and steals it? What if, God forbid, he has to use it?*

Doug protected me from worry, just as I believe he was prepared to protect me—us—with the hidden Glock. Worry, the fear of danger, is my biggest enemy. Although nothing had really changed, when he deployed a week later, I somehow felt safer when I thought about him evacuating with the hidden gun, prepared to protect us from whatever danger was out there, and from what my mind could conjure. As artificial as that safety may be, it's easier to sleep knowing the supporter and defender of the nation still has a thought left for you.

CHAPTER 13

Dear Doug,

Hey, it's me again. I sent you an email earlier today while I was on my planning period, but I really miss you right now, so I thought I'd say hi. Louie's right here with me too, just snoring away, nothing new there. It's a quiet night. I'm watching TV and grading papers. Might read a book, might go to bed early. What else is there to do?

~~Actually, I have a question: do you guys know about the *San Juan*? Have they told you about the missing sub? I know the rules, at least, as they apply to me, as they've been explained to me at all those Pre-Deployment meetings.~~

~~I know not to expect emails every day. You're busy; you're working around the clock. I know there are censors on the boat reading my every word for tone and subtext (hah, *sub*text, get it?), checking to make sure we aren't writing in codes, and I know about the computer programs that would scan and throw out entire emails if they contained buzzwords like *death, dying, cancer, pregnant, miscarriage,* or *divorce*. No bad news. That command alone—*no bad news*—appears several times in the 90s edition of the *Navy Spouses' Guide* and at least half a dozen times in the *Georgia* deployment handbook.~~

~~I know I'm supposed to be careful too, about sending news that sounds "good" to me but might depress or distract you. That rule made no sense to me for the longest time. What good does it do a sailor who's already so physically distant from his family to be cut off emotionally too? Wouldn't a~~

140

~~father want to know that little Timmy learned to ride his bike today?~~ ~~Wouldn't that make him happy? We debated that for a while, I remember,~~ ~~before deciding that it didn't matter what would make who happy if the Navy~~ ~~didn't think it supported the mission. If the news that little Timmy learned~~ ~~to ride his bike made his deployed father sad to be missing it, he could be~~ ~~distracted on the job. That's a danger to everyone.~~

~~Do you remember the speech your captain gave at Pre-Deployment~~ ~~night? *That* speech. Hell of a speech. Remember? *We are the Silent Service for a*~~ ~~*reason. Not just because of us, the crew, but because of you.* He said so much about~~ ~~the importance of OPSEC and PERSEC, but what he said that stuck with~~ ~~me, that I couldn't stop replaying in my head, was that our email~~ ~~communications were one of the biggest safety threats to the boat. He talked~~ ~~about how when you guys, the sailors, get off watch or have a free minute in~~ ~~the day, you're glued to the computer, clicking and refreshing for any sort of~~ ~~communication—*comms*, he called them—from home. Bad news, distracting~~ ~~news, even, was how people got hurt, how limbs got lost. How men, in this~~ ~~age of relative submarine safety, got killed while underway. (Do you think~~ ~~that guy on the gold crew who got his hand chopped off in the trash~~ ~~compactor was thinking about news from home? It's possible, right?)~~

~~Anyone, he said, who was found to be causing distress or distraction to~~ ~~their sailor with their messages would be kicked off email and blocked from~~ ~~the boat indefinitely. Being cut off from you seemed like the worst possible~~ ~~consequence.~~

~~But now, I'm wondering, is that so different from what we're doing now?~~

~~There is a submarine and her entire crew missing, presumed lost. Your~~ ~~boat has been silent almost as long as the *San Juan* has been missing, and I~~ ~~don't think you know a thing about it.~~

~~I've followed every rule. I've locked down my social media. I've deleted~~ ~~every hashtag that ties me to you and you to the Navy (#navywifelife,~~

#submarinersdoitdeeper, #fuckdeployment). I changed my profile picture to a selfie of us at a Blues game, instead of one with you in your camos. I don't post anything about you being gone, being quiet, or even being on a boat anymore. These changes, we were told, would keep "foreign radicals" from using our posts, or the posts of Navy groups we're tied to, to glean information on the boat and her whereabouts, her possible missions and movements. It happens more often than we'd think, the captain said, NCIS gets involved—it's very serious. I believe him; I have no reason not to.

I don't like these rules, but I understand they're meant to keep you safe. I'm struggling with that right now though.

There's a submarine out there *missing*, Doug. *Missing*. A groaning, chugging hunk of steel full of motors, gears, torpedoes, and forty-four living, breathing human souls is *missing* and I haven't heard from you in over two weeks. Two weeks. Do you know?

Do you remember what else the captain stressed at Pre-Deployment night? In that auditorium in front of all of us? He stressed the importance of marriage and of family. The importance of a strong *homefront*.

My job is to support you, but how can I support you if I can't even speak to you?

Our entire relationship, from the time we were fifteen until now, has been built on communication. Since the beginning, we've talked about *everything*. No matter how hard I try, I cannot think of a secret I've kept from you, until now, until the San Juan disappeared.

Secrets are heavy, Doug. Enough to make me sink.

How am I supposed to keep quiet about this? I want to call my mom and cry, but I can't. I want to text all my friends, but that's not allowed either. I want to write a big angry Facebook status about how ridiculously hard it is to wait, wait, wait in this murky void of not-knowing, just to see if anyone out in the internet-world there has some words of wisdom and strength. I'm

~~grateful for the sub wives. I can talk to them, but we don't linger on it. It's~~
~~too scary for all of us, I guess. Too sad. More than any of them, though, I~~
~~want to talk to you. I want to hear you say whatever reassuring things you~~
~~can. You know the language of submarines and the language of me. Translate~~
~~for me, Doug.~~

~~Married couples—strong ones—are supposed to communicate, even~~
~~about the tough stuff. Your possible death is very tough stuff. Are the censors~~
~~who scan our emails alive? Am I actually being screened at all or is this email~~
~~going to zoom off to nowhere?~~

~~If you read this, I know you'd tell me to chill out, to not panic.~~
~~But will you read this?? Will they let you? Do you know?~~

~~Again, I know you'll call me crazy, but Doug, this is real. For the families~~
~~of the forty-four on the *San Juan*—this nightmare is *real*. There are forty-four~~
~~families that just lost someone at sea. That's forty-four wreaths of flowers~~
~~tossed out into the ocean, forty-four burials at sea.~~

~~Doug, I don't want to bury you at sea. I don't want to bury you anywhere,~~
~~ever.~~

~~Not talking to you about this disaster, this panic, has me feeling like I'm~~
~~lying to you—something a spouse should never feel.~~

~~I want to tell you the truth, Doug. Always. But the submarine force won't~~
~~let me. I am supposed to lie to keep you safe. It is a hard line to walk, when~~
~~doing what we must to feed our marriage—communicate—is one of the~~
~~most dangerous things to do when your life and the lives of all your crew, are~~
~~hanging in the balance.~~

~~Where are you, Doug? Where are you all? Why aren't you answering?~~

So, I don't know where to go from here. Like I said, quiet night. Maybe
this one will be the email that finally gets to you or gets a reply. Maybe you're
just really busy. Maybe you guys know about the *San Juan* and you're telling
me to be calm about it telepathically, or something. If you are, the signal's

weak. I'm so worried, Doug.

I'm thinking about you a lot—that's an understatement, but it's true. It's about the only true thing they'll let me tell you at this point.

Love you; Miss you. Write back soon.

Love,

Sam

CHAPTER 14

Wife Stuff, Two

For weeks after our first Hail and Farewell with the *USS Georgia* in December, 2016, I thought about the other officer wives I'd met. I wondered about them. The deployment timeframe had been announced—were they also unable to sleep? Had they cried when they saw their husbands' packing lists sitting on the kitchen counter?

Doug had been instructed by his higher-ups to inform me of that month's Family Readiness Group—FRG—meeting. He encouraged me to attend: "Maybe you'll meet the wives of some of the guys in my division?" While the wardroom event we'd attended was strictly for officers and their spouses, the FRG comprised the spouses and families of the entire crew, both officers and enlisted alike. I'd read about FRGs on some of the military spouse blogs I'd fixated on in the months leading up to our arrival. Maybe I'd make a connection or meet someone else new; maybe I'd learn more about deployment or how to survive.

I expected a packed gymnasium of family members of all ages at tables, laughing, eating, talking, working on cards or posters for their sailors. Instead, it was ten or so wives gathered in a preschool classroom behind the base chapel, no children. There was a Valentine's Day banner to sign for the upcoming deployment and a tray of cookies by the door. A young wife, younger than me, with a swollen pregnant belly introduced herself and asked if this was my first meeting. I told her it was and she smiled sweetly. "Oh, great! What division is your husband in?"

"Uhh…I'm not sure."

"Well, what rate is he?" An uncomfortable pause followed.

"Rate?"

She looked at me with one eyebrow raised, then glanced toward another wife nearby who was also looking at me like I'd just asked the stupidest question possible.

"We just got here from Charleston," I said, hoping to clear things up.

"Oh, so he's a Nuke!"

That was a familiar term. "Yes, yes! A Nuke. He's a Nuke."

"Is he an officer?" Asked the other wife in a lower tone.

"Yeah." It felt like the wrong answer.

"Oh. Ok."

It was the wrong answer. They smiled again, said they were glad I came, and drifted away. No one else spoke to me the rest of the meeting. Instead, we waited around for a member of the command triad to show up and answer questions but, when no one did, the president reminded everyone that they were very, very busy preparing for deployment so we shouldn't expect them to stop by for us—nearly scolding us for seeing their names on the meeting agenda. I signed the Valentine's banner before I left, but learned it was going to be hung in the crew's mess so Doug might never see it at all.

When I got home told Doug about my humiliating conversation with the two FRG wives he shook his head and laughed. I yelled at him for sending me in without ever telling me what a rate was or explaining that he didn't have one. Humiliated didn't even begin to cover it. How was I supposed to make friends now? They all thought I was a "snobby dumbass," I told him.

"Don't worry, Sam," he said. "You've still got that wardroom craft night coming up, right? You'll meet someone there. It'll be fine."

By the time craft night rolled around, about three weeks before Doug's first deployment, I was a pale, quivering shell of myself. I'd spent Christmas, New Year's, and all the weeks in between agonizing over both the deployment and my first official wardroom wives-only event. We'd be making halfway boxes and placemats for our husbands' months underway. Just as the email from the executive officer's wife suggested, I brought craft supplies to share: stickers, scrapbook paper, a rainbow of Sharpies, and a little bundle of pictures I'd had printed at Walgreens of Doug and I and our gangly mutt Louie. Still immersed in embarrassment from the FRG meeting, I'd also mentally brought my "categories"—all the "types" of sailors' wives I'd been viewing like a set of molds, trying to fit myself into one of them in order to survive this Navy life.

When I arrived, the XO's scrappy terrier announced my presence before the doorbell, yapping loudly until a tall, thin barefooted woman swooshed him aside at the door.

"Jack, enough!" Her smile was wide and welcoming. "You must be Samantha?"

I nodded sheepishly, "Yeah, Sam, actually."

"Come on in, Sam. Welcome to the party!" When she stepped aside Jack, the terrier, bounded at my knees. I'd brought flowers as a hostess gift so he helped himself to an enthusiastic sniff. "Hey everyone," the XO's wife called out, "Sam is here! This is Sam!"

To my left was the dining room where she'd set up a colorful array of scrapbook paper, stickers, and colored markers. One of the wives I'd met at the Hail and Farewell was setting up a laminator in the corner—she waved, "Hey good to see you again!" Another wife was unpacking a tote bag of unfolded flat-rate boxes from the post office. Across the foyer, to my right, three toddler boys alternated playing with plastic dump trucks, and pushing each other into a bean bag chair, laughing and screeching. In the living room, a pair of preteens scrolled through Netflix and their phones simultaneously. A timer went off in the kitchen and the XO's wife jogged to pull something out of the oven. More wives were there around her, talking, chopping vegetables, and pouring wine. Someone had plugged in their phone and started playing music over the happy din. This didn't seem right at all.

Our husbands were days away from deploying, from heading off to war. Possibly never to be seen again. We were barreling toward goodbyes and loneliness, toward months and months of nothing but waiting for their return. I had expected a morose, somber cast over things and talk of the dreaded separation. Instead, I heard one pair talking about a new yoga teacher on base, another about their gardens.

"Sam, right? White or red?" One of the wives extended two glasses to me, I took the red and we clinked our glasses. "Welcome to the wardroom." Her smile was wide and bright. I relaxed a little and lent a hand with the veggie tray.

There were twelve wardroom spouses; ten were wives, two were husbands still in the service, stationed elsewhere. Of the seven wives attending that night, I was the only one without a child, save for the captain's wife who was a seasoned stepmom of teenagers, so I couldn't contribute to their gripes about potty-training or learners' permits, but I was glad to listen and slowly become acclimated. All the moving, all the frequent changing of duty stations and wardrooms made these women all cheerful, easy conversationalists.

"How are you liking things so far? Are you all unpacked?" the XO's wife asked.

I nodded, "Yeah, all good on that front."

"That's a big hurdle, bet you're glad it's over. Have you been up to base yet?"

"Just to the commissary a couple of times, and the last FRG meeting."

Though I'd vowed to myself never to tell another soul about the FRG meeting disaster, I suddenly found myself confessing: "I had no idea what a rate was! No one warned me!"

The other wives laughed and laughed. Apparently, publicly screwing up your husband's rank or job title was an unofficial rite of passage. "Congratulations." One of the women raised her glass. "You're one of us now." In no time, I forgot all about trying to categorize them and simply enjoyed their company.

But even if I'd tried to, I couldn't have fit them into the "types" I'd thought so much about before: Super Moms, Winos, Worriers, and the like. None of them put off the airs of women who waited around for their sailor husbands. From stay-at-home moms, to career women, they all had and were proud of the lives they led in addition to the role of "sub wife." The Navy did not seem to define them, only strung them together like pearls on a strand. They barely ever mentioned deployment except for a handful of times when they referred to the different underways in passing like old episodes of *Friends: The One Where They Broke Down for Three Months, The One With the Buoy, The One With the Food Poisoning, The One Where They Ran Out Of Potatoes.*

After a little while, when we'd moved into the dining room, in a side conversation with one of the wives I'd met at the Hail and Farewell, I mentioned that this would be my first deployment. She gave a tiny gasp, squeezed my arm, and repeated what I'd said a little louder so everyone at the table heard:

"Guys, this is Sam's first deployment."

The next-newest spouse already had three or four under her belt, she couldn't remember exactly. After that, each woman started dropping little hints here and there about deployment, about what they did to help get themselves through:

"I have *so* many of these little Rubbermaid containers. I freeze at least half of what I make when he's home so I don't have to worry about cooking as often when he's gone. They're only, like, fifteen dollars for a set at Target, I think. One less thing to worry about, you know?"

"Hey, speaking of Target, anyone been to the Dollar Spot lately? I've already started buying welcome home gifts; it's my favorite way to pass the time."

"No, but I changed the propane tank on the grill this week without blowing up the house. Added it to the journal. I keep this list in a notebook of new things I do when he's not around. Kinda cool to look back on over the years."

"I can't decide what my *project* should be this time. Every deployment needs a project. I'm split between building some new garden beds for the backyard or putting up a pallet wall in the bedroom like Joanna Gaines does on *Fixer Upper*. Maybe both? I don't know."

A few of the more veteran wives suggested I take the Military 101 class offered at the Family Resource Center on base. It was designed for new spouses and covered all the ins and outs of marrying into the service from rank identification, to navigating the healthcare system, to the many procedural how-tos of getting things done while the guys were away—even solo moving, if the sailor wouldn't be around to transfer duty stations. Anyone who took the class walked away with a thick binder covering everything they could possibly need to know in just about any situation the Navy could conjure. Several of the other wives nodded emphatically and listed all the times they'd been "saved by the book."

"When the baby was sick…"

"When I had to sell our camper…"

"When we had to move the dogs to Pearl Harbor…"

I made a mental note to sign up for the class as soon as humanly possible.

When we got to the crafting portion of the evening, they explained to me that the placemats and boxes we were decorating would be given out on

Halfway Night—the celebration of reaching the halfway point of the deployment. With all our communal art supplies spread out over the dining room table, it could've been a children's holiday party we were hosting. However, we had gathered our glitter heart stickers for Valentine's, cut-out shamrocks for St. Patty's, and craft-foam Easter eggs not to celebrate but to reinforce the bond between home and sea.

I happen to have a knack for arts and crafts—it's a talent that serves little purpose except in situations such as this. My placemat—a picture collage of our dog begging for Doug's food—was a veritable work of art. The halfway box, a small USPS flat rate box, I transformed into a construction paper version of The Beatles' Yellow Submarine, then stuffed it with more pictures, some crossword puzzles, and a box of Milk Duds, his favorite candy. I learned later packing candy was a rookie mistake. In the heat of where they deployed to, the Milk Duds melted and solidified into one sticky block inside the box. None of the other wives put candy in their boxes. Instead, they included things like protein bars, powdered drink mixes, and roasted espresso beans. All the while, I listened, sponge-like, trying to learn how to be less like me and more like them.

Just as I remembered from before, they all seemed so capable and confident. The sub wives could handle toddlers, teens, their own jobs, their own lives, and throwing in the upcoming deployment didn't seem to faze them. One had battled breast cancer solo while her husband was at sea; another was raising a son with special needs and fighting for his school's funding before the state legislature. Many of them volunteered for various organizations or religious groups, and nearly everyone had their own health and fitness regimen that could put their sailors' healthy habits to shame (including, but not limited to, marathons and Ironmans.) And it wasn't as if the wives were inhuman. They all freely admitted annoyances and difficulties, but regardless, they were able to speak of deployment dismissively: "Deployment is,"—*shrug*—"eh."

I longed for an *eh*; there was nothing I desired more than to think of deployment and not cry or lose sleep, not panic or get sick to my stomach, but just shrug and *eh*—dismiss it. *Eh* was confident, *eh* was strong. *Eh* didn't care what deployment brought because *eh* could handle anything. In short, *eh* was kind of a badass.

But I wasn't anywhere close to finding an *eh*, and I wasn't sure I ever would.

I left craft night feeling light and buoyant—happier than I'd been since we moved. My phone was full of new contacts, and we'd even started making plans for get-togethers after the boat left. I didn't want to sleep immediately, I wanted to wait up and tell Doug all about this new world I was on the brink of discovering. He came home after midnight, drained from a day being evaluated in the trainers. All he wanted to do was shower and sleep. "Tell me everything this weekend, ok?" I said I would, but he was already asleep. All my excitement faded away.

The closer it got, the more deployment was drowning me. I couldn't complete the simplest of tasks without breaking down. Even laundry was enough to bring me to tears: soon I wouldn't be folding his shirts next to mine anymore, or accidentally mixing my socks with his. Doug wasn't ignorant to my struggles. He sat beside me at home, rubbing the space between my shoulder blades while I wept, trying to say comforting things but knowing how useless it was, because what did he know about being left? He was the one doing the leaving. Crying in front of him, showing my innumerable weaknesses, made me feel like I was less of a wife than I ought to be, that I wasn't fit for the military lifestyle and marrying into it was a gigantic mistake.

"You should've found someone better," I'd say to him. "Anyone else would have been better than me."

Even more, it was easy to feel second place to the submarine itself, the crew, and all the attention both required. They demanded every second of Doug's time and every last ounce of his energy. Oftentimes, when he came home from base, he'd be asleep, face-down on the carpet before he could unlace his boots. He'd wake up just long enough for dinner, mumble his thanks, then nod off on the couch until shuffling to bed an hour later. I'd stay up a little longer to pack his lunch for the next day or pick up his camos and hang them over the back of a chair. A lot of the time, it felt like I was only there to fill spaces the Navy couldn't reach.

Deployment came a few weeks later and I was still far, far from *eh*. For two weeks, I cried whenever I drove to or from work, struggled to get out of bed, and altered my routine to extremes to eliminate as many reminders of Doug as possible. I walked the dog three times a day to avoid sitting on the couch next to Doug's empty spot and carried a radio in one hand to escape the silence (talk shows only, love songs were too brutal.) I couldn't watch TV shows that we'd watched together or buy groceries for *me* that I would have bought for *us*. Junk mail came with his name on it and I'd wilt just reading *Mr. Douglas P. Brown* on the envelope. I'm embarrassed to say I grieved Doug's absence like he'd died, something I didn't realize until later when I happened to read Sheryl Sandberg's *Option B*, a book she penned after her husband's sudden passing, and found myself nodding emphatically with each turn of the page, but stopping when I remembered this was not a military spouse's deployment memoir.

I tried to break out of my *funk* by getting to know my new coworkers at the school where I was teaching, but I struggled to make friendly connections. It was as if I was too lonely to break out of the loneliness. Worse still, when I reached out to friends or family, I'd get angry and snap at those who loved me for no reason other than they tried to offer some sort of reassurance or comfort by telling me *it will be ok. You'll be fine.* But none of them had ever sent a spouse off to war or out to sea. What the hell did they know?

When I was finally able to sleep for more than a few minutes at a time, I'd wake up gasping because I'd dreamt Doug was in bed beside me, or out watching TV in the living room and, when I reached over for him or opened the bedroom door, had to discover all over again that he was, in fact, still gone, somewhere out under the waves.

I spent a few sleepless nights sitting outside on the back porch with my radio, wrapped up in a quilt, nursing a mug of hot water, looking up at the stars, while Louie ran circles around the yard. Orion, the hunter, the son of Poseidon, is the only constellation I've ever been able to find easily without searching, even as a child. I'd find his belt, then his sword, and then squint for his head.

When it comes to forever, it was always going to be Doug.

I don't pretend to live an epiphany-driven life. Realization and acceptance of change come slowly for me. It was only in the case of Doug where I felt strongly that God or some other cosmic force among the stars had intervened. He was it; he was the much-storied *one.* There was nothing I could have done to escape this separation, the repeated deployments, I knew. Even if we didn't marry, if I'd broken up with him (which would have been its own type of losing him) I would've been watching for this day, waiting for it from a distance, quietly asking God to return him safely. He was too much a part of me to let go, so I carried on, hell-bent on making the time pass quickly.

I tried to do the things the other sub wives had suggested. I started refinishing furniture in the garage and cooking large meals in the crock pot to freeze for later even though I had no one to share them with. From the library, I checked out copious numbers of books, determined to polish off my entire life's reading list, and I started running again, for the first time since moving to Florida. In an old journal, I started a list like the one another wife said she kept, filled with things I did for the first time while the boat was out:

1. Mowed and weed-whacked lawn
2. Fixed falling fence
3. Filed taxes

Only, after a few lines of actual accomplishments, I started listing out my many intimate moments with the Curse of Deployment—the subtext of Murphy's Law that states, quite clearly, that, in a military household, anything that can go wrong will go wrong, but only when the deployable spouse is deployed:

26. Government shut down—worried about not getting his paycheck, no emails to or from boat
27. Power out—opened garage door manually, propped up with ladder to back car out
28. Emergency after-hours dentist appointment for cracked tooth
29. Forgot to close gate, Louie escaped into neighborhood
30. Louie rolled in poop, required bath.

On that first deployment, Doug's crew was joined by five officer riders from the *Georgia's* sister boat, the USS *Florida* which was in dry dock for maintenance. They augmented the watch bill and worked alongside the other unqualified junior officers, like Doug, to get their fish—the gold dolphin warfare insignia worn on the left breast, awarded upon completion of their onboard qualifications, making them official submariners. I became close friends with one of the rider's wives, Laura. Doug and her husband had studied together at submarine school in Groton. They'd already left the States before she and I finally met (an "oversight on my part," Doug called it, feeling guilty that he hadn't introduced us before.) She and I started texting hours after the crew left, checking in on each other and making plans on weekends. We were in similar places when it came to coping with the deployment. Which is to say, we weren't.

"Can't get up. Don't wanna get up. This sucks."

"Same. I'm like a slug or a really, really, really sad zombie."

"I throw up every time I try to eat."

"I keep having nightmares. I'm scared to sleep."

"Does this get better?"

"Don't know. Tell me if you figure it out?"

Together, we tried to feel better or, at least, normal. We went to the beach or out for coffee, laughing at each other's stories of things we'd done to pass the time: organized cabinets, rearranged bookshelves, lots and lots of yard work. We sent one another pictures of our respective pets, my dog, her cat, and even went to a few FRG meetings together, sitting at a table by ourselves, but no longer alone.

Having another person there who understood what it was like to live in a state of *not OK*, made it measurably easier to get by—much more so than the frozen meals, projects, or lists. While I knew I could talk to any of the other wives in the FRG or wardroom alike, it was comforting to go through the first time with someone else also on their first.

Later, as I became one of the "older" junior officer wives, that would be the advice I passed along to the incoming junior officers' spouses on their first deployments: find your person, or your few people, and cling to one another. Hold on for dear life if you have to. That and, buy a reliable smart watch (one that sends alerts for messages or calls no matter where you are so you don't have to worry about missing one last communication from your husband before they run a startup and go back out to sea.) Even beyond the wardroom, when I happened to meet future or new military spouses through my graduate program or teaching, I was able to feel compassion and offer a hand, if they wanted it, remembering what it was like to feel so overwhelmed and disoriented, needing anything anyone could give. I wish I'd counted the number of times I gave out my number or email attached to the reassurance that any time was a good time. "Call whenever. Ask anything. I'm here for you." Even if I still wasn't sure how I got there, to a place where I felt I could help.

I continued to attend wardroom dinners, outings, and meetings as they came. We shared recipes, book recommendations, and bottles of wine. The mothers swapped stories and advice while I screamed with laughter, wiping tears from my eyes, knowing I'd pay for it in karma one day if I ever had kids of my own. We wept together when relatives passed away or babies were miscarried, guarding one another as much as we could from all the world outside, the world that didn't understand what it was like to do these things while so distant from your partner. In more ways than I can count, the wardroom felt like an accidental family. Many I never would have met otherwise, but now it was hard to imagine life without them.

A popular topic often circled back to was *busy-ness*. Keeping busy, I learned, was practically a commandment to the thriving military spouse. It was the currency that determined your ability to survive a deployment. It was the opposite of waiting—which still felt like the shameful, submissive path. The busier you were, the less time you'd have to take a breath and let the all the scary, lonely, overwhelming things about deployment creep in and throw your momentum to a screeching halt. While the guys were out fighting terrorism, we were on the homefront, fighting downtime. Some wives used their children, others, their jobs or volunteer work on base. A few more were in school or training programs to pass the extra hours. If I was good at one thing as a sub wife, it was keeping busy. It was practically my religion. During Doug's first year on the *Georgia*, I started teaching middle school reading—a job for which I not only had to plan lessons, document accommodations, and maintain extensive contact logs with parents, but also certify in, since my background was in English, not Education. When I wasn't in my classroom, I was taking professional development classes and studying for exams to put toward my teaching certificate (which, by my calculations, I would earn three months before it was time to move to a new state that would likely require new or additional certification). On top of it all, I was still working in the evenings and on weekends to earn my Master's in Creative Writing through the low residency program I'd started while Doug was in Power School. If I'd had a child at the time, I could have cornered the market on *busy*. I never wanted to admit that, through all the classes and essays, and papers to grade, it was never enough to fill the emptiness, but at least it made for good conversation—something not about the submarine.

Laura struggled with lack of busy-ness during our one deployment together. She lived further north, in rural Georgia by the base where housing is more affordable, but jobs are hard to come by regardless of education, experience, or availability. I won't pretend to understand the height of her elation when, before her husband's next deployment, she was offered a front desk position at a nearby veterinary hospital. "This one is going to be *so* much easier. I'm not even dreading it as much," she said. And even though the job turned out to be grueling and her boss was unapologetically rude and misogynistic, she didn't quit. It was still better than just waiting.

When the sub wives were together, nights stretched long and the burden of deployment felt lifted from my shoulders. For just a little while, I could float again.

By Doug's second deployment, Laura's husband was off our boat and back to his but two more twenty-somethings without children joined the wardroom: Michelle and Emma. Michelle was the new bride of one of Doug's closest friends on the *Georgia*. Emma was the long-time girlfriend of the newest junior officer.

I don't remember the specific first times we met, but our bond was instant. Weekends became "girl time" where the three of us would meet at each other's houses for brunch or bring our dogs together so they could run circles around someone's backyard while we talked about work, family, and the always-elusive return date which, on that deployment, changed three times in the first two weeks. The frozen meals I made now filled their plates as well as mine. We had a group text and a Snapchat group to keep in touch during the week and share the mundane details of the day that we'd normally share with our guys. Most importantly, we encouraged each other to take care of ourselves. *Do you wanna bring the dog over and walk? Are you eating dinner? I have soup on, come over.*

Many of the wives who'd been married into the Navy longer commented on how "good" our wardroom was. *Un-catty*, was the word tossed around. No one held grudges against one another or spread nasty rumors like other wardrooms they'd been a part of. When I asked what made our wardroom different, one wife attributed it to everyone "having their shit together." We were all normal women with jobs, children, and lives that carried on largely without outside drama. No one needed that sort of entertainment to pass the time. The *Georgia's* wardroom hadn't been a friendly place just a few years prior, around the time the sub ran aground while transiting in Kings Bay. There had been some sort of disagreement between a couple of the wives that had ended in numerous visits from the police. Their ugliness trickled down through the ranks, poisoning friendships in the Family Readiness Group, where crew spouses and children were supposed to be forming those same bonds that carry us all through the long days of separation. Bad wardrooms though, I'm told, are far more of an anomaly than good ones. Many wardroom friendships, they reassured me, are the kind that last lifetimes, no matter how far you inevitably move from one another. Many women organize annual trips to stay connected with their wardroom friends, even after the Navy years are over.

I was surprised at first, but learned from Laura over subsequent deployments, after her husband rejoined the USS *Florida* that, indeed, not all wardrooms are as harmonious as ours was. The wives of her wardroom turned on one another based on rumors of infidelity spread by some of their own.

In sub life, information from the crew about dates, movements, mission status, or even group morale, is infrequent and fragmented at best. Waiting for that information, with no promise of its arrival, is a powerless fight. Spreading a rumor, regardless of its veracity, might at least make you feel like you hold one card in a game where no hand will ever be dealt to you. Bad rumors can be frightening, especially if overthought. But the wives together could muck through them, figure them out, and, as a veteran spouse put it on a different occasion, "blow that poisonous shit out of the water."

There was, and still is, an immense amount of power in those friendships. If I credit the Navy with anything, it's making me into a better friend. Where before, I may have been inclined to dismiss or look past an opportunity to do something nice, I found myself now clipping out magazine articles on driving in the snow for Laura—a native Floridian—after a winter ice storm terrified her into skipping work for fear of black ice. I folded the article into a greeting card and put it in the mail because I understood how it multiplies joy to receive an unexpected card. For Michelle, I spent a Saturday helping unpack boxes and reorganizing after the flooring company finished in December, a repair that they'd started after a pipe burst in her home in August. If a group of us were meeting somewhere, we'd pick up each other's Starbucks orders and never expect to be repaid.

They made me want to be better, to try harder, to endure another day as the wife of the deployed. Through their example, and the example of all the other wives in the wardroom, I started to understand the power and role of the wife in a military partnership which is to give hope and create stability, to be the stars and signal beacons by which they navigate, and to remind the sailors of the life waiting for them when they get home; within that life, keeping it all moving forward, is someone who loves them enough to carry on. Waiting became less of an act of submission, and more an act of love, endured alongside those who know what it's like to honor that unique type of sacrifice.

The craft nights and dinners may have been what we did most often as a group of sub wives, but the support we provided one another, that was *wife stuff*. Being there for each other when the roof leaked, engines sputtered, colds were caught, bosses were jerks, or a first referral was given to a fertility specialist, that was *wife stuff*. And *wife stuff* mattered immensely. Even as the wardroom demographics changed with moves and marriages, including the addition of more husbands and same-sex partners, the *wife stuff* remained constant.

When Halfway Night rolled around on Doug's first deployment, the wives celebrated a few days after the sailors did underwater, reading out what our husbands had written about opening their halfway boxes that we'd decorated at craft night all those months before.

"I loved the card. Read it ten times, at least."

"Thank you for all the pictures. I hung them where I see them every night."

"I cut the Milk Duds up with a knife and ate them. Easily the best thing I've had in months."—that was Doug. No melting candy next time, I reminded myself.

"It made me smile my whole watch."

"It was like seeing the sun again."

"I miss you more every minute."

"I didn't know a funny little box like that would be the highlight of my week."—that was Doug too. When I read that, being a sub wife felt like holding the key to the universe.

Chapter 15

The Call

The ring my mother-in-law, Sue, wore on her pinky when she was alive was her grandmother's engagement ring, the story used to go. I can still see Sue, sitting in her reddish-brown recliner in the living room, recounting the history, shriveled fingers clutching a crumpled tissue she'd use to cover her mouth when seized by her deep smoker's cough. She'd have to push the back of the chair with all her strength to pop up the footrest beneath her feet—always wearing her favorite sherpa-lined pink Crocs. Most of her family was long dead and gone, but her eyes glimmered and creased at the corners when she talked about them. It made her look happy. She never missed a chance to reminisce and tell stories—a tendency that drove Doug crazy.

The first time I heard the story of the ring was also the first time she'd invited me over for dinner when I was about sixteen. Doug was in the kitchen. When he heard me ask where the ring came from, what the story was, he threw his head back as if he'd just been shot in the face, dramatically pantomiming his demise behind her back in the doorway. Sue wasn't known for being a brief storyteller, but she was a good one.

Jim proposed to his sweetheart, Mary, just a few days before the United States entered World War I. He loved her, he said. Would do anything for her. Wanted to marry her and raise a family with her. And, he told her, he wanted to enlist and have the wedding before boot camp.

Jim planned to join the Navy, the United States Submarine force. He heard the call to serve his country and had decided to answer it.

It wouldn't be until the next World War that submarines became colloquially known as *iron coffins*, but the danger predated the name. Men who went to war on submarines were as good as dead: hulls had weak spots, torpedoes misfired, and radio codes were easy to hear and easier to crack. Wives of submariners knew they were likely widows the moment the boat left port. Many sailors married in the hours before shipping out so their brides would receive survivor's benefits when the boat went down, taking its crew of young sailors with it. Entombed forever between torn steel and sediment, slowly becoming part of the sea floor—the Eternal Patrol, submariners call it.

Mary loved Jim and wanted to support him. But she wrestled with the knowledge that his call to serve might also be a call to die. Why did he have to answer? Why was *this* the song he heard? She struggled to accept his proposal with the weight of his choice hanging over her head. It was a predicament I'd be intimately familiar with about ninety years later.

Mary's father was an influential man who moved in high circles and she was his favorite daughter, perhaps only daughter—Sue could never remember. When Jim signed his name over to the armed services, Mary's father had his commission changed from Navy to Army and Jim was sent to France where he spent a year in the trenches. Somehow, his odds were better that way.

Just before he left, Mary gave him her engagement ring and ordered him to bring it home and put it on her finger at the end of his tour overseas. I always liked Mary for her decisiveness here.

The ring was a dainty thing with four tiny rubies on a white gold signet, all smoldering antique-cuts. Sue said that Jim wore it on his pinky finger while he manned a Howitzer, somehow dodging serious injury with every assault his battalion endured. By the time he shipped home, the ring had lost two of its rubies. Of the remaining stones, one was cracked in the setting, the other cloudy with scratches. The soft gold returned thin and misshapen.

Jim came home with shellshock, but his family and, eventually his children and grandchildren, would rarely speak of it for what it was. *Father is just tired today. Pour Father his drink, he needs his drink or he gets jumpy. Quiet down now, Grandpa doesn't like loud noises.* Sometimes he would lose focus and stare for hours at nothing—slack jawed, blue eyes wide at the whites.

Mary wore the broken ring until the day she and Jim died in a car accident in 1966 on a rural road somewhere near Wheeling, West Virginia, a month before Christmas. They were headed to visit their young grandchildren, the car full of gifts. No one can say for sure what caused the crash, but those who knew him remember how Jim could fall into one of his spells without warning. It had happened with the kids in the car before, but Mary had simply grabbed the wheel and yelled in his ear until he snapped out of it. The police report cites black ice.

Anytime my mother-in-law wanted to talk about her family's military history, she always started with Jim and Mary—Grandma and Grandpa Potter, her voice a little louder than in normal conversation. The broken ring was her gateway into talking about how the men on her side of the family were made to serve, born to answer the call of duty. Sue likened them to steel and iron and all manner of things that, in her mind, were completely unbreakable. When asked about service members on her estranged husband's side though, Doug's father's side, she would reply that they were all flat-footed cowards—all medically disqualified from serving whenever they were drafted. I believed her because I had no reason not to, though years later I learned that Doug's Grandpa Brown—his paternal grandfather—flew Bombers. She was never able to acknowledge that her son, my husband, had half their "coward" blood. The same son who yawned through all her stories over the years. I always wondered how many times he'd heard them before I came into the picture.

To Sue, the ring was made better for being broken, and Doug was predestined to be the next man of her kin to go off, serve his country, and return home a hero.

A drunk man once accosted my husband in a Taco Bell while we were eating with friends after a University of Missouri football game. The man crashed into the chair across from Doug with such force he shook the bolted-down table. He swayed on the seat, holding his gut for a moment before leaning forward and pointing one finger at the bridge of Doug's nose.

"*You.*" He burped, still swaying, blinking slowly. "You've got that *thousand-yard stare.* You should be a *Marine.*" He threw heavy emphasis on every word, inching the finger closer and closer. His breath stank of Bud Light and there were little shards of nacho chip stuck in his whiskers. Doug leaned back, laughing uncomfortably with the rest of us. We watched the middle-aged man squint at Doug's face as if trying to read it, mumbling to himself.

When our inebriated interloper finally wandered away after a few more minutes of swaying at our table, none of us could stop laughing. Doug's roommate wiped tears from his eyes, his face almost as pink as the drunk's.

"The fuck is a *thousand-yard stare?*" He coughed violently through heaves of laughter, choking momentarily on a piece of taco shell.

"It's what soldiers had when they came back from war—the look they had when they were in shock." I gave the answer no one was really looking for, remembering it from a book I'd read on trauma for my psychology class. Shellshock being the term used during the World Wars, before Post-Traumatic Stress Disorder entered the national lexicon.

"Oh yeah," another friend said, slamming his hands on the table for effect. "Doug has *seen* some shit." All of them were freshmen ROTC midshipmen and cadets—the worst they'd seen were the fake, rubber battle wounds they put on one another for training exercises: gashed-to-the-bone stick-on bandages and head-trauma swim caps. They were collectively about as weathered as an unopened umbrella.

Doug did look the part of war-weathered veteran, though, more than his baby-faced companions. His face is naturally angular and sharp, his jaw, strong and square. He's worn his hair in a buzz cut as long as I can remember. His build is broad and muscular, even though he rarely lifts weights. His manners, his calculated way of moving, even his posture, the way he sits and stands, suggest strict discipline and boot camp, when really it's just years of marching band and his mother nagging him to sit up straight, say *yes sir* and *no sir*. My grandfather used to call him "poster boy" because he looked so much like the square-faced sailors on old recruitment posters.

We decided, in the end, that the drunk man probably just liked Doug's eyes. They're an unnaturally icy blue, bright aquarium blue. His end-of-summer tan and dark eyebrows made them look even more vivid. In the right light, his eyes seemed to pop right out at you. Stare you down. We joked that night that his eyes were *full of freedom*. Through no fault or intention of his own, my husband has always looked like a man who serves.

For many years, I blamed Doug's desire to join the Navy on his mother. To me, it always seemed she'd goaded her son into serving to prove he was more like her heroic side of the family than the flat-footed, draft-dodging Browns. She wanted to place him at the forefront of the family hagiography.

In the nine years I knew her before she died, every birthday and every Christmas she would explain to Doug that, as part of his gift, she was putting together a scrapbook for him of all his family's military history, dating back to *at least* the Civil War, she'd say. Then she'd launch into another telling of her grandfather's days in the trenches, or her brother who served in Germany during Vietnam.

When she told her stories, her eyes always got misty. She'd gaze upon the son she'd raised by herself since he was six years old. He'd sit there, nodding, staring off into space, and waiting for it to be over.

She never minced words about it: she expected him to serve, expected all to serve, because it's *what good men do*. Whenever she said that, she always looked me up and down. Sue knew I wanted a different type of life. One where my husband would come home from work each night so we could share the evening together and talk about our days. If we needed to move, I wanted it to be a choice we made together, not an order from the government. I still dreamed of cities and job opportunities for a writer but, eventually, I wanted to make St. Louis our home and go hiking or camping together by the Missouri River on weekends. I wanted the changing seasons and all the familiar places we grew up at: the Zoo, Bush Stadium, Forest Park, Grant's Farm. If we had children, I wanted Doug to be there for all their firsts: first smiles, first steps, first Little League games at the same fields we played at as kids.

Sue knew I was drawn to big universities and big cities with jobs for writers. Once, years before we were engaged, I confessed those desires to Sue while Doug was out at sea for NROTC training cruise and I was struggling with his absence. I'd opened up hoping she'd have some sort of reassurance or advice, perhaps an anecdote about a strong military spouse in her family, maybe Mary herself. Without so much as a pause, Sue told me to leave her son, if I didn't want the Navy lifestyle.

"You aren't worthy of him if you can't handle it, so end it when he comes home." She said it sitting in her red armchair, coffee in hand, sipping away like she hadn't just told me to get lost.

If blood was where the call to serve came from, then mine was weak, pathetic blood.

Before my mother met my father, she dated the son of a two-star Army general. They were, per her description, *pretty hot and heavy* (ew, Mom!). But she says she never considered marrying him because she didn't want to be a military wife—the prospect of long, repeated separations and relocations wasn't something she envisioned for herself. She broke up with the general's son a few weeks after my father faked a fist fight with his friend in English class so he could sit next to the cheerleader, my mother, in the second row, per his arrangement with their teacher beforehand. He knew he wanted to marry her; he knew it then.

When they were dating, he promised he wouldn't marry her until he could support them with a job that paid the bills. He and his cousin, only a month apart in age, were approached by an Army recruiter during their senior year of high school. The recruiter talked to them about duty, honor, and a $100-a-week paycheck, plus benefits—a tempting offer in the early 80s. His cousin took the deal, but my father turned it down because he knew it wouldn't be worth the pain he'd cause my mother. He'd have to go about it another way. He went to work developing airplane parts the day after high school graduation and finished his undergraduate degree in three years so they could marry.

For years, this was a source of bitter friction between Doug and me. If my father turned down the call to serve for my mother, why couldn't Doug do it for me? Because he wouldn't, I determined that Doug didn't love me. Just as his mother said, I was unworthy.

My parents raised my brother and me to have a hefty respect for the armed forces. Whenever my dad's cousin deployed to the Middle East, we sent him care packages filled with candy for the men in his unit and toys for the children in the villages they were stationed near. At sporting events, when the anthem played, we always removed our hats and covered our hearts with our right hands. He taught us how to fold the flag. My grandfathers on both sides served in the Army for a few years—one, an officer who never got deployed overseas, the other earned a Bronze Star in Korea. By the time grandkids came along, the military memories were old, tired, and rarely talked about except during reruns of M*A*S*H.

I respected their service and the service of all those sworn to protect the country, but I couldn't understand why Doug seemed to want to serve more than he wanted to make memories with me or be there for our children someday.

So when I found myself hopelessly in love with my own high school sweetheart, a man bound by oath to support and defend the Constitution of the United States of America, I was both heartbroken and hopeful. His first oath came before we started college, when he swore into the Naval ROTC program that gave him his full-ride scholarship. The second oath, the day after graduation, when he was commissioned as an officer. Like my mother, I knew I wasn't cut out to be a military wife. The love and pull of home was extraordinarily powerful. But I'd resolved to try my hardest to be the partner Doug needed and, if I couldn't in the end, he would surely change his plans for me. Right?

We tormented one another with years of fighting between the two oaths. I begged him to quit the Navy before he commissioned so he wouldn't repeatedly leave me. I longed for the safety of monotony, of falling asleep next to him each night. He argued that I was making a bigger deal of it than it was—many couples did it every day and were fine. I'd already started to realize that while, yes, it would be difficult to establish myself as a writer through all the moving and changes, there was no rule saying I couldn't write anywhere we ended up. I'd always argue back, however, that changing jobs was far easier than changing who you were, and I was not strong enough to be a military wife. He wanted children one day, but I rejected having them at the thought of raising them alone in the chaos we were creating.

Sheer stubbornness kept us from breaking up, I think. Neither of us wanted to admit that while our love was strong, our aversion to the other's dream was verging on stronger.

I did not understand, could not comprehend, his need to serve. To me it often seemed like an ego trip—to prove himself to his mother or his never-there father, or even to himself. I implored him to try to explain to me why this was the only future he could imagine but he, the left-brained engineer who has no way with words, could never get much further than *it's just something I've got to do, Sam.*

Every time he rejected my pleas, I broke down further. Drowning in doubt, asking him why he couldn't change his plans like my father had for my mother. What could be more important than the commitments we make to the people we love, I asked?

The only conclusion I could draw was that I was simply not enough, just like Sue had said. I was unworthy of the whole of his love and would have to settle with being second place for the rest of my life if I wanted to spend any of it with him. Silver medal. Red ribbon. Through all the fighting, second-place love was still enough to sustain us, and we got married three months after his commissioning ceremony.

We never saw Doug's mother's military scrapbook or any of the newspaper clippings, award citations, or photographs of her relatives in uniform that she'd talked so much about. She died unexpectedly eleven months into our marriage and, during the long process of clearing out closets and sifting through scrap boxes in the basement, we never found more than a few creased photos of a boy headed to boot camp. The images were so sun-bleached and worn they could have been any number of Doug's relatives from her side—they all had that angular, military look about them. There was no name or date visible on the back. The grinning teenager could have been anyone's.

She left Doug everything in her will, including the four rings she'd worn up until they laid her in the casket: three sizable diamond baubles, traced back to her mother, and one dainty ruby ring, still bent out of round, and now holding two little diamonds where the missing rubies had once been set. She'd added the stones a few months before our wedding; I remembered seeing them at the rehearsal dinner when she showed the newly set diamonds to her brother.

I tasked myself with individually bagging and labeling all the antique jewelry before we locked it in our safe so, when we pulled the pieces out decades in the future to give to the next generation, we'd be able to tell them where each one came from, what its history was. I conferred with Doug's uncle for most of it, emailing pictures of each piece and relying on him and his connection to Doug's 90-something-year-old Great Uncle, the self-appointed family historian, brother to long-dead Grandpa Jim, to supply the backstory: *that one was Juliann's anniversary ring, that one's the original wedding ring.*

When we got to the ruby ring, the WWI ring, I asked specifically to hear the story again about the young lovers and the ring's incredible journey through the trenches of France to make its way back to Mary's finger. I was excited to hear it retold, especially by Doug's relatives who were so enthusiastic about remembering their family's past. I planned to write it all down and store it with the ring.

When the reply came, none of the relatives, not even the historian great uncle had ever heard of any war story attached to the ring. I asked them to check again and related to them the story exactly as I'd heard it probably a dozen times. They said they remembered his shellshock and the accident, but that was all. They weren't even sure the ring had come from Jim and Mary. One of them supposed it may have been a sixteenth birthday gift to Sue from one of their aunts who loved antiques, or something she picked up from a pawn shop as a newlywed. But certainly no connection to the Great War that either of them could verify.

I was dumbfounded. Had I been mistaken all these years? Had Sue? Her signatures were on some of the receipts for jewelry repairs; they were filed in files labeled in her handwriting. The ring was one of the only antiques without a paper trail.

Doug struggled to believe what seemed to be the most evident explanation: that his mother had made up the story about submarines and Howitzers. An apocryphal account that, coupled with the missing articles and citations, made me doubt the veracity of everything I'd been told.

After learning that her ring's history was nothing but fiction, still elbows-deep in sifting through her estate, we discovered that her prized Eastlake bedroom set—the one she said was brought over to the States by her great grandparents on a boat from Germany when they immigrated—was purchased by her parents from a reproductionist in upstate New York in the late 40s. Her silver flatware set was from Dillard's, not Denmark, and her vilified husband, whether or not he had been terrible in his day, wasn't much more now than a tired old man, moving back into his own home for the first time in twenty years. He'd returned to the picture in the last few weeks of Sue's life when there was no one left to care for her. The Navy had sent Doug to Charleston by then and she'd fired all the help insurance paid for after the open-heart surgery that was supposed to save her life. For a while, friends and neighbors, my mother, even Doug's often-absent older sister stopped by to help, but no one lasted very long. Doug's father drove from his studio apartment just a few miles away when she'd called about a fallen cabinet. He refused to leave after he watched Sue nodding off in the red leather chair, cigarette still burning in her hand. By then, she had no energy left to fight him and died in her sleep on Valentine's Day.

Doug's father was friendly and kind to us when we were in town for the funeral. He deferred to Doug on every decision and never once tried to steal or sell any of her antiques like Sue used to say he would. Doug and his father's relationship prior to this was almost nonexistent. I'd only seen his father twice before Sue passed, each for only the most fleeting of moments. It was through a kitchen-table conversation with Doug's father that I learned the sapphire bracelet Sue loaned me for my wedding day, the one she said belonged to her mother, Jim and Mary's daughter, had actually been a gift from her own mother-in-law who'd modeled jewelry for a department store in the 50s.

Doug was there in the room for that conversation and so many others, but he always seemed to be busy with something else: reading old bank statements or rustling around in a potato chip bag, taking a break between file drawers of saved receipts and tax forms. It was hard to blame him for shutting us out, grief alone is overwhelming enough.

I watched and waited for my husband to unravel with the knowledge that his mother may have been lying to him about so much of his childhood. I braced for anger and outbursts with my most soothing reassurances and embraces. With his new knowledge, I worried that he may now doubt his choice of career—to which he was contractually bound for another four years at least. There was no getting out or giving up his commission, and I wasn't upset by that, to my own surprise. He'd come so far, and I'd started to see how well-suited he was for the job after all. He was acing exams and, in one overinstruct's words, "killing it" on the watch bill. In just a few months' time, he'd be joining the fleet. I couldn't imagine a more horrible moment for doubt to sink in. I rooted for him. As much as I still hated the Navy, I didn't want Doug to suffer any more. We were long past the point of turning around.

He got frustrated over the furniture and annoyed by his father's pronounced hearing loss. It was hard enough for them to converse without Doug having to shout and repeat himself all the time. But he never once brought up the Navy. Never mentioned second thoughts or regrets. If anything, his zeal grew. His goals now in close sight, riding somewhere on the sail of a submarine.

Shortly after Doug joined *the Good Ship Georgia,* I became a middle school Reading teacher. The main feature of my classroom, the pièce *de résistance,* was the library: two tall oak bookshelves bolted to the wall and filled with copies of *The Hunger Games, Holes,* and several dozen discarded Read 180 novellas from the school's former curriculum. During my first weeks at the school, other teachers carted over boxes of old or unwanted books. A few friends in the area combed though Goodwill book bins on weekends, helping me build a collection that would entice my students into picking up a chapter book and enjoying it before they realized they were reading.

As the shelves filled with more and more titles, many students would finish their work and automatically grab a book—a *Harry Potter* or *Junie B. Jones*—so they could pick up where they left off the previous class—their place marked by a Post It with their name on it. Other students preferred the smaller novellas, or books of vignettes. Reading was easier for them in small bites. I told them they "could read the back of a Froot Loops box for all I cared," they just needed to be reading. They loved jokes like that.

A small faction of boys in one class was fascinated by my collection of *Worst Case Survival Handbooks.* They would assign one another sections to read then, after a set amount of time, would present their findings to one another.

"Ok, *so.* If you're caught in zip ties…"

"Gators, man. You gotta zig zag if you don't wanna be lunch."

"Don't touch the third rail or you're literally toast."

One of those days, they were reading through a section on armed assailants. A smaller, more timid boy of the *Survival Handbook* group raised his hand to get my attention. I walked over and sat on top of an empty desk beside him.

"Mrs. Brown, what happens if someone with a gun comes in the school?"

I remember lowering my brows, as if in concentrated thought, and scrunching my lips to the side. "Jayden, you know that would never happen." I didn't mean to lie to him, because it absolutely could happen, but my knee-jerk reaction was to reassure by any means necessary.

He glanced down at the illustration in the book: a masked man with a handgun, aiming it directly at a faceless victim. Arrows directed the faceless man which way he should dive to have the best chance at—literally—dodging the bullet.

"But…what if it did?"

I wanted to shake my head and rattle off statistics of how unlikely a shooting would be in our small-town middle-senior high, but his eyes were too wide for that, too unblinking and afraid. Looking around, so were the eyes of his companions: a gangly redhead and two Navy brats who bussed in from the base to the south. All of them were fixated on me, their teacher. The rest of our small class, just six or seven more students, was listening. I could hear their side conversation about Snapchat sputter to a halt.

"Then I'd protect you." I addressed them all. It wasn't good enough.

"How?"

The students had done drills of what they were to do if an intruder entered the school, but it was in August, long before I'd arrived the following January. They didn't know if *I* knew what to do. The student asking gestured to the row of windows behind him. First floor windows, easily broken into or jumped out of.

"I'd put you all in my office and shut the door." My office—the walk-in closet I'd dragged my desk into so the library could be installed.

They all snapped their heads to look at the closet, cluttered with papers, boxes of empty binders, and stacks of old curriculum novels, all coated in a thick layer of gray dust.

"I have granola bars in there, you could have a party!" I said, smiling to break the tension. A few of them laughed. One asked what kind.

"Peanut butter and chocolate."

"Would we all even fit?" It was one of the girls this time.

"Definitely. Look!" I pointed through the doorway. "One of you could hang out up there on the old bookshelf. Another two of three on the desk. There's plenty of space. You guys are such a small class. It's roomier than you think in there!"

"Would you be in there too?"

"Probably not. Someone has to be out here to tell the police we're safe." A few nodded, following the logic.

"So, you'd stay out here and keep us in there?"

"Mmhm."

"Who could open the door?"

I held up the jangling keys on my lanyard. "Just me."

No one pointed out the obvious: *Mrs. Brown, what if the bad guy shot you and took your keys?* They all just stared warily at the closet-office, whose door I had decorated with a beach-scene shower curtain from Walmart. This class of twelve would easily fit. Of that I had no doubt.

"So, you'd protect us?" The original student spoke slowly, surveying with his question.

"Yes." That wasn't enough. "To get anywhere near you, they would have to get through me first. They will not get through me."

The words came easily, effortlessly. Absolutely. Without thought or reconsideration. The students could tell. They relaxed a little in their seats and returned to their books and worksheets.

I think I understood then, for a sliver of a moment, why Doug chose to serve. Why he said it was something he *had* to do and could never offer a more specific reason. There was no ulterior motive, no family pride or heavy legacy. No love greater than the one he had for me. It was just something that said, "Yes, I'd die for you." Words he had said to me years ago under the cover of young love and darkness. Words he'd sworn to the entire nation in the oath he'd taken when he became an ensign

Words I said to my students not because it was my job, not because it was the right or wrong thing to do, but words I said because it's what teachers do, and I am a teacher. Teachers protect their students just as sailors protect their country. There is no desire to be saintly or measure up to any parent's expectations. Just a need, an instinct. Looking around the room, I knew I'd never let any of those kids be harmed while under my watch.

Of course I would round up my students and stuff them in a closet. Of course I'd bar the door with tables and desks and the library itself if I had the sudden superhuman strength to unbolt it from the wall. Of course I'd hide the keys before any intruder could get near them. Of course I'd go first if—God forbid—the intruder did. Of course.

Most revelatory for me was that this didn't mean I loved my husband any less. I knew he would understand if they found me lifeless and bloody in front of a locked closet where my students remained safe and alive. The same way I'd now feel if the hull of Doug's submarine failed, or a tomahawk misfired, tearing the steel like wet tissue. *It's just something I've got to do, Sam.*

It was a feeling he never could have explained to me. I had to know it to understand it.

Doug was out on his first deployment when I had this exchange with my students. I couldn't drive home and talk to him about it after work over diner. He was still deployed when I penned the conversation on paper in bed that night and deployed when I typed them for the first and second drafts. I couldn't ask him if this is the feeling he has, or if he answers the call because it's just who he is. But I know it is.

177

CHAPTER 16

Eight Days of Silence

"While the ARA San Juan carried enough food, oxygen and fuel for the crew to survive about 90 days on the sea's surface, it had only enough oxygen to last seven days if submerged." -ABC News, 21 Nov 2017

Refresh.

Refresh.

Refresh.

Refresh.

Refresh.

Refresh.

Refresh.

Refresh.

Refresh.

Refresh.

Refresh.

Refresh.

Refresh.

Refresh.

Refresh.

Refresh.

Refresh.

Refresh.

Refresh.

Refresh.

Refresh.

Refresh.

Refresh.

Refresh.

For the love of God.

Refresh.

Refresh.

Refresh

CHAPTER 17

Messages

In January 2017, not long before Doug's first deployment, I was at Queens University in Charlotte, North Carolina, attending my second on-campus residency as an MFA candidate. While I was there, I received a Facebook message from my second cousin's wife, a military spouse of over twenty years.

I received the notification just before sitting down in a workshop and didn't have time to read it until much later, when I was on my way to that evening's readings. The message was long and hard to follow—one of those copy-paste chains that get passed around inboxes like the common cold. It appeared to be an extended explanation of what "makes" a military wife: she moves from place to place, she waits, she supports, she laughs in the face of upheaval. She is stoic in the face of disaster and always puts others first. Her world revolves around her husband in uniform and she would have it no other way. His sacrifice gives her life meaning. She is the epitome of resilience and grace. At the end, the message left instructions to *copy and paste if you're a proud military wife* and sealed itself with a sparkling heart emoji.

I did not copy and paste but, after rereading the message twice more, I took a series of screenshots and fired them off to some friends with no introduction other than *look at this shit!*

My grip on the phone was so tight as I tapped, I popped it out of its case unintentionally, barely catching it against my chest before it shattered on the sidewalk.

After Doug's and my freshman year at Mizzou, six years before I began pursuing my master's degree at Queens, as a part of his Naval ROTC scholarship, Doug was sent to a month-long summer program called CORTRAMID—Career Orientation and Training for Midshipmen. He, along with dozens of other future naval officers spent the month on the East coast learning about the different career paths available to them after commissioning. They crawled through obstacle courses at Camp Lejeune, flew down the waterline in Ospreys, spent the night on a submarine, and boarded surface ships where they fired mounted machine guns into the empty open ocean.

Doug called me from Norfolk, Virginia on one of his liberty days. He had just eaten lunch and was killing time by walking laps around the NEX. I remember asking him what a NEX was. I'd never seen one nor heard the acronym for *Navy Exchange*. He described it as "a giant Sears with no taxes." Designer handbags and brand-name sports apparel one or two aisles away from sundries and large appliances. I still couldn't quite picture it. Even the most common military places and practices were still disorienting and foreign to me back then. PCS didn't yet mean *Permanent Change of Station,* a move to a new duty-station; his digital camouflage blouse and trousers I just called *camos,* not yet knowing their official name: *Navy Working Uniform*—or, *NWUs.* When Doug mentioned PT, my mind would immediately leap to *part-time* or *physical therapy,* not *physical training*—mandatory workouts done as a battalion, like the ones he would wake up early for during the school year in preparation for the semi-annual PRT—*Physical Readiness Test.* It was all an entirely new language.

We'd been fighting a lot since he'd left so I was surprised he'd called at all. The same fight as always, just over the phone instead of in person. Arguing over his commitment to the Navy and what it meant for our future. He was optimistic; I was not.

Just as I couldn't grasp the acronyms, he couldn't understand how my dreams depended largely on geographic flexibility that the Navy would never be able to accommodate if we wanted to live together—which we did. I still wanted to teach at a university, I wanted to find a tenure-track position. I'd also started applying for "backup" jobs grant writing for nonprofit organizations— a practical application of my writing degree. Not many submarine bases are in close distance to writing programs or big nonprofits in general. They are known instead for being middle-of-nowhere bases largely for security's sake—it's good practice to put distance between big cities and big warheads. Even the bases "in" big cities like Jacksonville, Seattle, San Diego, and Pearl Harbor, are situated miles away from the main hubs of civilization. I was also still a little bit of a homebody and hated the idea of living so far from my large, exuberant family: my parents, my brother, grandparents, aunts, uncles, and cousins— most of them lived within a few miles of one another and, as we all got older, had grown closer and closer as a family unit. The closest submarine base was a thirteen-hour drive from mine and Doug's childhood homes in St. Louis, from all that was loved and familiar.

But the day Doug called from Norfolk, he wasn't testy. He was in a good mood, chatty even. He talked and talked and talked about power outages on base, walking to McDonald's, and the other midshipmen he met during training. He counted out how many of them had girlfriends—his way of trying to help me see that yes, I could do this. If all these other girls can plan to move far away from home and follow their sweethearts base to base, then surely, I could too. I felt he was generalizing my worries on one hand and holding me to too high a standard on the other.

I remember that I was lying on my bedroom floor when we talked. I'd just gotten off from my lifeguarding job at the pool I'd worked at every summer since high school, and I didn't care much about Doug's efforts counting girlfriends.

Jokingly, sleepily, I asked Doug what he was shopping for at the *NEX* or what he was bringing back for me. He made thinking sounds for a few seconds.

"Hmmm. Ahh. *Ehhh.*"

In my mind's eye, I could see him stroking his chin and squinting like he always does when he thinks for an audience. After a few more seconds of *hmmm*-ing, he spoke again.

"Check your texts. I just sent you a picture."

He'd snapped a shot of a Hello Kitty clothing display in the women's department. Garish tees, jackets, and tank tops with the cartoon cat dressed in pink camo, wearing dog tags, and winking. Slogans in glitter. *I Love My Sailor! Proud Navy Girlfriend!* Little rhinestones on the trim.

"So," His voice crackled over the line. "Which one?" I couldn't tell if he was joking or serious.

"Oh, you know me best." I drenched my words in sarcasm he didn't pick up on.

"So, uh…tank top?"

"Um, no."

"T-shirt?"

"No, no thanks. Not quite my style."

He was quiet. I could hear him shuffling the phone around on his shoulder.

"The glitter or the *love my sailor*?" His voice was quieter and less cheerful than before, all the levity, gone.

I couldn't answer him because I wasn't sure which was worse: glitter or labeling myself in terms of my boyfriend's future.

We used to laugh at couples like that. Couples at our high school who branded themselves as belonging to one another with novelty t-shirts sporting kitschy slogans: *I'm with sexy!* It seemed so superficial to display love so publicly. It was starkly at odds with the quiet way we were.

Just because I was dating Doug the Sailor now didn't mean I wanted to wear pride across my chest in glitter. I didn't feel the need to advertise my feelings about my *other* in order to be a dutiful partner.

I am proud of Doug every day. I am proud of more than his choice to serve, and I love him for more than his oath to the Navy. I love him for his person, for the way he talks in his sleep and can sing more commercial jingles than songs on the radio. I love his facial expressions, his charming smile, and the way he rocks side to side when he walks, sometimes bumping walls in narrow hallways, making picture frames tilt sideways. His pragmatism and placidity are enviably steady like a drumbeat, like a march. He's strong, fair, and kindhearted with a soft spot for dogs and laughing babies.

Before he raised his right hand and swore to support and defend the Constitution of the United States of America, he never suggested I wear an *I Love My Boyfriend* t-shirt. Why would he? From the get-go we'd been an exclusive couple. I was his first girlfriend and none of my exes ever slunk back into the picture to cause trouble, save for a few bad memories. No reason to be jealous or doubt the way the other felt. Certainly there was no reason to wear our feelings in writing on our shirts. Back then, before the Navy, we laughed behind the backs of couples who wore matching clothes that declared how much they loved one another, or whom was with *sexy*. It was very opposite of who we were: reserved and quiet. Our relationship had its foundations in whispers and passed notes, never loud declarations or writing across the sky. We held hands in the very back of rooms, never participating in loud, romantic gestures other couples our age tried to emulate because they'd seen them passed around the internet: prom-posals and choreographed flash mobs dedicated to their significant other.

When he entered the world of the Navy freshman year of college, even in those very early days, I made an effort to meet the other girlfriends of Doug's battalion at Mizzou. I wanted to find someone who understood what it felt like to be so early-on committed to a man in the service, who could perhaps relate to my anxieties about altering my own goals in favor of his. But we were freshmen in college then, a time when romantic partners of friends changed by the weekend or were on and off like electricity in a storm. The coming and going relationships were too much for me to keep up with, so I just watched them happen, waited for the long-term couples to find us instead. On the rare occasion they did, my counterpart, the girlfriend or fiancé, had more flexible career aspirations like nursing or occupational therapy—there are hospitals and medical centers all over the world. I frequently cursed my aversions to needles and blood. In an effort to make conversation, I'd ask the girlfriend or fiancé about her studies, which would always lead back to me explaining that I hoped to get my Master's, so I could teach writing or English at a university. There'd be a few polite "Oh I sees" or a "That's cool." No one would ask the most obvious thing out loud: How are you going to do that with all the moving? Sometimes, someone would bring up teaching secondary as a "back up plan", since there are middle and high schools all over the country. Eventually, that's what I'd end up doing, but even then, it meant working at breakneck pace to get through certification courses and endorsement classes in time to certify before the next move to a new location, which was guaranteed to need some new type of certificate or qualification I didn't possess.

In my years spent watching, I noticed that, in the steadier couples, those who were on the marriage path, like we were, the girls wore their *Navy*

Girlfriend clothing often, or they displayed the unofficial title on a necklace, a bracelet. They stuck it to the back window of their car, or let it jangle around on a keychain. Screensavers, phone cases, and, in one instance, a wrist-wrapping tattoo. I had no aversion to decals or logos, but I resisted the idea of branding myself a *Navy* anything.

Sometimes, when we hung out in groups, I wondered if anyone else noticed that I was the only one unadorned with Navy pride. I wanted to love my boyfriend, my future spouse, for who he was as a person, not a sailor or midshipman.

Doug would never ask me to wear a special shirt or put a decal on my car window to make him feel more secure in our relationship. Freshman year of college, I took his PT sweatshirt as my own. I wore it all the time around my apartment because it was warm and smelled like him. Sometimes, I'd wear it grocery shopping when it was the only thing clean. But when he asked me on the phone a few months after I took the sweatshirt, whether or not I'd wear a sparkly cat shirt that advertised my status as a Navy Girlfriend, I recoiled because we were once the people who laughed at those people, until those people became the norm. I recoiled until quiet love and quiet pride weren't enough and, the closer he got to active duty, I felt, neither was I.

Ours was the first wedding in either of our families in decades. It was going to be a very large, very traditional, Catholic affair in St. Louis, Missouri, where we both grew up. Ceremony in the Old Cathedral under the Arch, reception at sunset overlooking a golf course green. String quartet and a big band for the guest list that spanned continents.

He was twenty-three years old, I, twenty-two. Young by most standards, but in love as ever and ready to commit before our loved ones and God. He commissioned as an officer in late December, the day after he received his engineering degree and three months prior to our wedding day, so we had a stable paycheck to get us started, and I planned to find work somewhere in Charleston after the move—our first PCS.

I would wear ivory satin and lace; the bridesmaids were in blue chiffon—*navy* blue, by coincidence—and milky pearls. The flowers were pink and white roses, hydrangeas, viburnum, and green hypericum berries, all tied in satin ribbons. The gentlemen rented tuxedos and dress shoes. My cathedral length veil and fingertip blusher, I beaded by hand.

I hadn't enjoyed shopping for my wedding dress as much as I thought I would. I have the body shape of a flabby, inverted triangle, and it took a long time to find a gown that flattered it. I was more than relieved when it came time to pick Doug's tuxedo. What could be hard about that?

Doug and I had agreed that he would wear civilian attire on the wedding day: one of the rented black tuxedos with a bow tie and vest. We picked it at a shop next to the grocery store by his mother's house—she'd recommended it early on in the planning process. We didn't even think to tell her when we went, we just walked in one day when we had nothing else to do, Doug tried on a few jackets, and they took his measurements. We left without a second thought.

About six weeks out from the wedding, I was at Doug's mother's house waiting for him to finish showering so we could go to a friend's birthday party. I sat at the kitchen table while his mom busied herself at the counter, sorting through mail.

"Sam," she said without looking up, "I meant to ask you, have the guys all ordered their tuxedos?"

"Yeah! Everyone's got their measurements in, last I checked. We used the place you recommended, down by Schnucks."

"Even Michael?" She mentioned Doug's college roommate, a fellow NROTC graduate, I wasn't sure why.

"Yep, think so."

"Won't Michael be wearing his uniform too?" Now she was looking at me. I still didn't follow.

"He's wearing a tux, like all the other groomsmen. They're all wearing tuxes." My future mother-in-law didn't move.

"Doug's tux is free because all the guys are renting through them."

She turned her back to me, rotating slowly toward the counter, hunching over it. My heart started racing fast and my face flushed red. Had Doug not told her that he wasn't wearing his dress uniform for the wedding?

At first, I wasn't even sure what happened, I just saw a flash of white then a pile of magazines and envelopes on the floor. Sue had whipped the stack of mail off the counter and flung it across the kitchen where it collided with the oven, snapping so loudly it scared their nearly-deaf Boston Terrier. He sprinted through the house and hid somewhere in the dining room.

I didn't move though. How could I? There's no protocol for what to do when your future mother-in-law flings mail because of a choice you made months ago—one of the few choices Doug and I actually made and felt unanimously about. He didn't want to wear his dress uniform for our wedding and I didn't want him to either, so he wouldn't. Easy choice. Still frozen, I listened hard, willing Doug to finish getting ready and come save me before she threw something sharper. She was breathing hard through her nostrils, still not looking at me.

"He's going to wear the choker whites for our engagement shoot, so there will be plenty of pictures." I didn't wait for her to respond to our compromise, I kept on talking even though I wished I could just shut up. "He wanted it. Doug wanted it. He likes the tux. It fits him well." I was practically stammering. "The engagement pictures will be so nice, you'll love them." Sue was a fierce woman. I'd never been on the receiving end of one of her outbursts.

But, flustered as I was, I had to stick up for myself. Doug's wedding tux was so much more to me than just a jacket and bow tie.

She was the only person who threw something, but not the only one who didn't understand. The closer we got to the wedding day most everyone reacted with raised eyebrows and stumbled over what to say next.

The reasons we opted for black-tie civilian attire were manifold. A sailor, or any member of the armed forces, does not get to choose which uniform he'd like to wear on any given day. Uniforms are dictated by the command to which the service member is attached and tend to rotate with the seasons. With the date of our wedding falling in the earliest part of spring, the dress uniform mandated would not be the swoon-worthy officer whites of Richard Gere and Tom Cruise fame, it would still be Service Dress Blues: a black wool suit with a black bow tie and stately combination cover with gold piping, the officer crest, and shiny, polished brim—Doug's least favorite uniform. It was scratchy, unflattering, and hot. That alone was enough to convince him to don a civilian tux, but he respected my list of additional reasons enough not to argue.

If he wore his uniform, then the one other sailor in the wedding party would have to wear his too—making the groomsmen side of the party visually unbalanced—something that annoyed me for no good reason. If those two wore their uniforms, the dress code for the entire wedding would have to be elevated accordingly. Military guests would be expected to show up in dress uniform—an inconvenience for those traveling from afar, particularly his ROTC friends from college who weren't supposed to get drunk in uniform but struggled to practice moderation when presented with an open bar.

Doug wearing a uniform made it a *Navy* wedding, meaning we'd be expected to add seafaring rituals and customs to our already tradition-heavy Polish-Catholic nuptials. The saber arch, the drinking songs, the invocations, bugle cries, and calls to attention. If we went by the book, Doug's commanding officers would be given priority seating in the cathedral, sitting alongside our parents and in front of the rest of our relatives, and given an honored table at the reception, seated with the same level of importance as those who raised us. It seemed ideologically wrong to me, disrespectful even, to demote our extended families that way.

And, of course, the comedic reason, the one I offered to the majority of inquiring invitees, was that Doug's dress whites were *white,* and he was the messiest eater I'd ever met. I had visions of spending my wedding night scrubbing béarnaise stains from his jacket and slacks. I'd tell guests that draping him in a plastic poncho during dinner was not out of the question, even in the rental tuxedo.

But all those details were secondary to me; in my heart, there was only one explanation that mattered at all. The un-surrenderable reason I wanted Doug to wear a tuxedo instead of his choker whites was personal: I was marrying *him*, not the Navy. Marrying his blue eyes, his bright smile, his heart stretched seaward—the heart I'd vowed to follow as far as I could, as far as the edge of the shore. The dream my own hopes had been placed behind time and time again, even so early in his service. By the month of our wedding, I'd turned down three full-time job offers to write for nonprofits I adored because, just like my preferred creative writing programs, they all required I move to cities far, far from submarine bases. Doug was always encouraging, saying there would *something somewhere,* but we both knew that the areas supporting sub bases were too rarely the same as the ones supporting writers and his job paid the bills far more consistently than mine.

After a year of our engagement, I'd already begun to feel the keen sting of other surfacing *wants* I had that the Navy made impossible: a stable home in one place, a predictable schedule, a husband who came home in the evenings and on weekends, the freedom to drive somewhere for a couple of days and not have to submit leave forms weeks in advance. I wanted to live somewhere idyllic and quiet, where we could walk from our home to parks and cafes or sit on a bench and people-watch for hours like we used to. I feared even more keenly than before that he would miss the births and milestones of any future children while out on deployment and it would create distance in our family and our marriage. Doug called it "picket fence living" and he was right. My vision of the future was vanilla and boring, but it was safe and what I knew best and it certainly was not going to be a reality for however many years he planned to stay in the service. If the Navy wanted him on mission, it would never matter how much I needed him at home. So just this once, for one day, our wedding day, I wanted the Navy to come second, even if only symbolically. Even if only in a garment.

It became clear that when people asked me if the groom was going to wear his uniform, they weren't asking at all. They were seeking to confirm what they expected to see because, after all, I'd be a dutiful Navy wife in just a matter of months, or weeks. I'd offer one or two of my reasons, saving the most personal for my closest friends. But the reason never mattered.

Friends who objected would groan and exclaim how *amazing* it'd be to kiss a man in uniform, forgetting I have that privilege almost every day. They'd goad me by saying I'd have the most beautiful pictures to Instagram later—*all* uniforms photograph so well, they'd say. Middle aged women, friends of the family, would smile knowingly and ask if I'd ever seen *An Officer and a Gentleman* or *Top Gun*. Then they'd insist I watch them again because that would *definitely* change my mind. Aunts gasped and gave each other sideways glances whenever they were reminded. My future mother-in-law called me a bitch under her breath at least twice on major holidays while I hand-washed her china in the sink.

No matter my reason, no matter how superficial, neurotic, or gut wrenchingly personal, the consensus was the same: *You're going to be a Navy Wife, so start following the rules.*

When we left Doug's house the day Sue threw the mail, I didn't tell him what had gone down between us while he was in the shower. He didn't ask why there were magazines and envelopes all over the kitchen floor, or why his mother didn't say goodbye when we left, just turned her back and stared out the window, still practically snarling with each breath. In the car though, I was fired up internally, and more than a little proud: I'd asserted myself over the Navy, over her and her love for it. Just this once, I *won*.

Delayed start-dates and hold-time included, Doug spent about a year and a half in the Navy's Nuclear Training Pipeline before he joined the crew of the USS *Georgia*, based in Kings Bay, Georgia. Unlike the NROTC training command in college and the nuclear training units in Charleston and Groton, where significant others remained on the periphery, in Kings Bay, the USS *Georgia*'s home port, I was welcomed almost immediately by the spouses of Doug's fellow officers—the *Wardroom Wives*, the Facebook group said (although technically our roster included two husbands.) There were ten of us wives, myself included, but only six or seven lived in the area when I joined. We made our homes all over the map, from north of the base in Kingsland and Saint Marys, Georgia, all the way down to south Jacksonville—some called our spread-out region *Florgia* to better encompass the cross-border commuting we all partook in. I lived in north Jacksonville which meant a lot of driving in the weeks before the crew deployed, when the wives met to decorate placemats, cards, and calendar pages for our husbands and the unmarried officers whom we divvied amongst ourselves, so no sailor felt uncared for during the dreary months underwater. And when the boat was out, the group met once a month to celebrate birthdays or holidays, share a meal, and sip cocktails on someone's back porch.

I relished my time with the wardroom wives, absorbing all the advice they spouted: everything gets easier after the first two weeks, buy a fresh tube of Neosporin for him and make him put it somewhere he can find easily—cuts and burns don't heal well in the low-oxygen submarine air. They told me never to apologize for my feelings nor feel bad for pouring myself a drink; "You're an officer's wife! You're going to need it."

As a group, the spouses of the wardroom didn't have much in common in terms of interests, or at least, not in the ways I thought we would. Sure, many of us were dog people and a lot of us liked yoga, but most of them I never would have met were it not for our one commonality: the love of a sailor. That spousal love begat our bonds. What I loved the most was that no one was afraid to voice their negative opinions about the Navy, the frustrations of deployment and the heartlessness of the bureaucratic systems that dictated both our spouses' lives and our own. So many struggled to find work that meshed with prior-earned certificates and degrees. Many times, an evening with the wardroom wives would start with heavy venting about whatever was weighing us down that day. It didn't sound like it'd be a good time, but hearing others complain about the same things that were burdening me was like coming up for air after nearly-drowning.

We talked about keeping busy and how we liked to pass the time when we had too much to spare: reading, running, watching *Fixer Upper*. That being said, of the local wardroom spouses on that first deployment, I was the only one without children and I never felt like I should complain about being too busy at home or too stressed at work when the only life that depended on mine was the dog's. I still felt like an outsider sometimes, even from the inside.

Regardless, it was comforting to hear that not every Navy spouse wants everything that comes with a Navy life. We don't all want to move and uproot; we don't all enjoy that brand of adventure. We don't all want to say goodbye every few months and then carry on with our daily lives, our children and our jobs as if the balance of home hasn't changed at all. Some enjoy it more than others, some like the months of independence, but not all. Not every Navy spouse feels more pride than exhaustion day to day. Sometimes, we want one day where deployment, orders, ceremonies, and uniforms don't factor into a conversation or decision with our spouses, family, and friends alike. One day to just *be*.

But the military's is a culture of obedience. It's taught to the sailors, we marry the sailors, and their lifestyle bleeds into ours in big ways and small. It stains and changes us. Even then, I could mark the changes in me just by surveying my closet. Where I used to have just one Navy sweatshirt—the one I stole from Doug back in college—I now had a second Navy sweatshirt I'd picked out myself, a few generic Navy tees from fundraisers, a zippered jacket with the *Georgia*'s emblem, and a pair of novelty submarine-print leggings I pulled out for fundraiser 5ks on the base. At an estate sale I happened upon by chance, I bought a sapphire blue intaglio pendant with the submariner dolphins etched on it in gold and wore it sometimes to Family Readiness Group—FRG—events put on by a board of sailors' wives. I noticed at one of those events, a "50% Night" dinner to celebrate the boat being halfway through its deployment, each one of the officers' wives also had on some sort of gold-toned trinket bearing an anchor or the old-timey dolphin warfare insignia of nuclear submariners. I'd become more like them without even meaning to.

Later, when the *Georgia's* captain changed commands, he gifted each spouse in the wardroom with a gold pendant engraved with the *Georgia's* crest on one side and the submarine warfare insignia on the other—a traditional gift for departing Commanding Officers to present, the older wives explained. I wore it almost every day.

Where I used to reject labeling myself as attached to the Navy at all, now I was a little more willing if it supported Doug or his boat. I could accept wearing a shirt or a necklace if it made him smile, or if it connected me in some way to these other spouses who seemed so knowledgeable and strong—because really, I came to decide, in the grand scheme the sweatshirt or the necklace were such small things. Still, I could never go as far as glitter or Hello Kitty.

The big changes, the ones that go beyond clothing and car decals, come more slowly, and aren't all that noticeable until you do something that goes against the hundreds of years of traditions like throwing a civilian wedding or pursuing your own goals rather than staying home, raising children, and waiting quietly, patiently for the sailors' safe return. The circulating social media posts that inform you, other spouses, future spouses, and civilians alike how things should and should not be, like the Facebook message I received at Queens. That tell people, often incorrectly, what's normal and what is not.

On our wedding day, I wore, as brides are wont to, all the items in the old rhyme: something old, new, borrowed, and blue, and a silver sixpence in my shoe. On the inside of my train, I'd had Doug's Navy-issued name tape sewn in. It had been removed from a worn-out pair of his blue coveralls: the uniform he'd wear on the sub while it was underway. Embroidered down the tape in gold block letters was my new last name—*BROWN*—representing my new life as the wife of a sailor, pushing me further and further away from anything familiar. Further out to sea.

I hadn't seen the second cousin's wife who sent me the Facebook message since her daughters were in early elementary school. Now they were both in college. The wife lived overseas, where her husband, a retired Army pilot, worked flying helicopters for the über-wealthy. The most contact I had with her was occasionally liking her daughters' posts on Instagram. Her message and the lack of context with which it was sent, felt like an invasion of the near-sacred space I'd claimed for myself in Charlotte. Charlotte was my *place*. It wasn't just where I went to graduate school for two weeks a year; it wasn't just where I liked to write. It was my tooth-and-nail fight to hold onto my dream of getting my Master's in Fine Arts so I could one day teach for a university.

Accepting my spot in the graduate creative writing program at Queens had been a leap of logistics, timing, and pride. In Doug's short time in the Navy, I'd already accumulated a lengthy list of temporary jobs and dropped careers: Lifeguard, Swim Coach, Donor Relations Liaison, Web Forms Specialist, Jewelry Sales Associate, and Swim Coach, again. When I applied for Queens, there was another PCS move approaching, but we were still waiting for the official orders telling us what city we'd call home next. We had no idea where we might be sent next and whether travel to and from my program in Charlotte would be feasible. I didn't know if I would have a job that could support the expenses of attending the one-week residency twice a year—like dog boarding, plane tickets, room, board, and lost time at work. I didn't even know if I'd have a job that would allow me so much time off. I worried how the program's workload would impact the dwindling time I had left with Doug before he started to deploy. Could I manage our home, our finances, our families, a new job, a new city, and grad school at the same time? Not to mention the dog, the lawn, the cooking and cleaning, the car repairs, keeping up the house, and the move itself to name a handful—all of which I'd be doing solo.

I was seven months into the program when Doug joined the *Georgia* and I met the wardroom wives. They seemed genuinely happy for me and were kind enough to ask about Queens: what it entailed and what I wanted to do with my MFA after earning it. I'd get excited and detail my loose plans to, one day, earn my PhD and teach at the college level, while writing and publishing books. That was still my dream, to which I clung tightly. The wardroom wives, infinitely more familiar with the ways the Navy often forced plans like mine to change, answered often with raised eyebrows. My civilian friends who asked usually just said *yikes*. More high eyebrows. At least both worlds had that in common.

But I couldn't say no to graduate school. I couldn't turn down the chance to earn the degree, to work with other writers, to finally have a conversation again about the things *I* was passionate about, conversations I hadn't had since college, when groups of undergrads from the English department would hole up together in someone's apartment to read for classes or write papers, bouncing ideas off one another for new poems, essays, or stories. It was our own writers' colony, centered around trips to Shakespeare's Pizza and Tropical Liquors for spiked peach Bellini slushies, and I missed it horribly from the end of capstone until I was accepted into Queens University of Charlotte a year later. Once I got to Queens, I found a similar camaraderie. No one at residency talked about missions or deployments outside of my workshops, where they were not an impending life event, but a narrative element. We had animated evening discussions over sushi and beer about prose, craft, and criticism. Never uniform care, nuclear reactors, or physical training requirements.

When I picture heaven, a little part of it looks like Charlotte because, for two weeks a year, I didn't have to live like a Navy wife: dutiful and determined and painfully pragmatic. I didn't have to be resilient. In the morning, I could drink a cup of coffee while reading a book at a patio table and listening to the Beatles in the sun without once feeling guilty that I wasn't cleaning the house, working on projects for his underway, or running yet another inventory of the deployment packing list which always sat on the coffee table in plain, unignorable sight.

Juggling my life with the program hadn't been as difficult as I'd first thought. It got more complicated when I accepted a job teaching middle school and had to start the two-year certification process, but still, it was doable. It took me a long time to articulate it, but I was proud of myself for being able to still work toward my own goals after marrying into the Navy way of life where personal sacrifice, not individual success, is the norm.

But then I got the message. In the middle of my happiness, the Facebook message. The list of every stereotype about the Navy Wife. Moving, drifting, inconsistent. Smiling, understanding, grinning-and-bearing. Martyr. The only thing missing was *uniform chaser*.

Look at this shit! I sent to everyone I thought would care.

My first thought directed at the message-sender was, *how dare she*. How dare this woman who I'd met three, maybe four times in my life send me this soliloquy, this reductive and insulting grammatically atrocious ballad of military wife life. I was disgusted.

Then I was curious and wanted to know why she sent it. Did she think I'd find it funny? A satire? Was it supposed make me feel better about something? Who said I needed to feel better at all? Did my status as an active duty military spouse automatically mark me as unhappy? Things weren't always peachy, but they were ok now, stable—better than they had been in years past. My focus on graduate school and connections with the other wives had helped alleviate some of the stressors of the Navy. I wasn't always unhappy, just anxious.

The friends I texted reacted in slow succession.

Uh, wow.

That's...something.

Spellcheck, much?

Not one of them noted the heinousness of the message beyond it being another copy-paste chain with as one friend commented "a confusing relationship to capital letters." *Send me to five contacts or a clown will murder your family*—it was just junk mail fodder to them and, indeed, wasn't written with any attention to grammar. My friends were all civilians who'd only ever dated civilians—I'm not sure how I expected them to see in it what I saw. I supposed I could have sent it to a few of the wardroom wives, but I didn't feel enough closeness with them yet—or perhaps I feared they'd respond with affirmation and agreement with the message, or worse, that they'd think I agreed with it. I didn't want to feel more trapped in the message's narrow idea of a military spouse than I already was.

That night, when I returned to the hotel, I tried to go to the gym but found it closed. Ice coated the streets outside, so I ran stairs in the fire escape, wanting to burn away the message, rereading itself aloud in my subconscious. It bothered me how much of myself I saw in the message, and how much I didn't see.

Of course, I thought, of course it started out with moving. Who could think of a military spouse and not think about the moving?

> *Lots of moving... Moving... Moving... Moving far from home... Moving two cars, 3 kids, 2 dogs, all riding with HER of course. Moving sofas to basements because they won't go in THIS house; Moving curtains that won't fit; Moving jobs and certifications and licenses. Moving away from friends; Moving toward new friends; Moving her most important luggage: her trunk full of memories.*

Like the message says, I have a "trunk," a Rubbermaid box, of memories that travels in the car with me anytime we PCS. It sits beside the dog in the backseat, full of old letters from high school and tokens from our wedding day. Oddly enough, for all my aversion to uncertainty and change, I've grown to like moving. The long process of choosing a new place and completing it with what old furniture and photographs we have is cathartic and gives me some sense of purpose in those tumultuous first weeks under each new roof: make a home, make it nice.

Then it talked about how strong military wives are, how *independent*. As a woman, it's a sentiment I appreciate but, when applied to my role as a sub wife, almost always feels condescending because more often than not, it applies only to the running of the household and social lives of the family:

> *They call her 'Military Dependent', but she knows better: She is fiercely In-Dependent. She can balance a check book; Handle the yard work; Fix a noisy toilet; Bury the family pet... She is intimately familiar with drywall anchors and toggle bolts. She can file the taxes; Sell a house; Buy a car; Or set up a move...all with ONE Power of Attorney.*

> *Military Wives are somewhat hasty... They leap into: Decorating, Leadership, Volunteering, Career alternatives, Churches, And friendships. They don't have 15 years to get to know people. Their roots are short but flexible. They plant annuals for themselves and perennials for those who come after them.*

In a new house, I am lethal with a scratch awl and some drywall anchors. My eye for decorating and redecorating is keen and flexible. Taxes are no biggie now and the storied Power of Attorney I keep while Doug is gone isn't as powerful as the name would have you believe—many institutions can refuse to honor it, leaving spouses of the deployed high and dry in times of crisis.

I wondered why "leaping" into new projects and friendships was characterized as *hasty* and not *ambitious* or *outgoing*. *Hasty* is a nasty word I've often heard applied to the youngest of military marriages—the ones where the service member is a newly-enlisted eighteen-year-old and the spouse is barely out of high school. No one wants to be called *hasty*, especially when they're trying to be brave.

> *Military Wives have a common bond: The Military Wife has a husband unlike other husbands; his commitment is unique. He doesn't have a 'JOB' He has a 'MISSION' that he can't just decide to quit... He's on-call for his country 24/7. But for her, he's the most unreliable guy in town! His language is foreign TDY PCS OPR SOS ACC BDU ACU BAR CIB TAD EPR (well maybe not so foreign to me) And so, a Military Wife is a translator for her family and his. She is the long-distance link to keep them informed; the glue that holds them together.*

Again, like the message, I do translate for our families: each fractured branch receiving their own watered-down version of what Doug is doing or when he's going, when I can tell them at all. Most of the time it's just me, the holder of all knowledge, all order, all secrets, somewhere out there alone, save for the kinship I've found amongst the other wives who know what it's like to be frustrated to spend birthdays, holidays, and anniversaries alone, or to show up to a wedding with duty as your plus-one instead of your husband because the boat needed him more than you.

On the eleventh floor of the hotel stairwell, it occurred to me that perhaps the wife of the distant cousin was offering a hand of companionship, a connection. She probably sent the message to tell me I wasn't alone and that she understood—that was all. To a small degree, in that moment, I appreciated it. From what I remembered of her, she was kind and sweet. My mother loved visiting with her when they were in town. Friendship and understanding, distant mentorship, was probably all she meant to convey.

But still, it stung. There were too many things in those paragraphs, too many descriptions that didn't fit me at all, but I'd more than once felt pressured to become.

> *Often waiting... Waiting... Waiting... Waiting for housing. Waiting for orders. Waiting for deployments. Waiting for phone calls. Waiting for reunions. Waiting for the new curtains to arrive. Waiting for him to come home, For dinner...AGAIN!*

It's hardly worth repeating: I can't stand waiting. Waiting, to me, implies sitting around and doing nothing, or meek submission and subservience. I don't wait for phone calls when he's gone. I tell him not to make them. But still, whenever Doug leaves, I check my phone compulsively for an email, hoping one from his secure boat account will appear each time I refresh the screen. I don't want to be a wait-er for I fear it will drive me insane. In the early days, waiting for a man, albeit my husband, made me feel like less of a woman and more like a servant.

A Military Wife has her moments: She wants to wring his neck; Dye his uniform pink; Refuse to move to Siberia; But she pulls herself together. Give her a few days, A Bible, A travel brochure, A long hot bath, A pledge to the flag, A wedding picture, And she goes. She packs. She moves. She follows.

In my *moments*, as the message called them, I have never gotten angry enough to want to dye Doug's uniforms pink—the man looks far too good in pink, for one. But I have threatened to leave. I have pulled down my suitcases and started packing in the middle of the night, hoping to be at the state line by morning. Sometimes running away entirely feels like the only way to escape the obligations I never could have been prepared for when I married him: the frustrations of never sharing dates and locations with even the most trusted family members or correcting those who assume that because Doug serves on a submarine, he's completely out of harm's way, so I have no reason to worry. There's immense frustration in speaking a different language than them and having to adapt to live by a different set of rules and realities. There's also the exhaustion of often being the only present-party in a two-person relationship.

Typically, I don't welcome unwelcoming neighbors like the message says wives do, or should:

She welcomes neighbors that don't welcome her. She reinvents her career with every PCS; Locates a house in the desert, The Arctic, Or the deep beautiful south. And learns to call them all 'home'. She MAKES them all home.

I don't really meet any neighbors at all beyond *Hello, how are you,* and *yes, the dog is friendly* It's more of a safety precaution than an antisocial tendency. When Doug is gone for months at a time, I don't want anyone to know. Perhaps the neighbors are friendly, but maybe their nephew visiting from

Boston isn't? Maybe he'd like to break into a house where the wife is home alone, presumably defenseless. The Navy calls that PERSEC—personal security—and they require all family members adhere to it strictly. When Doug is gone, I drive both cars, wash both cars. I leave lights on in different rooms on different days and keep a radio on when I'm out of the house.

Sometimes the only thing that lifts you up is having a connection to others in the same situation.

> *Military Wives quickly learn to value each other: They connect over coffee, Rely on the spouse network, Accept offers of friendship and favors. Record addresses in pencil...*

But I don't record addresses in pencil. I use an Excel spreadsheet, like most people of this century with knowledge of computers and Cloud drives. When someone moves, I highlight their row in yellow and, when the time comes to send out Christmas cards, I text them and update accordingly. Of course, the pencil mentioned in the message is a figure of speech but *come on.* Enough of the Navy is stuck in the past as it is, why make a pointless metaphor out of it? The message's narrative was needlessly retro and made me feel guilty for the admittedly traditional housekeeper role I play in our marriage which I have no reason to be ashamed of at all. When we started living together in the year before the wedding, Doug offered to help with the chores, with the cooking, with the cleaning, but I asked him to let me do it all myself. Any help he gave me then would be help I missed when he was gone—a catalyst for bitterness.

I still wear my hand-me-down Navy sweatshirt around the house. It's going threadbare around the wrists and neck, but I can't let go of those years of softness and good memories worked into the fabric—memories of slipping it on in the middle of winter and it still smelling faintly of Doug: Old Spice and powdered Tide. I try not to wear it out to the store anymore. I know I'm not supposed to since it's not just a sweatshirt but part of his uniform. But sometimes I don't realize I have it on until I'm at the checkout at Sam's Club, buying protein bars and toothpaste in bulk for his next deployment.

When I'm upset because of the Navy, I don't look to a bubble bath or a Bible, and God knows I don't recite the pledge. I get angry and start yelling. I yell at my husband and I tell him without mincing that the problem we are facing is a direct result of his job. I tell him when it is his fault and I tell him when I'm sick of the Navy talk, the Navy parties, the Navy obligations, and sitting through his long, semi-compulsory evening meetings when I have to be at work early the next morning—the ones where I don't *have* to go, but it makes him look better if I do. His rank, low as it is amongst officers, and how I preform in relation to it, can set him up for success or failure should he choose to continue on in the Navy after his required service is up. The submarine officer community is relatively small, and word of unsupportive wives travels quickly. But I don't lay my own ambitions on the altar of his duties. I go for a run or a swim, or a long walk with the dog and, when I come back, I tell him that we're just going to have to make both ways work. Even if it doesn't always work.

I do things differently, as most spouses do in their own ways, some big, some small. In the Navy, that's not something often celebrated, let alone acknowledged.

The friends I've made since Doug commissioned are priceless to me because I never expected to find such companionship in this often-isolating lifestyle. We can laugh over drinks, sharing anecdotes about last-minute moves and shrunken uniforms. But the second the conversation among the wives turns to sanctifying the sailor sides of our husbands, I shut down. I can't contribute. Many days, I worry that this signifies some sort of defect within me, or that I don't love my husband as much as I think I do or should.

Is there something in my genetic makeup that precludes me from being a thriving, successful Navy wife? I worry that my threats of leaving Doug will come to fruition because I can't keep my mouth shut. I can't put a halo above my sailor's head or erase the things he puts us through for the sake of his oath, his holy oath, that supersedes the one we made together at the altar in the cathedral beneath the Arch on the second day of spring.

> *Why? What for? How come? You may think it is because she has lost her mind........actually it is because she has lost her heart. It was stolen from her by a man, a wonderful and dedicated man, Who puts duty first, Who longs to deploy, Who salutes the flag, And whose boots in the doorway remind her that as long as he is her Military Husband, She will remain his military wife. And would have it NO other way."*

> *~Copy and paste if you're a proud military wife!~*

Lost wasn't a bad choice of word for the message. Sometimes, as a spouse, it's easy to feel lost, like an afterthought, in the sea of military life. But if military life is a sea, oftentimes a *rough* sea, you have to know how to swim if you hope to survive. There is more than one way to swim, is there not? So why does the message remain that there is only one way to be a proud military spouse? Can't I be proud without copying and pasting?

CHAPTER 18

The Cook Off

The December 2017 staff meeting at the school where I taught in Florida was one of the most anticipated events of the entire year. The last faculty gathering of the semester happened a few days before winter break when all the mid-year scrimmage testing was finished and included about fifteen minutes of actual work, then a chili and dessert cook-off. We were a small-town school. Most of the recipes submitted to the contest had been in teachers' families for generations. The smell of the cafeteria that day was warm, meaty, and overpowering.

I sat at a round cafeteria table with a few of the other middle school teachers, all excited for the meeting to wrap up so we could start eating. Most of them knew my husband was in the Navy and deployed, though it wasn't something I talked about much at work. It was nice to be in a place where the Navy did not make up the whole of my identity. Amongst ourselves we chatted about assignments and exam grades, never deployment extensions or missions gone awry.

Today though, I wished I could. I wished I were close enough with my colleagues to just break down there at the table and sob.

I still hadn't heard from Doug. We were edging close to three weeks without word, though I hadn't spoken about it to anyone outside of Michelle and Emma since the Christmas party. More than once I considered messaging the few crew wives I was friends with on Facebook and asking if they'd gotten anything from their sailors, but I knew that was the wrong thing to do. It could cause panic, or worse, rumors.

The San Juan and her crew remained missing as well, and the news cycle covering them was relentless. Every hour "updates" aired with no new information at all, adding in more pictures of the grieving families gathered with their signs, calling for answers: *te estamos esperando*. Two nights after the wardroom Christmas party, I hit my limit. I'd unplugged the TV in our bedroom and started charging my phone in the bathroom instead of on my nightstand so I wouldn't be tempted to stay up all night reading myself further into worry. I kept replaying the XO's wife's words over in my head; *You get used to it eventually*. How soon was eventually, I wanted to ask? How much longer would I be waiting to hear if our husbands are alive or dead? Would the all-consuming dread subside eventually? Whenever I could, I'd send my students into transition and rush to my desk to check my phone for word—but nothing.

Waiting, waiting, waiting still.

Georgia's silence was deafening. I was supposed to be driving home to St. Louis that weekend for the break, to celebrate Christmas. I'd bugged my coworkers for audiobook recommendations for the sixteen-hour drive, partially for entertainment, but also because there was no way I wanted to be alone with my thoughts for that long without some sort of paltry distraction. I'd gone with *Devil in the White City* because serial dismemberment and gore sounded like just the balm I needed.

Calling the staff meeting to order from her podium, the principal asked us to pull up our laptops and verify that we had submitted grades, updated our accommodation logs, and a handful of other tasks due before the semester ended. There was a din of bags unzipping and computers chiming awake; fingers tapped out passwords. Once we'd finished that and signed off on the Google doc, she said, we were free to go through the food line. The typing got faster.

I am not a big chili lover, so I walked through the line with two coworkers and waited for their recommendations.

"Mrs. Brown, what do you like?" Asked the eighth-grade English teacher.

"We never make chili at home. I don't know!"

"Never?" Answered the seventh-grade math teacher. "God, we make it every weekend during deer season. Have you never had venison chili?"

"Nope."

"Ok, then you have to try this one. He uses fresh venison and his wife grows the vegetables." She handed me the ladle, before walking down the line and laying out the backstory of each teacher's recipe.

I ended up with three or four other chili varieties on my plate and a cup of the school secretary's legendary banana pudding. Right as we sat down with our ballots to start tasting, my phone vibrated in my back pocket. As I shifted to grab it, I fumbled it onto the floor where the vibrating amplified against the metal leg of a chair. I laughed and snatched it up, and then my stomach dropped.

Three missed calls from Michelle, two from Emma. My school was miles away from civilization—our cell service was terrible. I hadn't felt it buzz at all. Text notifications started filling my screen, but my ancient phone froze as I tried to unlock it. I couldn't read the texts.

"*Fuuuck, fuck, fuck,*" I hissed, slouching low with the phone in my lap, my forehead nearly on the table.

"You ok, Brown?"

I nodded, not looking up. "Yeah, uh. Phone thing." After fifteen excruciating seconds my phone unfroze and I entered my password.

It opened straight to email and I swiped down to refresh. Then again. New messages, highlighted in bold, began to appear:

LTJG BROWN, Douglas P. USS GEORGIA BLUE (SSGN 729-B). 30 Nov 2017, 6:53 AM

LTJG BROWN, Douglas P. USS GEORGIA BLUE (SSGN 729-B). 1 Dec 2017, 5:34 AM

LTJG BROWN, Douglas P. USS GEORGIA BLUE (SSGN 729-B). 2 Dec 2017, 6:07 AM

And they didn't stop. Every few seconds a new message from Doug loaded into my inbox. I could hardly breathe. Finally, the upload completed with the arrival of an email sent just that morning. I opened it:

> *Hey again, it's me. Got your message but sounds like you haven't heard from me in a while still. Hopefully that changes soon? Nothing's different here. Everything sucks lol. Glad your students are done testing. Bet they're glad too. Drive safe on your way to St. Louis. That's soon right? I don't remember exactly when you said break starts. Will you stop to sleep somewhere? Tell everyone I said hi!*

I squealed and slapped my hand on the table repeatedly, then sighed and grinned from ear to ear, reading and rereading what he'd written. My face was hot and flushed and for a few seconds I couldn't stop giggling. *The Georgia is ok! Doug's alive!*

"Brown?"

"Yeah?" I smiled at my tablemates. "Sorry, sorry. I just got an email from Doug. It's been like, three weeks."

"Oh, that's great!"

I nodded enthusiastically, but they were already back to their chili. *That's great* didn't even begin to cover it.

Three-ish months later, when the deployment was over and Doug was safely home, we would disagree about the length of time he was out of contact. He claimed it was less than a week that they'd been unable to transmit communications. Why then, I'd ask, did it take so much longer to hear from you? He didn't know. We tried to figure it out using the time stamps on the messages I'd saved versus the few he could access from his secure boat email. Most messages from the three weeks of silence had a disparity of four or five days. We had no reliable way to account for the incongruencies. When I talked to other sailors and their wives, they had no better luck figuring out the dates either. Was it a time zone issue? Or was this the amount of time each message had spent waiting to be censored? Some couples emailed each other only every few weeks, or only when they had pressing news to share, so they barely registered the *Georgia*'s silence at all. We've never been able to nail down an exact number of days without contact.

Rather than dive into my email right there in the meeting, I chose to save them for when I got home. Instead, I swiped over to the texts from Michelle and Emma.

Holy shit. Holy shit. Holy shit!

Guys I'm crying, I'm so happy.

We're not widows!

Fuck it, I'm leaving work early. Anyone wanna meet for drinks?

I can't leave till six, have one for me or I'll meet you later!

I said I'd be down for a drink as soon as my meeting let out. Some teachers were already leaving so I scarfed down the chili and made a quick exit out the back doors of the cafeteria, practically running to my car. All I wanted was to be with Michelle and Emma, with the sub wives who'd been there too, who knew what hell we'd just emerged from. I wanted to hug them and cry and then get very, very drunk.

On my way off the highway, I drove over a shard of metal and got a flat tire. With my long road trip coming that weekend, I had to ditch drinks to get it fixed. But I wasn't upset. How could I be? My husband was safe and alive! He wasn't in a crushed can at the bottom of the ocean! I'd been able to read words he'd written just that very morning. I texted my regrets to the wardroom and waited on roadside assistance, practically dancing with joy.

"Ma'am, you're in a very good mood for just getting a flat," the man from AAA said as he put on my spare.

"It's almost Christmas!" I said half of what I felt: *it's almost Christmas and my husband is alive!*

In the waiting room of Firestone, I went through each of Doug's emails one by one, savoring them like a smorgasbord of the rarest delicacies. True to his word, he'd sent something every single day. Some days he was happy and optimistic: he'd passed a board, they'd gone on a swim call, he'd eaten his favorite meal after watch. Other days he was blue: quals were taking forever, he hadn't slept in days, he was still really, really upset that he had no Christmas music to listen to. He asked about our dog, about my students, and how my grad school writing was coming along. He told me stories about his division and recalled sweet memories of our newlywed days that made me smile bigger each time.

I drank in every word—it was better than wine. Reading Doug's words was the next best thing to having him right there with me and, after so long without him, the joy felt nearly equal to a reunion. Surprisingly, I even felt a little woozy after a while and chose to put my phone down for a few minutes to rest my eyes. I'd left my reading glasses in the car which was now lifted ten feet off the ground for a replacement tire. Then I broke out in a cold sweat. It rapidly became evident that I wasn't woozy from happiness, but some kind of stomach bug. I spent the next thirty minutes locked in the tire shop's tiny bathroom, sick as a dog. I texted one of my coworkers and asked if any of the chilies had included ginger. "Probably," was her reply. I am allergic to ginger.

By the time I emerged, my car was done and the mechanic who came to find me looked worried. "You look really pale, Ma'am." He offered me a

Sprite from the vending machine and asked if I wanted to call someone to drive me home.

A year ago, before Doug had begun to deploy, getting a flat tire alone would've been the kind of minor tragedy that sent me spiraling. Having an allergic reaction in an unfamiliar waiting room without any close family or my spouse to call for help would have felt like the end of me. A year ago, being a Navy wife meant, to me, that I would have to deal with everything by myself. That no one would want to help me because, as a sub wife, I should be able to do it all alone.

Now, the idea seemed laughable. I could've called Emma or Michelle or any of the sub wives, and I know they would've come in an instant to drive me home. Thanks to the pre-deployment meetings and regular briefs from the Family Readiness Group, I knew all the resources available to me when emergencies happened. I even knew my school's principal lived just a few miles down the road from the Firestone. Her son was in the Army; she wouldn't hesitate if I called. Help, when I needed it, was abundant and given without condition—not unlike the love of a spouse.

Being at my weakest and lowest, while still knowing I was supported and protected, was exactly the growth medium I needed. At that time, about halfway through Doug's second deployment—sick, weak, and completely elated, was the first time I'd ever felt that the Navy, and all the people who'd come into my life because of it, had made me stronger and better than I'd ever been. I knew I had a submarine's worth of people to help me, to get me through what was sure to be a long, unpleasant night. But at the same time, I knew I did not need it to survive. I would not die without it. I was capable, even when slightly incapacitated.

"Thank you, but I'll be alright," I told the mechanic, accepting my keys and his skeptical gaze.

My husband is alive, and I'll be alright! Not because he lives or is present with me, but because of where he's brought me—because of the opportunity the *Georgia* gave me.

That night, after a few more hours on the bathroom floor, I plugged in the bedroom TV again and let it play in the background while I wrote to Doug. I told him about the chili cook-off and about the tire. I told him about my allergic reaction at Firestone and the kind mechanic who'd insisted I take the Sprite. I assured him our dog was doing well and that we'd drive safe on our way to St. Louis that weekend. I told him over and over how happy I was to finally hear from him, how relieved I was to know he was safe. Did he know when he was coming home yet, I asked, knowing he would have no answer.

The news was still on when I finished writing. Immediately I felt bad for asking when he'd be home because there, on the screen again, were the dozens of families in Argentina wondering the same thing, still waiting for the silence to break.

CHAPTER 19

Wife Stuff, Three

I spoke my first *eh*, my first vocalization of Naval-apathy, or something near it, one week before Doug's second deployment in September 2017, while getting ready for my college roommate's wedding, in which I was a bridesmaid. It was the morning of the ceremony, at the salon where we were having our hair done. Forced by the stylist to sit still, my friend the bride wanted to talk about anything to get her mind off her nerves. She asked about Doug and, as it is with everyone we know who is not part of the sub-world when they ask about Doug, they ask about the Navy.

"He leaves pretty soon, yeah?"

"Yeah." It was against OPSEC—Operational Security—for me to tell her just how soon so, for emphasis, I added, "*soon*, soon."

In reality, he was scheduled to leave in four days.

"I don't know how you do it; I feel like he just got home."

She was right. It had been just over two months since he'd returned from the previous underway.

"Deployment is..." I started. It was still hard to say it out loud and accept it was already happening again. But when I could have said *terrible*, or *miserable*, when I had the chance to say I was devastated, I didn't. "It's...whatever. It ends eventually." I laughed a little and shrugged. "Eh."

It was even harder to believe those words had come out of my mouth, and even more, that I meant them. No sarcasm, no bitterness or defensive joking. No tears. Only weary honesty—and, as I'd hoped, it did feel a little bit badass.

I was thankful to have Doug there for the weekend of the wedding. It was a miracle he'd been allowed to take leave so close to the flyout date what with all the trainers, work-ups, and certifications the crew was going through. He grinned at me from the pews at the ceremony, swapped my high heels for flats at the reception, and had Chinese food waiting for us in the hotel room when we returned after midnight, drunk and laughing. We shared sesame chicken and danced barefoot in front of the bed to a few more slow songs he played from his iPad, like we used to in college, which was almost certainly a lifetime ago. As I pulled bobby pins from my hair and slipped out of my bridesmaid's gown, our buzz faded into yawns and long embraces. He held me up through exhaustion as I tried to do the same for him, giving him everything I could before losing him again.

I had several more *eh*s after the *eh* at the wedding and after he left: at work, over holidays, when visiting with old friends.

"Yeah, he leaves soon."

"No big deal."

"I've got enough to keep me busy."

"*Eh,* it's not so bad. Not anymore."

They were all just as genuine as the first and came from that same, small place of strength—like some new second backbone that I never expected to be there. But I knew enough then to understand that the backbone was temporary, that *eh* is just a place you visit, not a place you live.

Two weekends after Doug left for that second deployment, my parents came down to visit. The deployment was supposed to be a short four-month stint that would end with Doug's crew bringing the *Georgia* back to Kings Bay for the first time in three years for dry dock and major maintenance. The hope was they'd be home in time for Christmas and, if not that, shortly after New Year's. Oddly enough, while I was still measurably upset and weepy over his departure, I wasn't consumed. I had a plan this time and a marginally better idea of what it was like to be alone. Every weekend between the start of the deployment and mid-January was fully booked. While my students were working on projects that kept me as busy as them, I had a thesis to write, teaching certification classes to take, and a stack of books to devour for grad school. I had Michelle and Emma, my newest wardroom friends who'd just arrived to the boat, to help pass the time. The boat was projected to be home by the end of January—slightly later than the original before-Christmas estimate, but that was still ok. Everything was going to be fine this time. Better, even.

I was with my parents at Topgolf, finishing up our game and getting ready to leave, when my phone started to flash and buzz—messages in the group text with Michelle and Emma. I could barely keep up with the string of messages as they poured in, one more quickly than the next.

What the shit! This is insane!

What the fuck happened?

They just left and now this? This! This is bullshit!

What in the actual fuck.

I butted in, asking what was wrong.

The deployment got extended. Something with the Florida being off-schedule. What the shit.

It wasn't an official message from the command, they told me. Not yet, at least. The *Georgia* was back in port for unexpected repairs and the captain had announced a several-month delay at an all-hands call due to the *Florida's* delays back in the States. The *Georgia* would now require a crew change in mid-April. Their guys had messaged them on Facebook while the boat internet was still open and Michelle let me know Doug should be on soon since her husband was about to relieve him off watch.

I joined in their exclamations. *Holy fuck! No fucking way. They cannot be gone that long. No! Fuck!* It felt like all the hard work I'd done to prepare myself had come crashing down.

Within a minute, before my parents noticed that I was starting to breathe too fast or that my face was burning, Doug was on Facebook, telling me what the captain had said: on top of the *Georgia's* own need for repairs, the USS *Florida*, the *Georgia's* sister ship had failed part of her sea trials and was being sent back to port in the US for more maintenance. She would not be able to cross the Atlantic to relieve the *Georgia* in December as planned. Doug's four months at sea were now likely six, possibly more. The boat and all its crew wouldn't be coming home in January, or even by early spring the way things looked.

I was devastated. All the forward momentum I'd gathered, all the plans, all the preparations, all the busy-ness I'd so carefully cultivated was, in my eyes, dead in the water. Jettisoned, I slipped instantly into rage and channeled it all right at Doug. *You asshole. You selfish bastard. How could you do this to me? This is your fault.* And of course, he wasn't being selfish. And of course, the delay wasn't his fault. He was following orders, doing his job. But his job wasn't like other jobs. The *Georgia* and I couldn't peacefully coexist. It didn't matter how much I pleaded or prayed. She came first—to Hell with what I thought I needed, which was him, home. We fought blindly, so blindly, typing furiously back and forth in all-capital letters, unable to scream at each other, solving nothing because there was nothing to be solved. I was the monster that time, howling in grief over more time lost.

The deployment he'd just begun would end up being the longest SSGN deployment in the platform's history.

In the parking lot of Topgolf, loading our clubs into the trunk, I sobbed uncontrollably, telling my parents about the extension, wanting comfort, but receiving only criticism. "Sam, he's serving his country," my father said, not incorrectly.

They told me to stop fighting with Doug, not on the grounds that it wouldn't change anything, but because it was only going to make it harder for *him* and make *him* feel lonelier. My dad brought up how he used to feel when he traveled for work, but I didn't want to hear it. For the first time in my life, I told my parents to back off. Their intentions were good, they always are, but I was incapable of acting with grace, patience, or understanding. I was impetuous and cruel. I told them I didn't care what my attitude did to Doug (although I did) and that they had absolutely no way of knowing what this was like for me. None at all.

But the sub wives did. We each confessed to our own breakdowns in relation to the extension: one got drunk on cheap grocery store wine, another went shopping and bought a hundred dollars' worth of new clothes and shoes. Some stayed in bed. I was fueled by rage and couldn't stop berating my husband with the most hateful bile I could spew. The fight went on for days.

I had failed again, repeatedly, at my one job as a sub wife: to support my sailor without question or condition. Every time, when I thought I'd found the deepest trench in the whole ocean, I'd blow out all my ballasts and sink even lower.

A veteran spouse I talked to a few months later, during a casual wardroom shopping trip where I owned up to my failure, called it *hitting the wall*—when you get to the point in a deployment where you can't handle another curveball, and then another one comes flying at your head. You shut down, losing all reason and control. "Even ten days in?" I asked.

"You have to fall apart. You *have* to. Without a breakdown, you can't repair and move on."

It had been less than a year since Doug had arrived on the *Georgia*, but if I met the version of myself who showed up at the Hail and Farewell that first night, I wouldn't have known her, nor would I have liked her. All I'd focused on was categorizing the wives—collar flippers, super moms, winos, helicopters, *Hooya*s, and so on—thinking of them more like caricatures than actual living, breathing women, like myself. Not once did it occur to me that it didn't matter what "type" of wife each was. I was so afraid of losing my husband to the cogs of the military, I had scoffed at the one thing all the wives had in common: the submarine. For all the ripping apart it did, the *Georgia* did a fair amount of bringing together too. As lonely and desperate as I felt coping with the deployment extension, now I had a dozen other women who were dealing with it too. It didn't matter if they drank a lot of wine, or poured their energy into their kids, or wore shirts and bracelets with "Navy Wife" on them. For all our personalities, we were all sub wives. Differences beyond that faded away when we were all faced with the same challenge.

Even more fascinating, was how little I cared now about being the "waiting woman"—an idea that transfixed me as far back as high school. I'd felt ashamed to be the one left behind, like Doug going off to war and leaving me to wait, made me less of a woman, or less of a wife. After coping with the deployment extension, then the disappearance of the *San Juan* in the company of all the other sub wives, I learned from and absorbed their strength. I learned how to break down, without breaking apart, and how to remain strong for Doug's sake. Whenever I felt like I was flailing around, unsure of how to manage, or wanted to give in to the bubbling anger that resurfaced every time the Navy altered the deployment schedule, I leaned on the wardroom, on my friends, following their lead.

When I wanted to scream and sob and shout at the unfairness of it all like some petulant child, I learned to breathe past it. If someone outside the Navy—a friend, a relative, a prying coworker—wanted to ask about Doug, I learned to summon my "*ehs*" from a place of both indifference and strength. Yes, the Navy often made our lives difficult, but I was finished letting it control mine with anger. I wanted to be, at least. But, as I'd been told, sometimes you have to fall apart. *Eh* is a place you visit, not live—so I strove to make my sojourns there less frequent.

Before Doug joined, I remember wondering what kind of woman *does* this? Who willingly chooses to place her marriage in the hands of something so large, great, and unfeeling as the military? Slowly, I've started to understand.

Teachers, pharmacists, and social workers choose this. So do nurses, doctors, and lawyers. Financial analysts, accountants, waitresses, and bankers choose this. Loan officers, personal trainers, and pastry chefs choose this. Ultrasound technicians and bartenders choose this. Librarians choose this and so do realtors. Mothers choose this. Those without children choose this. Husbands choose this. Religious people choose this, and so do the secular. Foodies and runners choose this life. Yogis and Cross-Fitters too. The young choose it, the old choose it. Every day, we choose it. We have good days and we choose it; we have bad days and we choose it still. We are tall, short, thin, fat, smart, powerful, brave, hopeful, and hopeless all at once. Every spouse is different. All we have in common is love.

That's the only category that matters.

Waiting at home for a spouse gone off to war is not an act of submission or deference but one of the greatest acts of love. I would not know this were it not for the surrounding strength of my fellow sub wives. They knew the secret of the military spouse and shared it willingly so that I too might make it in this life so rigidly defined by the comings and goings of a great steel giant.

Michelle, Emma, and I got together near the tail end of the long deployment for one last girls-night before the guys came home, supposedly, in less than a day and a half, according to the command overseas. It was the end of February, 2017. I'd baked three dozen submarine-shaped sugar cookies for us to decorate, cooked dinner, and pulled out every bottle of wine left in my house so we could celebrate.

We'd all been in contact with our husbands by then, the first phone calls from land in several months. Michelle shared with us that her husband asked if she'd miss "hanging out with the girls" once he was home. We screamed with laughter that he thought their return would change the family we'd formed amongst ourselves.

"Is he crazy? Doesn't he know we're practically married now?"

"I'm almost a little sad, guys," I admitted. "It's a big change again, to have them back." I remembered how odd an adjustment it had been to have Doug back the first time, how it felt like living with a stranger. As much as I wanted to welcome him home effortlessly, we'd existed in separate worlds for too long. This family of women in the wardroom was what felt safe now, where I felt the most at home.

Fortunately, the somber moment passed quickly and we went back to drinking and decorating what were clearly too many cookies. We pressed on though, knowing how much the guys would appreciate homemade treats waiting for them when they arrived. We talked about bagging them up individually and handing them out on base when we went to meet the buses.

But at about eleven at night, a few minutes after icing the last submarine, we got a call from the command phone tree: the arrival was pushed back at least three days. We sealed the cookies tightly under saran wrap, knowing they'd be stale by the time they came home now. I took a few pictures for memory's sake and got back to preparing for homecoming.

As much as we dreamed of "wife nights" lasting forever, when the guys are home, the monthly official wardroom spouse events slow to a stop, and our impromptu dinner dates and hangouts don't happen as often as before. We text or snap, but not like we did when the guys were gone. There's no love lost or hurt feelings, in fact, it feels quite natural; everyone just wants to spend as much time together as a family as possible, the clock always ticking down until the next goodbye. The only time we're all together as a wardroom is for command meetings or, like when Doug and I first arrived, Hails and Farewells, but you'd never know we were the same group of people. It is hard to say goodbye to those moving on, especially those wives with whom you've endured some of the most difficult parts of your life. But military life gives little options for those who prefer to stay put, so the goodbyes are part and parcel. They're...*eh*.

When it's just us, just the wives, we form our own little universe. We drift together like moons around a planet, support one another, each on our own path but drawn together by the same gravity, by our marital connection to the Navy. But when the boat is home, the center shifts entirely, the tides all change, making the two worlds almost unrecognizable.

Walk into a room of sailors and their spouses and, at first, it looks like any room of people at a party: clusters here and there, some sitting, some standing, talking, laughing. Especially when they're dressed in civilian, there's nothing remarkable to see. Just a bunch of guys with the same haircut and their wives at an after-hours work function. But look closer, look for a minute longer, and you can spot the pairs: an arm around the waist, a hand hooked around an elbow, standing with shoulders pressed against one another.

I think a lot about my civilian friends who are married. All in our mid-twenties now, there is no shortage of them. Most of us had weddings within a year of one another but our marriages seem leagues and leagues apart. While they still seem like young newlyweds, we've been torpedoed forward in time and given weights for our pockets. Goodbyes, deployments, relentless separations. The velocity of it catapulted us out of the early days of unfettered bliss and into a weathered relationship full of unanswerable questions. *Are we strong enough? How much can we stand? Will we still know one another when all is said and done?*

Challenge-less marriages don't exist. But how I envy, sometimes, the hurdle of a two-week business trip, or the difficulty of choosing what city to live in. I want to butt heads about normal things like where to spend holidays, or when to take vacation. What if our biggest problems were allocating our budget or our in-laws? Who cooks dinner? Who writes the thank-you cards? Which one of us picks up the dirty socks? Shouldn't we both? Any little thing can put strain on a marriage, but there's nothing like *will you follow me anywhere* and *will I ever see you again* to stretch it to its limits.

Maybe I am wrong to wish for different problems. I chose the Navy as much as Doug did, knowing we'd take on challenges an all-civilian marriage wouldn't. But when a civilian-married friend says something like "I don't know how you do it," I want to run to the arms of a fellow sub wife because *they* are how I do it. The net of love and support provided by the sub wives is what has saved me time and time again when the pace and intensity of a military marriage seems just too much.

Women are strong. We know this to be a fact. But there is a double-edged fierceness to a woman like a sub wife. She is able to hold the word in her arms, and then let it go. She can thrive in the murk of unknowns. She's found the pride in choosing to wait for her love to return, holding its place while wading through the shifting tides.

CHAPTER 20

Sack of Wheat

"And now," said the Little Red Hen, "who will help me eat the bread?"

"I will!" said the duck.

"I will!" said the goose.

"I will!" said the pig.

"No, I will eat it myself!" said the Little Red Hen. And she did.

~Little Golden Book, Diane Muldrow, ed.

There is a website turned internet phenomenon called WelcomeHomeBlog which boasts thousands, maybe tens of thousands, of videos of surprise military homecomings. It first appeared in June 2010, right after Doug and I graduated from high school and just a few months before he began his NROTC training in college. I became aware of it almost immediately—its meteoric rise to popularity defined *viral*.

Videos from the site slowly, then very quickly appeared as forwarded chain email in inboxes and were featured in evening feel-good human-interest stories on every news outlet across the country. I distinctly remember a stretch of time over the summer before freshman year of college where almost every casual phone conversation between my mother and my aunts involved asking one another if they'd "seen the one where"...then describe any number of dramatic homecoming scenarios one could imagine.

A simple search on WelcomeHomeBlog will pull up a pages-long list of videos catering to the viewer's specific tastes: soldiers sneaking up on their wives at work, Marines ringing their mother's doorbells, airmen popping out of gift-wrapped refrigerator boxes at parties, sailors crossing thresholds, bearing balloons and armfuls of flowers. The surprisees scream and usually bawl. They jump up and down until the camera can't even keep up with them and they turn to a pixelated blur, catapulting into the arms of their loved ones, returned to them after so long.

With the volume up, you find yourself wondering if the sounds people make—the combined shrieking, laughing, and sobbing—are even of this world. Mothers howl and clutch at their faces. Young children shake and heave out their sobs, smashing their cherubic faces into their long-absent parent. Wives scream as if they are frightened, and who can blame them? Suddenly seeing a spouse after being apart that long is not unlike seeing a ghost. Then there's hysterical laughter, panicked stammering, blubbering, and fervent repetition of *Oh my Gods*. Only from a prime seat in the world's finest opera house can one garner a greater appreciation of the range and ability of the human voice, I'm sure of it. Many of the wives leap straight into their service member's arms as if drawn by a magnet. There's no shortage of venues either: birthday parties, family dinners, graduations, baseball games of both little and major leagues, airports, Christmas mornings, Passover Seders, Disneyland, Legoland, and dance recitals where the returning service member collapses like a Jenga tower at the sight of a pint-sized ballerina in her tutu, hitting his knees just in time to completely envelope her. There are special tags for surprise proposals, fathers meeting their babies for the first time, and reunions with pets—a favorite of mine because, along with being a dog lover, I used to be a bit of a WelcomeHomeBlog junkie myself. In college, it was my preferred method of procrastination when I had an essay to start or an upcoming exam (*just one more, then I'll go study...*) It took absolutely no effort to spend hours watching clip after clip, completely hooked on the happiness.

The blog is, in its essence, a celebration of service members, their families, and the payoff—the joyous reunions after long separations that some say make all the sacrifices worthwhile. It brought the homecoming into every home, inviting anyone, civilian and military alike, to share in that hard-earned moment of relief and joy.

WelcomeHomeBlog's popularity coincided perfectly with Doug's years in the University of Missouri's *Tiger Battalion* in Columbia, Missouri—the Naval Reserve Officer Training Corps program that granted him a full ride through college in exchange for tenure of service after graduation. He swore his first oath in August 2010 and, after a week-long "boot camp" of sorts with his fellow midshipmen, began an almost-normal college freshman schedule, punctuated by physical training three times a week and an extra class each semester on military history or leadership. Every now and then, he stood a flag detail for a sporting event or went on weekend-long field exercises in the woods. Since I attended Mizzou as well, at the same time, and had a front row seat to many of his events. I started to experience my first taste of waiting then: being cut off from him for short periods of time while he fulfilled his duties with the battalion, enjoying extra time with friends or on my own, but always waiting for the phone to buzz with a text, waiting to hear that they'd made it home safe. Small as his obligations were back then, it didn't take long for those in our lives, our family and friends, to start placing me in the role of dutiful, waiting spouse, although we were still many years from his commissioning and our marriage, from the *real* waiting.

During the first few years of college, my mom, aunts, uncles, grandparents, cousins, old friends from high school, and new friends from Mizzou all sent me videos from WelcomeHomeBlog, or called to tell me about a video they'd seen the night before: *did you see the one with the soldier-dad hiding behind Santa in the mall?* If I said I hadn't, they'd text it to me almost immediately so I could watch the little boys in sweater vests jump off Santa's lap when their father stepped out from behind the gilded candy cane throne. To me, especially as time went on and Doug's commitments to the program increased, it was a small, sweet way those closest to me showed their support, showed they'd be there for me when Doug did eventually join the fleet and start to deploy—an inevitability I dreaded with intensifying vehemence. Years out, it manifested in fights and bitterness toward him, where I'd say cruel, cutting things, trying to make him feel my pain: *You'll never know what it's like to be the one left behind* ("left behind" being a term he rejects on principle, believing it to be reserved only for Gold Star Families whose servicemembers gave their lives.) As the months leading up to his departure grew fewer, as the weeks ticked down, I simply grew despondent. I didn't want to talk any more about it. Just get it over with. Sometimes, when I was at my most fearful and fragile—anxious about all the unknowns of deployment: How long would it last? Would we be able to email? Would he come home the same person? Would I be able to handle the months and months of loneliness?—Doug would remind me of all the little ways our family and friends had already shown their support, assuring me, promising me, that although I'd be by myself, I'd never be alone when he was gone.

Our lives before Doug started deploying weren't vibrant or exciting. If they had been, it may have been easier to fill the void he left with nights out on the town, drinks with coworkers, or dressing up and going to loud parties with big groups of friends. But Doug and I are quiet people with small circles. We don't like to spruce up for expensive bars and trendy restaurants or go places so loud we can't hear one another talk. When we have time off together, we go hiking with the dog, walk on the beach, or run errands, splitting the shopping list in half and making it a competition to see who can get to the checkout first.

"And you have to look like a normal shopper," he says. "Don't like, sprint or power walk or anything."

Most often though, we camp out in front of the TV. He watches sports or home improvement shows while I read or grade papers, each of us stopping periodically to wrestle the dog for his squeaky toy or switch loads of laundry. Sometimes, I'll pester him to do yoga with me just so I can laugh and help him up when he inevitably loses his balance and topples over. We kiss for no reason; we dawdle with each other's fingers. That type of presence, that quiet coexistence, is hard to replace when he is gone.

We were living in Jacksonville, Florida, when Doug deployed for the first time in February, 2017. It was about a month before our second wedding anniversary, and as he said, my circle, our circle, was there to support me.

The crew left early on a Thursday morning and by Saturday I had two weekends' worth of dinner plans with his college roommate and a friend visiting from Connecticut. My mother flew down during my first spring break from teaching and, between shopping trips and leisurely mornings on the beach, she helped clean the entire house and strung over one hundred plastic eggs onto pipe cleaners so I could decorate the tree out front for Easter like we'd always done at home. And when that Easter came, one of my childhood friends who happened to live in the area invited me to dinner at her apartment with her fiancé and another couple. We drank sangria and played board games well into the evening. My dad and brother drove from St. Louis to Jacksonville near the last month of the deployment and, while I was at work, fixed every squeaking door hinge and started to turn my dying yard green again, filling in dirt and Bermuda seed where the sprinklers didn't reach and the grass had gone bare. It was a huge relief to have experienced hands available to teach me what I'd never had to learn until then. (If you ask them though, they'll say they did it so they could go to Topgolf.) Those who couldn't visit punctuated the months of Doug's absence with frequent calls and texts to check in, say hello, to ask how I was doing or, even better, fill me in on their own lives without mentioning the deployment at all.

When my beloved grandmother passed away in the middle of the first deployment, a friend from graduate school sent the largest bouquet of Peruvian lilies I've ever seen, and a card signed from her entire family, including the German shepherd. At their fullest peak, the flowers strained at the vase and bloomed out over the entire table. They thrived for almost three weeks before their wilt even began to show. When I looked them up later to see if their long lifespan was normal, I learned they were a symbol of strong bonds between friends. Between her gift and the flowers Doug had pre-ordered to be delivered on the holidays he'd miss, my house was only ever briefly without the damp, sweet smell of thoughtfulness.

All the kindness shown to me while Doug is gone has been a pattern repeated each time he leaves, whether it be for deployment, or sea trials, short cruises, or training schools out of state—a pattern for which I am so thankful I get teary-eyed thinking about it. I am not sure what those accumulated months, verging on years, would look like without the appearance of familiar faces for whom I can pull myself together, be it for a week, an evening, or just long enough to write a thank-you note and put it in the mail.

Because the truth of it is, I handle deployments with all the grace of a jumbo jet falling out of the sky. It doesn't take long for me to crash and burn. I'm nasty. There is a lot of sobbing, a lot of shouting in empty rooms, a lot of desperate, fruitless bargaining with God to make it end *now*, to bring him home safe *now*. There are many fervent, fruitless prayers to change something in the cosmic fabric of the universe so I can hear Doug's boots clomping through the door, to listen to him settle down on the carpet and doze off for ten minutes next to the dog, the way he always does. Not even to see him— just to hear him would be enough.

Between the visits and the phone calls there are days of struggling to get out of bed. For every dinner with a friend, there's dozens more spent alone, eating quickly at the counter so I can get through my work faster and reach the sleeping pills that are my gold medal for getting through another day: melatonin for the weekdays with early alarms, something stronger for weekends with nothing but time to fill. Sleep is the only time during a deployment that I can escape counting days in either direction. How many down? How many to go? How many more before I lose my grip?

Worst of all, there is always that small, nagging, ugly voice when I'm sitting across the table from an old friend or a roommate or any number of my most beloved family that says, *to you, it doesn't matter.* Not that Doug's deployment doesn't affect them, not that they don't sympathize or care, but that it doesn't consume them like it does me because none of them are his lawfully wedded spouse. True or not, reasonable or irrational, it's the chorus that prevails.

Their days continue the same no matter where the boat sails or which sailors make up the crew. No one but me, Doug's wife, feels his absence so acutely. As far as I know, no one else hyperventilates when they try to watch hockey on TV because it's what they've done with him every winter for more than a decade, no one clings to their phone, begging out loud for an email to come through, and no one else fights to keep the radio on when a song plays that reminds them of him, or, even worse, a commercial jingle that he sings in some goofy voice when he's home—which he isn't and almost everything I touch, hear, see, taste, and smell reminds me of that.

But deployments end. In fact, that's one of the few good things about them. As the weeks remaining tick down, my support circle starts to feel a little more like it did in college, when I first started assuming the role of a spouse—they send videos from WelcomeHomeBlog or any number of copycat websites that have cropped up since then. Each video comes with a sweet comment from the sender, meant to get me excited for Doug's approaching return:

"So sweet!"

"<3 <3 <3"

"You soon!?"

"Thought of you!"

"Can't wait to see this!"

"You'll have to let us know when he's back!"

"Keep us posted!"

Somewhere in those last few weeks of loneliness a slow shift occurs in my thinking, in my processing of the separation, like the grinding of tectonic plates. It's hardly noticeable at first, but after a while, the change is undeniable, destructive. The interior voice turns from ugly to unbearable. Those I love, those who have been nothing but supportive, are all at once detestable and I have to make an effort to keep myself from telling them all to kindly fuck off, like some snarling animal caught in a trap, in pain.

Stop texting, stop calling, stop asking about the date, time, place, of the sailors' arrival. In all likelihood, I'm not allowed to tell you but, if I could, I still wouldn't. Don't ask me to shoot a video or "take a good picture." And, for the love of God, don't ask if you can come see him get off the bus or off the plane, don't ask to stay in our guest room for the weekend to visit in exchange for *capturing the moment* with photographs, as several have expressed interest in doing.

Homecoming is so much more than a cute photo op or the perfect angle for a viral video. It's more than a celebration of a mission successfully completed.

Homecoming is the messy moment when those absent are finally returned to those they've left. For some, that means their parents or close siblings. Others, their children. For some, like Doug and I, it's just the two of us. A partnered pair, one coming back to the other. Some like the fanfare of homecoming and hang around the meeting point, watching everyone hug and cheering them on, while others just want to pick up their sea bags and leave.

For me, it's not a spectacle nor a circus. It's our family becoming whole again—a moment fought for over months by no one but the two of us. It doesn't happen in baseball stadiums or cozy Christmas dens. Sometimes it happens after seventeen hours of flight delays, in an empty parking lot at four in the morning. Sometimes, in the lobby of the on-base children's recreation center to entertain the children while we wait out yet another delay. Sometimes, in an effort to get home faster, wives will tell their husbands where they parked and to simply "meet me at the car." No balloons, no confetti or wrapped up refrigerator boxes for the sailors to hide in and pop out of at the perfect moment. Especially in the secretive submarine community, where boat movements and return dates are shared with the smallest possible number of people for the crew's safety, homecomings cannot be the grand fanfares so many expect. Just a caravan of buses full of pale and groggy sailors who tumble out weary and worn down from the long journey home.

Homecoming, the process of it, lasts far beyond the two and a half minutes of video posted online. For some, it's just as big of a mountain as all the time apart. Reintegration takes time and work. Rarely, if ever, does a service member come home and have things immediately pick up just as they left off. Children have grown, milestones reached and surpassed. Some have newly been born. The wives, even the ones like me who grieve their spouse's absence like a loss, have grown used to doing things on their own and don't ask for or want their sailor's input. When Doug comes home, within the first few days, he always has something to say about the way the lawn is mowed or makes snarky corrections to my shopping list. *How do you not remember what flavor yogurt I like? I've eaten it for like, three years.* It takes time to feel happily married again.

Still, those who don't understand want to be a part of it, want to place themselves square in the middle of Doug's and my reunion and the resettling weeks that follow. They see it as a way of celebrating all that Doug has accomplished, not comprehending what it means to us to have as much time as possible to ourselves before the process of preparing for the next deployment begins—usually within a few weeks' time when the crew goes back to trainers on base. While the help and support of loved ones has been immeasurable, I am the one who's weathered the emotional labor of the long separation, carried it around on my shoulders like a heavy sack of wheat for baking bread everyone will want, but only I get to eat. Not because I want to keep them from it, but because they did not marry *this* sailor, *my* sailor, *my* husband. They sow and reap different seeds: those of friendships or extended family. That doesn't make their crop any less important, it just cannot be made into homecoming bread.

Near the end of Doug's second deployment, a coworker invited me to his barbecue and I'd yet to RSVP.

"Can I pencil in as a maybe? Doug might be home by then."

My coworker *ooh*ed loudly and grinned wide. "Gonna need some privacy that weekend in casa Brown?"

"What?" I was caught off guard.

"Privacy! If he's gonna be home, you'll wanna get it on like Donkey Kong."

I rolled my eyes. "Knock it off. You sound like one of the students."

He wouldn't stop grinning. "You know I'm right though! This is exciting."

"Put me down as a maybe for the barbecue, ok?"

In reality, I knew it'd be at least a day before Doug and I did anything R-rated because, by the time he comes home, he will have been on a plane for over thirty hours. He'd need a shower and sleep more than he'd need anything from me. But why was it my job to explain that to my coworker?

Let closed doors be closed.

That comment about our sex-life was just another reminder of the gap between civilian understanding and military reality. How the romanticized idea of the übermensch warrior returning home virile and triumphant to a family who remained divinely resilient in his absence, obscures the reality of imperfect people who are called to extraordinary duty, each person in the picture carrying out their service to the country as best they can. Some with inspiring resolve, others, like me, with hobbled steps and much more help than they deserve.

I often think about starting a companion site to WelcomeHomeBlog, an anti-site—GoodbyeBlog. On it, spouses could submit their own videos from their hardest days of deployment. The videos could range from the light hearted and humorous (the day they caught their first lizard in the house) to the frustrating (the day everyone had the stomach flu, including the dog, who barfed up a pinecone on the living room carpet) to the sad (the death of a close friend or family member that your spouse won't be able to mourn for months) to the downright devastating (videos made in the hours after dropping off their spouses, knowing that in those awful moments, the deployment has just begun and all manner of things lie between them and their reunion.) There would be guilty, tearful rants about feeling horrible for having a fun night out while you know your spouse is having a miserable week underwater. Or trying to be happy enough to celebrate an engagement, a wedding, or a baby without feeling bitter because, while everyone else is over-the-moon, you can't even enjoy simple spousal companionship.

Maybe GoodbyeBlog, if it existed, could serve as a tool for those who want to understand the reality of the sacrifices families and spouses make for the good of their servicemember's mission, for those who would otherwise want to step into someone else's homecoming so they can experience the WelcomeHomeBlog sensation for themselves without knowing all things great and small it took to get there.

For me, the joy of Doug's homecomings isn't in the first hug, or the first sight off the bus. It isn't in jumping up and down and screaming, crying with a bundle of balloons (which, for the record, I've never done.) It's hours later, in his first sigh, the first settling back into the couch or the bed, where he lays down then sinks into the welcoming softness for the first sleep or first nap. He sighs, eyes barely held open, and smiles. Then, I have done my job. Then the deployment ends, for me. Weary as we may both still be, at least we are weary under the same roof again. It's a quiet, private joy I've only ever experienced alone, in my own heart, and I like it that way. I have crossed the finish line and received my sailor home safely, provided us both a sense of comfort, of peace, even if only for a little while.

"No, I will eat it myself!" said the Little Red Hen.
And she did.

CHAPTER 21

Fears

I've feared a lot of things over the years, things that have kept me awake, things that have consumed my mind, made me feel half-crazy: losing library books, quicksand, and being pulled over for speeding. I've feared airplanes, cars, reckless buses, trains, overcrowded subways, and submarines. Especially submarines. And especially deployments for more reasons than I can count. I've feared the consuming quiet of an empty house, feared Doug's spare glasses, accidentally left out on the nightstand before he went underway. What if putting them away made me miss him more, even though every time I looked at them during his absence, they broke my heart?

The first thing I remember fearing as a child was Plumpy—the squatty green troll on the Candyland game board, caretaker of the gingerbread plum trees—because he featured in a vivid nightmare I'd had in which he was hungry not for gingerbread plums, but my feet, and planned to get them by waiting in our basement and popping up through the floor to grab them. I remember crying, trembling, until my mother or father carried me into the safety of the kitchen, where I could hide my feet from Plumpy in the basement by sitting cross-legged on a kitchen chair.

In the third or fourth grade, I took a summer school science class on "crime solving." We learned the bare-boned basics of fingerprint dusting and how a criminal could be identified and arrested by just the tiniest sample of

DNA. Near the end of the summer, we were introduced to a pair of *real-life* police detectives from the city who helped us solve a "murder" we walked into at the beginning of class, the room zig-zagged with yellow crime scene tape around a white chalk outline of the victim's body on the floor. I grew distinctly afraid that my family would be murdered. I also feared plane crashes and car accidents to the point where I would get choked up any time I watched my dad's car pull out of the driveway to go to the airport. Back then, my mom attributed my budding fearfulness to my grandmother's recent cancer diagnosis (I heard her say as much to anyone she talked to on the phone) but, to me, the tendency toward fear was always there, and had always been there, floating somewhere beneath the surface—as much a part of my DNA as my eye or hair color.

When I started losing sleep, my parents let me listen to the radio at night, thinking that the music would be soothing. Instead, I spent half an hour every night listening to a show where sad listeners called in and asked the DJ to play songs dedicated to this or that loved one who had either left them for someone else or was dead. It confirmed what I feared most: loss is real.

Although I'm sure I should have, I never sought treatment for my intrusive thoughts because, past those late elementary school years, it didn't factor much into my daily life. That is, I got used to it. My grandmother survived her cancer, a promotion required my dad to travel less, and no one ever came to slaughter those I loved in cold blood. Things were good. Of course, certain events stripped back all the years of coping and deep breathing exercises I taught myself: study abroad trips in high school and college, anything that involved being in a plane, being out of contact with loved ones, and any sort of travel delay, or sudden change of plans.

So it was with bitter and laughable irony that I met, fell in love with, and married Doug, a sailor whose job would require me to live out more manifestations of my worst fears than I could ever have dreamed up. We've moved far from our childhood homes in St. Louis to Charleston, then farther to Jacksonville with more moves on the horizon. The geographical distance that separated us from home was nothing compared to the gulf created by being the only military couple in an all-civilian family. We became outsiders to them. Things weren't the same when we called home or went in to visit. Doug and I have lived apart for months at a time when he was sent to schools in other states that wouldn't allow accompanying spouses. And, by the time he'd spent a year attached to the USS *Georgia*, we'd gone almost as long without seeing one another at all or speaking freely as husband and wife without government censors checking our messages for bad news or bad moods. I had frequent anxiety attacks that brought on heart palpitations, tremors, and erratic moods that often turned dark and threatening, causing me to ideate ending my own life. And, as is the case with most mental illnesses, I did not suffer alone. Doug too, felt the ripple effects of every bad day, even when he was half a world away, underwater.

I was very alone the day I feared nail polish.

For years, painted nails were my thing. In college and especially when I was selling jewelry during the first year of our marriage, I had shades for all seasons and wore them in religious rotation: pastels for spring, bright corals and neon pinks in the summer, grays in the fall and winter, and deep, shimmery reds around Christmas to get customers in the spirit of buying strands of pearls and large diamond earrings. Every Sunday, in our little Charleston apartment, I balanced on the edge of the bathtub and painted each finger while Doug watched TV and prepared his uniform for the upcoming week. It was a ritual as familiar as church.

But I'd fallen out of the habit by the time our marriage hit a year and a half. We moved to Jacksonville and Doug attached to the *Georgia*. I hadn't felt any strong pull to keep my nails so pristine like I had before. Not only did I no longer sell jewelry, I was too busy spending time with him to sit and wait for each coat to dry while he was home, and just plain too busy when he was gone. On top of being almost halfway through graduate school, I started a new, much more demanding job teaching middle school and took on all the household tasks that had never come up in Charleston when we lived in the apartment instead of a house with a yard: taking care of both cars, keeping up an HOA-approved lawn, repairing the rotting fence after every major storm, and assembling or refinishing furniture for the bedrooms, to name a few. I didn't have time for pretty hands anymore; they were always working, always occupied or preoccupied. The box of polishes sat under the bed, collecting dust until the dwindling hours before Doug's return from his first deployment.

Painting my nails was supposed to be the relaxing end to all the preparations I'd undertaken for his homecoming. For a week, I worked in the sweltering yard, cutting tall grass and laying down seed in the places it had burned away, pulling weeds out of the mulch beds and concrete cracks. When it stormed, which it did almost every day, I'd use the rain and an old broom to scrub away dirt on the patio and driveway. Even the rarely-opened guest bedroom and the inside of our spare closet received a thorough detailing and reorganizing. If my anxiety issues have one silver lining, it's that they make me a fantastically meticulous cleaner. I dusted, vacuumed, soaped, laundered, and scoured every corner of our house. For the first time since he'd left, I picked up the pair of glasses he'd left on his nightstand and cleaned off the dust because soon he'd be home to wear them. Small as it was, I felt brave to hold them in my hand again because for many weeks, just the sight of them reduced me to tears. The end was close, so close. I threw out a browning succulent and replaced it with a new, greener fern. The sheets we got as a wedding gift that shrunk up dramatically in the wash I wrestled onto the mattress until they were flat and smooth, just the way Doug liked them. I had half a dozen gifts wrapped for him—one for every holiday or occasion he'd missed—each box I'd covered in plain, brown butcher paper, then hand-painted to match the missed occasion: Valentine's, St. Patrick's, our anniversary, the dog's birthday, and so on. There was a bottle of champagne chilling in the fridge. Doug was going to come home soon, and we were going to celebrate.

Not long after he left, I'd found a beautiful dress at a resale shop in town: a blue and white full-length sundress that made me feel like a million bucks (despite it costing only $17.) I knew immediately it would be what I wore for Doug's homecoming. It was a perfect fit when I bought it but months later, when I pulled it out of the closet, it looked bigger on the hanger than I remembered. The last six weeks or so had been the busiest of the deployment for me: wrapping up the school year with my students, taking two different certification courses through the district, and still sticking with my long-distance graduate program that I was hell-bent on finishing, even though the degree was in Creative Writing, not Education, all while grieving the death of my grandmother and fighting off two separate bouts of the flu. I lost almost twelve pounds that month alone and, when I tried on the dress, the once-flattering neckline now plunged below my bra. The fitted waist gaped, and the sleeves kept slipping off my shoulders.

I took a picture of myself in the dress in the bathroom mirror and texted it to a friend. "Does this look too big?"

"Yeah. Size down."

"It was resale, months ago."

"Crap. Can you get it tailored?"

"Not in time."

"In time?"

"Homecoming soon. But shhh."

"OMG!!! What the backup outfit? Are you going for pretty? Sexy? Nautical?"

I had no idea what "look" I was going for. Was I supposed to have a "look?" I'd just liked the dress!

By the time I'd ransacked the closet for another outfit, my breathing was already faster than normal. I didn't text more with my friend or call any other sub wives to ask what they were wearing. It was my first real homecoming, but I didn't want to seem too eager. My careful plans felt like they were falling apart in my hands.

My unpainted, unmanicured hands.

All the nail polish I'd accumulated over the years was stored in a small Rubbermaid I kept under my side of the bed—nearly two dozen shades that spanned the prismatic spectrum. But none of them were right. They were all wrong. Every single one of them; too bright, too dark, too pale, too garish.

It felt like the end, which it was, in a way—the end of one most dreaded life-event: the first separation from Doug, the miserable deployment. In not much longer, I'd be able to say I'd survived, I'd conquered my first deployment, my biggest fear to date. But had I really conquered it if thinking about it—even the end of it—still made me feel sick? I felt less like a warrior or conqueror and more like a wounded, battle-weary soldier, crawling across the carnage, using my last ounces of strength to wave the white flag. *I give up, deployment. I couldn't stop you, but we're both still here.* It may not have been pretty, but at least it was almost over. I hadn't won, but at least I was here to see the end of it.

That was, *if* I made it there, there was still time remaining—and I wasn't sure that I would survive it. As my heart began to skip beats, making it hard to catch my breath, I imagined my obituary, if I were to keel over in that exact moment, which I was truly thinking I might:

> *The deceased was found on her bedroom floor, wearing sweaty gym clothes and a topknot, surrounded by her favorite nail polish. She was clutching bottles of Cajun Shrimp, Charged Up Cherry, Bubble Bath, and Mint*

Candy Apple. On the closet door, she'd hung no less than six different sundresses. Shoes were scattered every which way. Investigators were unsure if they fell there, or if the deceased threw them in agitation. There were no signs of foul play and toxicology reports revealed no presence of drugs or alcohol in the system.

Maybe that was the problem. No drugs. I should have popped a Xanax before it got this far—a prescription I got for fear of flying that I tended to take for fear of separation or fear of change.

Deployment was a change. Homecoming was a bigger one. He'd been gone just over four months—a medium-length deployment for his class of submarine. No one was sure how many months they'd be home for. It was already being whispered amongst the other wives of the boat that it wouldn't be very long: three months, tops.

For all those gone-months, I'd battled reminders of the way things used to be: dinner together at the kitchen counter because we didn't have a table, sharing a bottle of beer because neither of us wanted the whole thing, hearing him fiddle with his glasses in the other room instead of wearing them, bickering over laundry, morning breath, painting my fingers while he rolled his camo sleeves and polished the toes of his heavy, black boots.

Now, I was supposed to let those things back in, let *him* back in. Our home was supposed to be perfect, and I wasn't supposed to bring up the hell I'd gone through to come within touching distance of the finish line. I wanted so badly to look whole, to look like the victor.

I don't think, in the fifteen years I've known Doug—from sixth grade well into adulthood—he's commented once on my nail color. By my calculation, we've attended more than enough school dances, proms, formals, Navy balls, family events, fundraisers, weddings, holidays, and anniversary dinners together to have given him an ample number of opportunities to say something about my nails, (which were always done for such occasions) not to mention my weekly ritual of keeping them immaculate for at least a year of our lives together when I worked for a jeweler who required it. He grew up, essentially, as an only child to a single mother who wore acrylics. His older sister moved out before he was old enough to observe or learn anything about the grooming rituals of young women. And he is, after all, an engineer through and through—his mind only focuses on what is necessary, and, to him, nail polish is certainly not necessary.

Yet, for some reason so dense it was altering the orbit of my universe, the thought of painting my nails *wrong* for him paralyzed me in those final, dwindling hours. They were who I used to be, before deployment, before I became so ragged and exhausted inside.

Should I paint them red, a nod to the patriotic occasion? Or perhaps, hot pink? But I had so many hot pinks to choose from; neon hot pinks, fuchsia hot pinks, peachy hot pinks. Too many. I considered a toned-down blushy-pink, almost nude, but put it away along with turquoise and lilac for being too spring-y. Nothing felt right.

I tried to picture our reunion, that first hard embrace, weeping with joy, my hands wrapping around his neck, fingers reaching up, feeling the familiar and long-missed softness of his hair, brushing his whiskers with the back of my hand—but *what color were my nails?*

How would he react when he saw me again?

I didn't know.

It had been so long since we'd been together, I felt like I didn't know much about my husband anymore. I hadn't seen him since we Skyped months ago when the boat stopped in port to resupply for a night or two. Even then, his face was too pixelated to say whether or not he'd changed. So had he?

For over four months, I had no idea where the boat and crew had been. I knew where they started and where they ended, the little sandbar island just south of the Equator, but the mission area was classified, as was the mission itself. What had Doug been doing all that time? What had he seen, if anything? Had people died as a result of the boat and her mission, would more die yet? Or were they saved? Did the *Georgia* gather enough intelligence to spare the innocents? What role did my husband play in all of this, what cog in which machine was he?

Would he still like the same things? Still have the same ambitions and plans? When he said the deployment "sucked" when we talked over Skype that once, did he mean it? Or would the exhilaration of a mission completed be enough to propel him into decades more of enthusiastic service? Did this time apart from me make him realize that the stress I cause him, the burden of my anxieties, wasn't worth the constant struggle? Was there a chance I would feel the same way—ready to leave the pain I suffered being married to someone who stoked my every fear?

I wondered if I'd look the same to him, or if the deployment had weathered me as much on the outside as I felt it had on the inside. He'd groaned to me in an email in the last few weeks of the underway that his hairline had receded even further, that he was starting to go gray behind his ears. I reminded myself not to laugh when I saw it and in doing that, I laughed out loud, to myself, on the floor of the bedroom I'd be sharing with him again in only a handful of hours. Would we even be able to sleep, or would his presence be too foreign?

Was I getting back the same Doug I'd always known—the one who's never cared about nail polish a day in his life, or some new version that paid attention to those things?

How powerful is the Navy? In two-and-a-half years, I'd already watched Doug turn from high school graduate, to eager midshipman, then from a newly sworn-in officer, all shiny and swelled-up with pride, to weary Nuke student, working ninety-hour weeks that left him hollow. The last time I'd seen Doug, he was an active duty sailor diving headlong into his first deployment with equal parts excitement and dread.

How much had they changed him now?

In the end, I cried for another half-hour and chose the patriotic red, but Doug did not come home the next morning, when he was supposed to. I got a call from the command phone tree just after I'd finished putting on top coat, informing me there'd been a delay. Six hours later, another delay call. Then another shortly after. The plane carrying the crew and all their gear was delayed a total of seventeen hours, added up on each leg of the journey. I stayed awake, too excited and nervous and nearly-nauseous with anticipation to sleep, spending most of the extra hours skimming old magazines, texting other wives, dusting again, wiping off clean counters, waiting for more updates through the phone tree, and, most of all, clinging to my phone, hoping for a text from him, if he found Wi-Fi in one of the many airports they got stuck waiting in.

The crew landed in the States around three in the morning on my twenty-fifth birthday—on Flag Day.

I didn't wear any of the dresses pulled from the closet. When the plane landed, I hadn't slept in almost two days. I threw on shorts and a sweatshirt and schlepped up to base where most of the wives looked like me but were holding pajama-clad, heavy-lidded toddlers on their hips to boot. A few families got dressed and made-up for the occasion, but they stood out as odd wearing cocktail dresses and pressed slacks in the muggy, pre-dawn air, night bugs buzzing all around. The original meeting point was supposed to be inside, at a building on base where kids could decorate signs for their returning parent and play in the ball-pit. Instead, it was one collective yawn in an empty parking lot near the off-crew buildings where the sailors trained and did paperwork when they were home.

The buses arrived, five in a caravan, and without warning or fanfare, the crew stumbled off. No ceremony, no send-off; just bags and sleepy bodies. They had been on the same plane for over thirty hours.

Doug was sixth off his bus. He didn't hug me so much as he collapsed on me, looking taller and thinner than when he left. We lingered less than a minute before hurrying to the car, hoping to beat the rush of traffic that would bottleneck out through the gates.

He remembered what day it was after ten or so miles on the highway and lifted my hand to kiss it while he drowsily hummed the tune to "Happy Birthday."

My red nails right in front of his face, and he didn't say a thing about them.

Chapter 22

Bless You From the Other Room

Pollen count is high in the South. It's always high, no matter what the season. The earth is dry, the air is heavy and sticky, and little particles of tree seed and dust float through it like a swarm of flies.

I sneeze.

I sneeze and, for the first time in a very long time, someone answers," "Bless you."

My husband answers, "Bless you."

His voice echoes from the living room, where he lays with the dog, to where I am, in the laundry room, folding his boat sheets into neat, stackable little parcels.

Homecoming is everything.

Before the buses even leave the parking lot on day-zero of deployment, homecoming is the ultimate goal. It is the day every family member and sailor alike circles on the calendar and what we all count down to for weeks and weeks and weeks, even if we don't mean to or try not to. We throw colorful parties to mark the halfway point with banners, music, and plastic leis, regardless of the time of year. When exhaustion sets in—the weed whacker is broken, the laundry's not done, and there are a million deadlines competing for your attention at work—homecoming is the proverbial carrot you dangle in front of yourself to keep moving forward, to keep you from spending days under the covers, as I often want to. Homecoming is the beacon over the water. It's hoped for, prayed for, and bargained for with the divine—*Please, God, let it get here faster.*

Of course, as with most things in the military, when homecoming nears, it's never quite how you planned. More often than not, homecoming is less of a singular event and more of a process drawn out over days. The crew turns over, hands off command of the boat to their replacements overseas, then disembarks to wait in hotels for a different command in the States to book and send a plane, which can take weeks, in the meantime enjoying their first full-sized beds and hot showers in months. On the plane, they usually spend more hours delayed on the tarmac at foreign airports than in flight—and they spend over thirty hours in the air, on a good trip, as they zig-zag back to the US from across the globe. They've stopped in Ireland, Germany, Kuwait, the UAE, and places where diplomatic relations aren't harmonious enough for the sailors to get off the plane and stretch their legs in the terminals.

At home, for the loved ones waiting, this translates to phone-tree calls that push the long-awaited day of homecoming back four hours here, seven there, eighteen here until suddenly the sheets I washed so Doug could spend his first night home in a freshly-made bed have been slept in three times, mercilessly twisted and wrinkled and sweat on. These are some of the longest days of the deployment, the delay days.

But just like the hundreds of days before them, the delay days also, eventually, end. The phone tree calls stop coming and the sailors' cell phones are back in service—they start to text and call as soon as the plane lands stateside, and we wives can trace their progress down the coastline until they land at the Air Station and board the buses that will transport them up to Kings Bay, where all the families are starting to gather with their handmade signs, balloons, and miniature American flags to wave.

The buses roll up in a line, the sailors disembark, and it's a few minutes of chaos as families reunite—those still looking for one another trying to navigate around hugging couples and jumping kids without accidentally stepping into someone else's embrace. All around us people are shrieking, screaming.

Doug finds me and we hug awkwardly, wobbling, not remembering where our arms go, or which way to turn so we don't knock heads. I don't cry; I'm more tired than anything else. We don't ever spend a lot of time at the meeting point—I don't even bring the sign I've made—and, in the car on the way back to our house, he holds my hand and flips through stations on the radio, pointing out each song and jingle that he's never heard before, all released while he was somewhere under the ocean, cut off from the outside world. That's the extent of the conversation. It's not that we have nothing to talk about; we have six months of catching up to do, but where do you start? Do you start with the big, the things you weren't allowed to send over the monitored email connection? *Doug, I went to the doctor and something is wrong with my eyes.* Or do you start with the small talk, the first date talk? *Weatherman says it's going to rain tomorrow.*

We always seem to choose neither. We choose the radio. It's strange to hear his voice again. The easy part is over.

Homecoming always starts out so calm, a trickle: Doug comes home, he's been on an airplane for days, he wants to shower and sleep. He rolls around on the floor with the dog for a few minutes, then makes a slow march toward the bedroom, a crawl, brushing his teeth along the way, and barely shucking off his shoes before passing out on top of the covers. It takes him, on average, about forty-five minutes of ugly, drooling, snoring sleep before he stirs, strips off his shirt and his pants, and works himself down into the creased-up sheets that I'd intended to leave so freshly cleaned.

Like you would with a newborn, I try to sleep when Doug sleeps those first few days. He's on submarine hours still and will be for a week or two at least—underwater jet leg, *boat lag*. A bomb could fall in the backyard and my fearsome warrior would be none the wiser.

I get in bed with him and he doesn't move. Sometimes, the dog wriggles up between us and whines for attention, and other times it is just Doug and I on the mattress we bought with our wedding money in Charleston—what now seems like ten lifetimes ago: a pair of newlyweds, up and down the aisles of display beds, lying stiff on showroom mattresses in an Ashley Furniture asking ourselves *pillowtop or gel? Queen or King sized?*

We chose the mattress we did because Doug could bounce up and down on one side while I lay on the other, and I hardly moved at all. Perfect, we thought, for all the nights where he'd be working late shifts or leaving early in the morning. I could sleep undisturbed through all his comings and goings. While Doug was gone, I stayed on my side of the bed for the most part, letting the dog take advantage of the open real estate on Doug's side so his return in that regard shouldn't have made any difference. But it made everything different. For the first few days of homecoming, I cannot sleep beside my husband. Although he sleeps on the side I've faithfully left empty, his presence fills the entire room. The mattress we once chose for its steadiness is older now and transmits his every stretch, every twitch, and every cough right to my side like Morse code. His breathing is loud and captivating—sound where there was none for so long. I could watch his chest make the blankets rise and fall for hours. More unnerving than anything is the return of his smell to our bedroom—Old Spice, Tide. It floods my senses, send shivers down my back. I grow tense, mostly because I didn't even know that this smell was something I missed, and now I am drowning in it.

Looking at him, sleeping soundly in our bed, I cry harder than I have in a long time. Probably as hard as I do each time I drop him off for deployment at the same parking lot where we meet the buses at the end of it.

Big, heaving parking lot tears, I cry in our bed, at a time when I'm supposed to be the happiest wife alive: *my husband is home safe from war.* These should be tears of joy, but they aren't. It's a flood of the most unnamable sort of salt water, tears I cannot stifle drenching me down to the neck of my shirt. Usually, Doug doesn't even stir but still, I move to the couch so I can sleep alone again.

Everything is strange those first few days.

Physically, Doug is unfamiliar to me and my mind can't process the visual of him moving around our house again: walking room to room, touching papers on the coffee table, reaching up into a cabinet for a water glass—although, after the first deployment, he had to ask me where we kept the glasses because he hadn't lived in the house long enough to remember.

If our house were a reef, he would be the man in a diving bell, moving slowly through an underwater world he's never come across before and doesn't know how to navigate. This world of water, in all irony, is mine and mine alone. I know it's every current and control its every wave.

Doug comes home looking taller and thinner, and he sounds different when he talks—his voice always seems to have dropped an octave or two. He no longer complains about the size of our shower or all the covers on the bed. They are spacious and soft compared to what he had on the sub. When he showers at home, he can leave the water running and lift his elbows to wash his hair without cracking them on the walls. The quilts on our bed that he used to hate because they made him sweat are still heavy and numerous, but they are better than the thin sheet and single fleece throw issued to him onboard. Things have changed.

The first time he was gone, I theorized that months walking through the sub's narrow passageways would train out his natural way of walking: rocking side to side like a wide-footed waddle. But I was wrong; he came home and still bumped a shoulder on every doorway and knocked picture frames crooked down the hallway. Thankfully, not everything changes and, although I find myself constantly straightening pictures, I am glad because it is familiar.

Countless military resource books, pamphlets, and websites covering "The Cycle of Deployment" call the first weeks (or, depending on the source, months) a service member is home the *honeymoon phase*, which always brings to my mind those mattress-shopping days, the giddy days after our wedding before we started butting heads again. We didn't have many of those good days, and I'm not sure we've had much more luck with homecomings. Perhaps, for us, there's too much weight placed on the days following upending, life-changing events. How could anyone be expected to carry on in starry-eyed bliss, when, in reality, all that was familiar and safe is now gone?

When Doug wakes after some double-digit hours of sleep, we start the dance of a couple that doesn't remember how to share space: struggling to split time in the bathroom, writing longer grocery lists, and clearing spots in the pantry for his protein bars and oatmeal, each of us parking too close to the other's car in the garage, me, because I'm not used to thinking about his driver's-side door, him, because he's not used to driving anything smaller than the length of two football fields. The sex is awkward and terrible.

Sometimes, he's so quiet going about his day I forget he's home at all so, when he strolls into the room, I gasp or scream.

Doug holds me then, laughing his head off. He thinks my skittishness is funny because he doesn't understand that, for me, there's still a stranger lurking in my home.

My temper then is shorter than usual:

"Shoes don't go here."

"*Close* the cabinet doors."

"You have to clean off his paws when it rains or he'll track mud all over— just like that."

"If the roll runs out...*replace it.*"

"Why'd you turn it off? I was watching that!" Even though I wasn't watching TV at all, I wasn't even in the room. I'm just used to leaving it on for the comfort of white noise.

He points out things to me too. I've let the blinds get dusty. The dog doesn't *need* a frozen Kong toy every day. I don't ever wipe up the taupe-colored shimmer on the edge of the sink where I tap my eyeshadow brush. Did I always used to put on three different moisturizers before bed?

His immune system is weak after so many months of isolation. Colds, stomach bugs, and fevers aren't uncommon in the first week home but can last for months after. We start to go out again, on "mini-dates" when his boat lag and health allow it. We walk the dog around the subdivision or go out to dinner near the beach. Hearing the waves reminds Doug of submarines, and then he wants to tell me all about the deployment, about his shipmates, about who pulled what pranks, and what nicknames they gave one another during *mids*—midnight watch—when the boat is quietest and most boring. Everything reminds him of something on the boat. Sometimes, he talks so much about it he chokes up on his own dry throat.

I'd rather listen to him coughing all night than have to hear another word about the damn boat, sometimes.

A better wife than me would be more understanding of my husband's desire to talk about his sub and shipmates. I have no way of truly grasping the level of isolation he and the crew have just emerged from. He laughs when he sees news stories or picture online of ground troops in the Middle East gathered around TVs watching Armed Forces Network football games. "Must be nice," he snickers before telling me again how he went without sporting events all this time, only getting the scores of major games every few weeks if command updates from shore allowed it. "They get bigger beds than we do too. Sure the situation is a little different—different mission and all—

but they get *beds*, Sam. *Beds.* The one thing that was good about my rack was how dark it got…" There's little he loves more than a good, dark bedroom.

When Doug gets starry-eyed about the deployments he claims to hate, even if it is just the darkness of his rack, my resentment toward him, toward the Navy that owns him, grows. *Aren't you tired? Haven't you had enough of them already?* It's unfair of me, I know, because it's the only thing he has to talk about. For months, the boat has been his world. But our marriage is never in more danger than in the joyous days of homecoming.

The sea bags don't usually come home until the crew has had a few days— at least a weekend—to rest with their families. Then, the following Monday, Doug drives up to base for an hour to collect his two duffels, marked with his last name and colorful duct tape on the straps for easier identification in the sea of green canvas. He brings them home and leaves them in the garage because nothing that's been on the sub gets carried over our threshold before it's been rid of *boat smell*. It's a rule not just in our house, but in the houses of submarine wives across the fleet.

You could ask ten people what *boat smell* is and you'd get at least ten different answers. Of those I've talked to, wives and sailors alike, I've heard "rotting meat," "old rubber boots," "sweat and cat piss," "wet dog," and "a trash can of diapers baking in the sun for a week." After his first ride on a submarine, sometime in college, Doug described it as "old cheeseburger and fart." The only real consensus is how terrible and pervasive it is.

To me, it smells overwhelmingly musty like mothballs or a stuffy, dark closet of old coats. Eau de Goodwill.

Boat smell is actually just amine: one of the chemicals used in the sub's atmospheric recirculation systems. It scrubs carbon dioxide from the air they breathe. In concentrated doses, it smells a lot like ammonia and is hard to get out of anything that it comes in contact with, especially fabrics. Mingled with no small amount of each sailor's personal body odor, it's an unforgettable combination.

Every wife I know has her own sworn-by methods of eradicating boat smell. The methods are as diverse as the women themselves. I've heard use of lemon juice, essential oils, vinegar, color-safe bleach, and, my personal favorite: car soap, a garden hose, and a push broom on the driveway.

I soak his clothes: the uniforms, coveralls, undershirts, socks, and boxers overnight in a sink of OxiClean and hot water. They've been washed on the boat a few times and Doug usually does a small load in the hotel laundromat when they reach port, but the smell lingers. After they soak, I run them through the wash twice with "sport grade" detergent and dry them with no less than three meadow-scented Bounce sheets. It's a lot of folding, a lot of socks to pair. Doing those first heavy loads of boat laundry is when I first feel the sting of lost independence. When I'm alone, at least there's only one person's worth of socks.

The sub issues Doug a set of bedsheets and blankets that, by his own admission, he never washes onboard. Those, I soak for days, until the water stops turning gray, then wash them with more capfuls of detergent and double the Bounce sheets. After the dryer, I spray them with Febreze and fold them up with coffee bean sachets between the layers. Everything gets stored in laundry baskets that I shove in the corner of our spare bedroom, ready for the next deployment—the countdown for which has already begun. He will report to base, to the off-crew facility, to train, study, and do paperwork for the next few months, like a normal nine-to-five job. But every day the crew is home is another day closer to leaving again, going back underway.

It takes a few weeks, but eventually we grow back into each other. We spend enough time together where we can have conversations about things we are both part of: weekend plans, buying him a new car, where next to hike with the dog. He takes medicine and gets over his first flu. He brings me lunch at work or sits beside me while I read. Every now and then, he pulls up lists of universities that have both creative writing programs where I could teach and Naval ROTC programs where he could serve his shore tour— places we could go for few years of compromise if the cards were dealt in our favor.

Doug's feet, when he comes home, are dry, cracked, peeling, and sharp when they brush against my legs in bed at night. I take him for a pedicure, which he groans about until I show him pictures from the sub wives' group text—every single one of his fellow officers ends up in a pedicure chair sometime that first week back, getting the dead skin sloughed off their feet for the sake of their wives. It's always fun to see who's laughing in the pictures, and who's just grumpy about it. Doug's usually some mixture of both while he's in the chair but concedes the end result is worth it.

I get disproportionately annoyed as he discovers "new" music on the radio, turns it up, and tries to sing along every time one of his "awesome new songs" come on. What is new to him, has been overplayed for months back here at home. When I say things like, *oh my God this has been in the Top 40 forever*, he sings along louder, making up the lyrics he'll never quite remember.

Most importantly, Doug and I are eventually able to form sentences that don't start, *Oh, this one time, during the underway*, or *By the way, while you were gone*.

I sneeze doing boat laundry and Doug blesses me from the other room where he's reclined on the couch, watching whatever's on TV, drifting off during the commercial breaks, even as the dog pushes toys at him, begging to play.

For all the support I have during deployments, all the friends and family who call to say hello, all the people who visit or make plans with me, having someone answer my sneeze is indicative of what I miss the most. Someone to share the mundane with: the shopping for beds and folding of sheets and simple pleasure of having a loved one sitting just one room away.

Sometimes I cry doing laundry too. Not because it's too much work, or because I think he should be doing it himself, but because I know, sooner than I'd like, he'll be packing his sea bags again and the process will repeat: parking lot tears, working myself to the bone to keep from feeling the absence, finding balance, then losing it to yet another homecoming, a loss as painful as it is wonderful.

Through it all, I would rather do boat laundry every day for the rest of my life than say goodbye again. But without goodbye there could be no boat laundry, no reunion, and no reason to press on through the most sorrowful days. Without deployment, I'd have no reason to laugh with Doug as he pilfers through the kitchen, looking for the cups, or take the time to be grateful, with each pair of socks I roll, that he's come home safely and there are socks to roll at all. That he's walked through the door, still mostly the man I remember.

Chapter 23

Sub Mom

"You, you did not know me then.
Know me then."
-Thomas Hornsby Ferril, "Basket"

I t started with a steak salad.

The salad was a celebration meal I made for myself after my first phone call with Doug since October: grilled skirt steak on a bed of romaine and tomatoes, with a homemade chimichurri dressing.

The *Georgia* had made a brief stop in port for supplies and allowed sailors a night of liberty just after New Year's. Unable to say anything for certain, Doug hinted the deployment might end by early March, rather than early May. All put together, the salad smelled peppery and divine. I wondered if Doug would like for me to make it for him when he finally came home— *home*. The word itself made me feel drunkenly happy.

But when I sat down to eat the salad, I had a hard time chewing. It wasn't the toughness of the steak or the heat of the chimichurri, but my jaw itself felt tight and bound. The more I chewed, the more and more it ached. I suppose I'd been clenching it at night, or in my stress. After a while, I gave up. I picked out the strips of steak, stored them in a Tupperware, and threw away the greens. My mouth was so sore but how could I be upset? In less than two months, I might have my husband back again!

Over the next few days, the discomfort in my jaw only grew. While I was teaching, my left ear throbbed dully, and my words came out muddled. If I accidentally clacked my teeth together while talking, I'd have to hiss through or hold a cold water bottle to my cheek. After eight days of pain, in the teacher's lounge at lunch, I tapped a plastic fork against my backmost molar and immediately doubled over in my chair. On the way home from work I called my dentist and begged for an emergency appointment.

The x-rays, he said, indicated I needed a root canal. I wasn't *happy*, so to speak, but at least the pain had a source and could be fixed. And on top of that? Doug was still in frequent contact and still projected to be home by March. We'd been able to email more frequently than before, gradually having more normal conversations where we mapped out trips to take with his post-deployment leave, among other things.

By the time I was in the examining chair I was practically bubbling with my private joy. The endodontist was young and chatty. For a medical appointment during which she was going to jab me full of numbing agents and drill out the inside of my molar, we got along quite well. So much so, the pain seemed to abate ever so slightly.

"Tricare insurance, yes?" She asked, and then continued. "Such great coverage. My sister is married to a Marine."

I nodded. "It gets the job done."

"So, a root canal, huh?" She poked her gloved fingers around my mouth. "Does this hurt? This? What about here?"

"Nuh uh, nuh uh. Nuh uh." She prodded around the offending tooth and gums. I'd been sticking to liquids since the fork incident and had taken care not to do anything to re-aggravate the tender nerve. But now I felt nothing— had the tooth died or something? "I don't feel *anything* you're doing."

She leaned in closer with a second lamp, "Everything looks really healthy, actually. No inflammation or anything. Gums are fine. But you were in pain?"

"*So* much pain." My eyes watered at the thought of it.

"I wonder if it's a cracked tooth…" The endodontist was speaking to herself, now kneading all along my cheek, neck, and up to my ear. "Well, either way, I don't love the x-rays they sent for you, so we're going to re-take those, if that's ok?"

"Absolutely, yeah."

"Ok, I'll go get that ordered. Unless, wait—are you pregnant?"

I shook my head and gulped a little. "Nope, not pregnant."

With Doug back in more regular contact, we'd been able to talk about trips and vacations, yes, but our conversations had also turned to our next big dream: starting a family.

Until Doug's first deployment, I didn't want children at all. We'd always talked about having them in a playful, hypothetical way, but once the possibility of a marriage *with* children presented itself, I balked. Why, I cannot remember specifically—which I'm sure is nature's clever way of keeping me from backpedaling. I know I had my reasons early on, and I had even more reasons when the gears of the Navy began grinding away at my time and patience with Doug. We fought too much in the beginning; we wanted and needed so much from one another that it consumed us. It was impossible to rationalize bringing another, needier person into our home. As wrong as it felt not to want a baby, when I closed my eyes and pictured the future, nothing looked clear and that wasn't the type of life I wanted to offer a child.

But then Doug left, and I didn't have to worry about children for a while.

He deployed, and I learned to manage on my own. I shouldered the immense, consuming heartache left by his absence while driving all my energy into teaching, writing, taking care of the house, and the dog who was, for all intents and purposes, clearly *our baby* himself. When I needed help, I started to recognize it and ask for it, and found deep friendships where I didn't know there were any to be made. Some days broke me, and others made me feel as if I were riding the crest of a tidal wave. I learned to love my husband through the leagues and leagues of ocean—and the cold hull of steel—that separated us. I will never be able to claim that I did it all alone, nor would I want to. But, for the most part, the reality is most of the long deployment days were spent between me and the ticking clock.

Over the years, over these pages, and in conversation, there are many, many ways I've described the Navy and Doug's commitment to it. Some of them are tame—an *honorable service*, a *selfless act*—and others should not be repeated in polite company. I've called it a *machine*, a *soul-sucking hellhole*, a *sadistic puppeteer*, a *clusterfuck*, and, more democratically, *an opportunity*. It was all those things, good and bad, all at the same time. But more than anything else, the Navy was our crucible.

Doug's deployments, our repeated separations, have set ablaze every bit of the selfish selves we carried into our young marriage. Which of us endures more for the other? Gone. Who did what to whom? Disappeared. Who's to blame for whose suffering? These deployments have melded us together, burning away everything that we once fought about, the things we once thought mattered.

I'm not sure if it's fair of me to say that we never would have figured things out without the Navy's intervention, but it sped things along in the way a forest fire clears out underbrush and opens the cones of pines so that they may seed and sprout. I can say, however, with no uncertainty, that the greatest gift the Navy has ever given us are the ashes of our relationship, all gathered into a neat little pile. *This is what matters now*, they seem to say. From this, something could grow. Doug and I stared at those ashes when he returned home from his first underway and it didn't take long for us to see that, after all the hurt, all the time apart, we still wanted one another. And we wanted to honor that love with a child of our own: the most wonderful thing we could possibly have borne out of the Navy years. After all we'd both put in, the want of a child was what the Navy gave us back.

But with that gift, came the curse of time. We did not try to conceive before he deployed, but we talked about it a lot. We talked about names and little toes and big round eyes and fat, rosy cheeks. We vaguely agreed to build shelves in the garage and clean out the spare bedroom so it could become a nursery. We talked about storybooks and kindergarten, and then jumped to prom and college. When he left on his second deployment of the year, instead of it being just me and the ticking clock, I was joined by thoughts of the family I'd hoped we'd already be growing, but weren't.

Until the very end, this deployment was one of multiple extensions that frustrated both the crew and those of us back home. It came with the added devastation that was not only pushing back the number of months I'd have to wait before seeing my husband again, but the number of months we'd have to wait before trying for a baby. There was far too much time left for thinking. When the *San Juan* disappeared and the *Georgia* slipped into silence for so many weeks, I grieved not only his absence, his potential demise, but the fact that any chance at having our child would have gone down with him.

Even during the years I didn't want children, Doug and I talked about what we would name our hypothetical kids if we had them. For a boy, we liked the names *Patrick* and *Cooper*. Cooper, we agreed on one day not long after we got engaged. Doug was watching an ESPN documentary on the Manning family. I was behind him in the kitchen of our college apartment, half watching the TV, half folding shirts on the counter. The documentary mentioned the eldest son of football legend Archie Manning, Cooper.

"I like the name Cooper for a little boy," I said, half to Doug, half to no one. "*Coop*."

"Me too." Doug tipped his head sideways over the back of our couch, grinning at me. I wanted to wink back, but I can't wink, so I scrunched my face at him and went back to folding.

Patrick is Doug's middle name. I've always liked it, even before I learned it was a family name: his father's middle name, his great uncle's first name, and some unknown number of male Browns' names before them. They're Catholic and there are a lot of them, so it's hard to keep track. When Doug and I talked casually, noncommittally, about the future children I still didn't want to have, we agreed that Patrick was in the running right alongside Cooper. After Doug's mother died though, we found a decades-old handwritten note in his baby book that expressed her hope that he would someday name a son Patrick to carry on the family tradition. Since then, Patrick has held the top spot for a boy's name without debate or contention.

In the 1970's, the Navy took a census of its submarine force and found that, of the Nukes—the sailors who manned the reactors and the engine room as Doug did (and all new officers do) for his first year onboard—those who had children had a remarkably higher number of daughters than sons compared to sailors who worked in other divisions on the boat. Since then, it's been known as the "Nuke's Curse" to beget nothing but daughters. There are online forums of next to no scientific validity that hypothesize this predisposition toward female children comes from the Nukes' proximity to sperm-killing radiation—where the sperm that are killed are the "weaker swimmers," often the male XY chromosomes. Some individuals on these forums claim the submariners' daughter-numbers correlate with the reproductive ratios of high-hours pilots and astronauts who would also be exposed to high levels of *rads* over years. But one quick head-count of the children in the *Georgia* Blue Crew's wardroom gives you four daughters to nine sons, including stepchildren fathered during other, now defunct marriages. The balance only tipped after our first two years on the boat when a new Captain assumed command of the *Georgia*, bringing along his four daughters, and three of the families with sons moved away and were replaced by sailors without children at all. Subsequent, more recent studies have shown no correlation between a sailor's job designation and the sex of his offspring, but the Navy continues to monitor its baby-numbers. The internet forums claim this balance of numbers is a result of all the safety protocols and radiation monitoring done on today's Nukes and any sailor on the sub, who wear thermo-luminescent dosimeters to monitor their exposure to radiation—*TLDs*. Periodically, the sailors receive a printout from Doc, the medical corpsman onboard, with data from their TLDs, detailing their rad-levels, which, according to Doug, remain lower than when I go to the beach and get a sun tan. But still, Doug says it's a *really, really big deal* if you're caught onboard without your TLD.

Doug and I have yet to agree on even one name for a potential daughter. We talked about it at length before he deployed and continued the conversation in email on and off the boat. He likes names like *Rebecca, Sarah, Haley,* and *Suzann*—his late mother's name. But I am a teacher and carry with me the annoying habit of attaching my students' characteristics, both positive and negative, to their names. I shoot down a lot of his suggestions because of this. Between his "Nuke's Curse" and my "Teacher's Curse," we often joke that we are doomed to have nothing but daughters who will go through life numbered instead of named.

"Daughter One, did you finish your homework?"

"Daughter Four, stop yelling at your sister. Two didn't take your sweater, Three did."

Our nonexistent "numbered" daughters have, on occasion, risen into the dozens—his unoriginal poking at my supposed Catholic obligation to overpopulate the world. It is from my Catholic side of the family that I get my middle name *Jean* after my grandparents Eugene and Jeanne, and my aunt, their first daughter, Mary Jean. Doug and I both agree it is an important name, but it will be challenging to integrate Jean into any future daughter's name simply because our last name and Jean both end with *n*s and putting two names together that both err on the nasal side of pronunciation doesn't sound as pleasant as we'd like. But I think all we need is the right first name to precede it.

I favor names that suggest colors: *Hazel, Violet, Rose,* and *Olive.* But with our last name already being a color, my top names get vetoed as well for fear our baby girl gets inadvertently named after a Pantone swatch.

Whatever we have—daughters, sons, or a mix of both—one thing is certain: it is unlikely they will ever know their father as a sailor.

This is one of the thoughts that occurred to me near the beginning of the deployment spent waiting, consumed by thoughts of the children we wanted, but hadn't yet gotten the chance to conceive.

Doug's remaining months on the *Georgia* are dwindling. When I do eventually get pregnant it will be sometime after Doug returns from deployment, which, at this point, will be when he has roughly sixteen months left attached to the submarine. The *Georgia*, piloted home by the opposite crew, is expected to return to Kings Bay a few months after Doug and his crew for dry dock maintenance which is scheduled to last fourteen months but will likely run over that timeframe because major maintenance periods always do. There is a chance Doug will never go out to sea again. But if he does, and we have our first child by that time, he or she will be too young to know he is gone. A few months old, at most.

After these next sixteen months, if we adhere to the plan we made in college, Doug will next report to a shore tour and spend around two more years in the service, the time during which we've more recently talked about planning for our second child. Then…that's it. He will join some sector of the civilian workforce, we will move to wherever his new job is, call it home, and the Navy years will be over. Our eldest, if born exactly nine months after Doug's return from deployment, will be about two and a half, give or take, when Doug leaves the Navy. Far too young to have any concrete memory of the years his or her daddy came home from work every night in camos, clomping around in heavy boots that he'd unlace and leave on the floor for the dog to smell and push around with his nose. Will they remember the stiffness of the camos against their cheeks when he scoops them up to cover their heads with kisses?

Our children will grow up with what I imagine will be only a peripheral knowledge of their father's years on the submarine. Not so different, I suppose, than the way all young children only barely recognize that their parents existed before they were parents. But still, the idea captivates me.

There's a picture from our engagement photo shoot in a boxy frame that I use as a bookend. Doug is all done up in his handsome high-necked dress whites, I, in a white shift dress, and we are smiling at one another, embracing as if about to lean in for a kiss. Our children might see that picture, that uniform, enough over the years to understand that their father was once in the military, or they may not.

They may notice that a few of his ties and dress socks have submarines on them, or cartoon periscopes peeking above waves. Among the wrapping paper and party supplies, will they notice the red, white, and blue "Welcome Home" banner I used to hang across the doorway when Doug returned from a deployment? Will we be making sugar cookies one day, the kids and I, and mixed in with the seasonal cookie cutters, will one of them find my old sub-shaped cookie cutter and ask, *What's this?* How long will it take them to notice all the submarine Christmas ornaments I've collected if they only get unboxed once a year? Will they ask about the funny looking gold dolphins on one ornament—the submarine warfare pin? Will they notice it is the same as the one on their father's favorite mug, on his golf towel, and on the belt I needlepointed for him as a qualification gift? When I wear my gold pendant, engraved with the same insignia, a gift from the *Georgia's* outgoing captain, will my children reach for it with their baby fingers? Will they smudge it with their tiny fingerprints?

As they get older, become more aware, will they notice things about us, their parents, about the ways we act, that they know are odd but don't know are the result of the Navy years? Will they see how their father can sleep without moving, like a corpse, the way he slept in his rack so long ago? What about the way he speaks, in what I call "boat-isms": *Request help with the lawnmower; request two ibuprofens.* Will they see the scars he has from injuries sustained underway that never healed properly in the oxygen-starved air of the sub? Will they tease their mother for calling a grocery store seven or eight different names—*Dierberg's, Schnuck's, Lucky's, HyVee, Harris Teeter, Piggly Wiggly, Winn Dixie, Publix*—before sometimes getting it right, other times landing on that strange, unfamiliar word: *commissary.* They may notice how their mother keeps the TV on, or has music playing, no matter what else she's doing or she gets jittery. Or they may not. They may just think that's the way it's always been.

By their preteen years, I'm sure they will understand that their father is a veteran, that he was in the Navy when they were born, and hopefully they will have a decent idea of what that means about him, but I doubt their understanding reaches as far as what it means about me. Maybe that's a good thing.

I worry we will be overly strict parents to our children. He, coming from the military, and I, from teaching struggling readers, each have strong parameters and beliefs about what behaviors are and are not acceptable. Will we learn how to soften and monitor ourselves so our home is a home, not a joint submarine-trainer-after-school-detention program? When Doug and I fight, will we have the sense not to fight like we did in those early Navy years when there were no young ears listening, when we were at our most vulnerable and unsure of all that was to come? Have we come far enough now to avoid sinking?

Will my children resent me, as they get older, for insisting they learn to do everything themselves? I want them to know how to change a flat, fix a fence, and take care of themselves when they're sick. They need to learn how to cook more than just scrambled eggs, how to budget, how to invest and save, and how to do their own taxes. It's non-negotiable that they be able to navigate through their health insurance and know what numbers to call in case of an emergency, be it a broken pipe or a broken bone. Better yet, they need to know what to do before calling anyone at all. Most of all, I need them to be good at making friends out of strangers, but equally content being alone. I don't want them to flounder or doubt themselves. They need to know not just *how* to do things, but that they *can*. Will they understand that I insist not out of cruelty, but out of love and the memory of the days when I thought I knew how to do so much until I had to do it all alone?

I want them to be strong like a sub wife. I want them to stare down their version of deployment, their biggest fears, and say *eh* from the get-go because they know it is not too much for them. I pray that, whatever walk of life they choose, they have their own version of sub wives to fall back on.

Already, I look back at the years I've spent tied to Doug's service and more than pride, more than grief, more than accomplishment, and more than loneliness, I feel exhaustion. As a mother, will I be spent too? Will the years of upheaval and chaotic goodbyes bleed into their childhoods? Thinking about deployments, about the mental, emotional, and physical distance the Navy put between us, makes my shoulders tense, and all the muscles in my back and arms start to ache as if they've taken up that heavy sack of wheat again to carry all alone. I feel brittle. I think about the parking lot where Doug and I said goodbye, where I sent him out to sea. *God, please, never make me do that again.* I want no more excitement out of life save the small but great joys of my children walking, talking, crying, growing up, going to school, having their first loves, first heartbreaks, first home runs, graduating, succeeding, failing, and becoming their own selves somewhere along the way. I want weekends of sitting around doing nothing but enjoying company and summer vacations that our someday-teenaged children will complain they have to go on. Does this make me boring? Probably. But I fear my capacity for adventure on a grand scale is dried up. Who knows though? Maybe in time it will refill itself, like fresh groundwater seeping up into a dry well. But for now, I just want to rest and hold my child who has not even had a chance to be made yet.

There are no statistics in front of me spelling out the number of service members who have a parent that served in the military. Although the numbers exist, I don't need to see them to know the correlation is strong. I always think back to Doug's Prototype graduation, on the USS *Yorktown* in Charleston, when the speaker, standing before hundreds of parents and relatives of the graduates, asked those who were actively serving, or had served their country in the past to stand, and a staggering number of those in attendance rose to their feet amidst a round of applause. It was at least half, probably more.

I cannot take my future children back in time to show them what it was like to be us—*Sam-and-Doug*—before we were Mom and Dad, when we lived under the Navy's thumb and had so little freedom to call our own shots because of Doug's commitment to fighting for that freedom itself. The only way my children will know sub life, or military life in general, is if they choose it for themselves like Doug did or, if they are like me, and fall in love with someone who has heard the call.

I understand my prayers for peace will only be granted for so long because it is likely one of my future children, maybe more than one, maybe all of them, will answer the call to serve the way their father did. Perhaps our son, our Patrick or our Cooper, will become the pilot Doug didn't, or maybe our daughter will be the one to join the *Silent Service* since, by then, the submarine forces will be fully integrated amongst the sexes and ranks—not just female officers onboard like there were in Doug's sub years. Maybe her Captain will be female too, one who served with Doug or near him when he was a junior officer, since Doug's boat was the second in the fleet fully outfitted to integrate both male and female sailors.

To any child of mine who joins the service, I have only generic, albeit heartfelt bits of, advice to offer: stay strong, be brave, call or email me whenever you can. Any more practical advice will have to come from their father. I am not a sailor, not a submariner, just his wife. I can be strong, but I cannot truly guide like he can, sailor to sailor.

The child who becomes a spouse though, I will hold until they don't want to be held anymore, and then remind them that it is ok to not always be *ok*. I will be there for them in the ways so many were there for me: talk on the phone as much as they want, visit often, take them to dinner, clean their home, fix their fence, send cards, say prayers—for both them and the other spouses who become their tribe. Maybe in time, I'll learn ways to make it easier for them than it was for me. I want them to know the strength, not the sorrow. But of course, one does not come without the other.

Whatever way it happens, if it happens, which I must prepare myself that it will, I will have no choice but to learn what it means to be the mother of a service member, to know an even deeper worry and fear than that which I knew as the twenty-two-year-old bride of a sailor. It feels almost inevitable that I will have to call up my memories of these sub wife days and find that old strength, that old magic, that gave me legs to stand on.

"Nope, not pregnant." I told the endodontist.

"Perfect! We'll be right back to get those x-rays."

In less than ten minutes I was draped in a lead vest with three spacers in my mouth to get the camera angle just right. The technician flipped her switches from outside the exam room and took back her vest and spacers. After she left, I twiddled my thumbs and read through a cooking magazine I'd taken from the waiting room. They had a two-page photo spread of herby green sauces on steak called "Spice Up Your Chimichurri"—*like hell I will.*

"Mrs. Brown?" The chatty endodontist was back. "I've got your x-rays."

"Oh?"

"Good news is you definitely don't need a root canal. Your tooth is fine, they all are."

"Really? I mean, that's great, but why was I in pain?"

The endodontist rolled her chair up to mine and began massaging her hands all over my jaws and neck. "We didn't see any cracked teeth or damaged fillings either." She rubbed her thumbs in circles along my gums, then on the hinge of my jaw. "Are you under a lot of stress?"

I almost snort-laughed inches from her face. "Sometimes," I understated.

"I think you might have done some nerve damage in your actual jaw muscles. Something must have aggravated it and that's what caused you all the pain. It happens sometimes with chronic jaw clenching. You might have touched an old filling a little too hard and that's why the one tooth was so sensitive too." She started to type behind my head while she talked. "It's probably something you're going to deal with to a degree forever."

I was almost disappointed there was no quick fix. When she laid it out, it made so much sense. The pain, the way it migrated from my teeth, to my jaw, to my neck, my ears. She raised my chair and I compulsively opened and closed my still-tight jaw, massaging it with my open hand. Six deployment extensions, one missing submarine, weeks and weeks of frightening silence, one husband still not home, and a family on the horizon, *maybe*, equals permanent nerve damage, I suppose. The endodontist told me to buy a heating pad from Walgreens to help relax the muscles and to see my primary care doctor to get a referral for a pain management specialist.

Anticipating a full root canal, I'd taken the day off work. It wasn't even noon when I left the office—a gorgeous, bright January day. I didn't want to spend it at the pharmacy or on the phone with Tricare. I knew exactly who I wanted to be with.

I pulled out my phone and texted the wives: "Hey! Good news! No root canal for me! I'm right across the parking lot from Cantina Louie. Anyone want to get lunch? Margaritas?"

It was the middle of a weekday, I doubted anyone would answer me, let alone drive out to meet me. But I was wrong.

"Woo-hoo! Yay for your teeth! I'll be there in ten minutes."

"I just finished up a call down the street from there—I can do lunch."

"I get my break in half an hour, so I'll join then—yay!"

"Can't turn down that queso—coming soon!"

I sat in my car in the parking lot with the windows down waiting for my group to arrive. The sound of cars coming over the bridge dissipated into a rushing noise, like a foamy wave washing up the sand. Far across the salt marsh, a storm rolled away, bruise-colored clouds tumbling down the A1A, towards the sea. Beside me, on the passenger seat, my phone continued to buzz, chime, and ding. A text, a reply, another text, and one more email from the deep.

ACKNOWLEDGMENTS

I t takes a village to write a memoir. (That's how the saying goes, right?) The first thanks of this acknowledgment section goes to the chiefess of my book's village, my mentor, turned agent, turned publisher, Tracy Crow. When I first met Tracy in June 2018 at an On Point Women Warriors Writing Workshop, she scared the shit out of me. She was professional, exacting, knowledgeable, and took the art of writing the military story very seriously. If you're a military writer, get a Tracy in your life ASAP. As president of MilSpeak Foundation and official revitalizer of MilSpeak Books, Tracy is giving the military community—from servicemembers, to family members, to caregivers—a whole new avenue to connect with each other and the civilian world. I am honored to have been chosen in the first group of writers the new MilSpeak Books is publishing. Thank you to the foundation, the board, and every other member of the MilSpeak village.

Thank you to Margaret MacInnis for editing the final revision of this book. When I was in fourth grade, my school district cut explicit grammar instruction from our curriculum. No one has felt that sting as keenly as Margaret did when she called out my every comma, every semicolon, and every questionable use of italics. I do so solemnly swear I will never start another sentence with *so* or *but*. Thank you for your careful eye.

The largest of thanks to the faculty of Queens University of Charlotte, especially Kathryn Rhett, Jon Pineda, Emily White, Robert Polito, Fred

Leebron, and Rebecca McClanahan. Without each of you, I'd still be twiddling my thumbs over a half-finished essay about a bridge and a cargo ship. Thank you for your guidance, your criticisms, and your mentorship. Thank you for keeping in touch. Endless affection to Melissa Bashor and Buffa Short for keeping my shit—all of our shit, really—in line so we didn't have to stress about the paperwork.

Heaps upon heaps of gratitude to my CNF cohorts and workshop groups who handled the first drafts of *Sub Wife*. Without your thoughtful feedback and confidence in my story, this book would never have happened. Without your friendships, I'd be a lonely, lonely memoirist. Extra special thanks to Liz Logan. Liz, you've been in my corner since day one and, if I'd died before *Sub Wife* was finished, I had it noted that you were the one I wanted to finish it. No pressure. Give Quinny a belly rub for me, ok?

And to my many wonderful non-writing friends, thank you for supporting and sustaining me as a human through the writing of this book. There are too many of you to name as I am disproportionately blessed. Thank you for calling, texting, coming to visit, and letting me visit you. Thank you for letting me pet your dogs (and appreciate your cats from afar.)

Thank you to Julija Šukys, Lauren Fath, and Elizabeth McConaghy for navigating my first forays into nonfiction at Mizzou. Thank you for recognizing and honoring my passion, always holding space for more discussion and questions. Thank you for giving me the proverbial balls to send out my first pieces and always being examples of strong women writing strong words. Thank you to the editors and staff of *The Missouri Review* for the experience of working in publishing, and for connecting me with Roxane Gay so I could ask her my piddly undergrad questions with confidence (before realizing I'd interacted with modern literary royalty.) Thank you, Roxane, for being a gracious sovereign.

My high school English teachers Jason Lovera and Lou Jobst taught me both discipline and love of the written word. The former coached me rigorously on the finer points of essaying and hosted before-school "Grammar Fridays" to remedy the curriculum's glaring gaps, the latter dressed up as Raskolnikov and played guitar in class a few times a week to take our minds off college application anxieties. Mr. Lovera, thank you for telling me what to do with my life. Mr. Jobst, thank you for teaching me how to live that life with unapologetic joy. Thank you to my swim coach Kevin Mabie for taking me on as an assistant to his freshman English class, giving me my first taste of teaching. One last teacher whom I must thank profusely is Ken Greathouse. He tried to teach me chemistry. Instead, he taught me how to fail with grace and prioritize my goals. Thank you for all your wisdom and patience (and for padding my exam scores so my GPA didn't disappear entirely.)

Early on in the writing process, I told a group of my own middle school students that I was writing a book. I owe them more appreciation than they'll ever know because every time I started losing steam or wondering if what I was writing really mattered to anyone but me, one of them would ask, "How's your book going Ms. Brown?" Love you guys. You make me proud. Keep making good choices. Pay attention. Take off your hats. Put your phones away. Wear a seatbelt. Yes, I can see the earbuds under your hair.

And while we're bringing up love, I owe the spouses of the *Georgia* Blue wardroom an ocean of it for their unwavering support through every season of our Navy years with the boat. When I started writing this, I knew there were only two parties who had the power to shut down the entire project: Doug and you, the sub wives. But from the second I brought it up, to the final punctuation mark, I've had your enthusiastic support. That has made all the difference. Thank you for trusting me to share our inner circle with a wider audience. Next time someone tells you that you "knew what you were getting into" when you married a sailor, show them *Sub Wife* and say, "Yeah asshole, but no one told me my friend would turn it into a book."

My family is large and loud and wonderful in all things. One side of the family, my dad's side, is made up of readers. They have fostered me as a writer for as long as I can remember—always providing new books or blank notebooks. My mom's side of the family is where the party's at (#TurnUpForTurek.) I won't take a Jäger shot for anyone but you guys. Thank you to my entire family for making me who I am and tolerating me accordingly.

Mom and Dad, thank you for supporting every single one of my dreams. Without you, I am nothing. Thank you for always answering the phone when I call and for sitting front and center at every reading, concert, and event my entire life. Thank you for continuing your loving ways with Palmer. You have blessed us beyond measure. Jacob, thanks for always being the cooler of the two of us—I don't know how you bear the burden.

Dougie Fresh, thank you for being the definition of "unconditional." I love you most, too.

Photographer credit: Joyce McCown, Moonshadow Press

ABOUT THE AUTHOR

Samantha Otto Brown holds a BA in English from the University of Missouri-Columbia and an MFA from Queens University of Charlotte. Her nonfiction work appears in PANK Magazine and Mizzou's EPIC. She lives with her husband, daughter, and dog in Lawrence, Kansas, and runs a blog, The Page & Print.

Thank you for supporting the creative works of veterans and military family members by purchasing this book. If you enjoyed your reading experience, we're certain you'll enjoy these other great reads.

SALMON IN THE SEINE
by Norris Comer

One moment 18-year-old Norris Comer is throwing his high school graduation cap in the air and setting off for Alaska to earn money, and the next he's comforting a wounded commercial fisherman who's desperate for the mercy of a rescue helicopter. From landlubber to deckhand, Comer's harrowing adventures at sea and during a solo search in the Denali backcountry for wolves provide a transformative bridge from adolescence to adulthood.

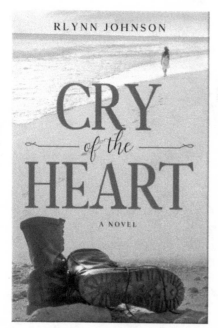

CRY OF THE HEART
by RLynn Johnson

After law school, a group of women calling themselves the Alphas embark on diverse legal careers— Pauline joins the Army as a Judge Advocate. For twenty years, the Alphas gather for annual weekend retreats where the shenanigans and truth-telling will test and transform the bonds of sisterhood.

BEYOND THEIR LIMITS OF LONGING
by Jennifer Orth-Veillon

The first collection of poetry, fiction, and nonfiction to reveal the important, yet often overlooked, influence of World War One on contemporary writers and scholars—many of them post-9ll veterans. Among the contributors are Pulitzer Prize-winning and National Book Award-winning authors.

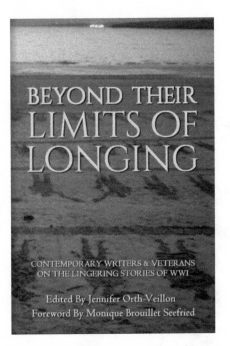

COLLATERAL DAMAGE 2ND EDITION
by Kevin C. Jones

These stories live in the real-world psychedelics of warfare, poverty, love, hate, and just trying to get by. Jones's evocative language, the high stakes, and heartfelt characters create worlds of wonder and grace. The explosions, real and psychological, have a burning effect on the reader. Nothing here is easy, but so much is gained.
—Anthony Swofford, author of Jarhead: A Marine's Chronicle of the Gulf War and Other Battles

CPSIA information can be obtained
at www.ICGtesting.com
Printed in the USA
LVHW011358120422
715979LV00004B/513